SOURCES OF INSPIRATION

Sources of Inspiration

15 Modern Religious Leaders

Edited by
Gene I. Maeroff

Sheed & Ward

Library of Congress Cataloging-in-Publication

Sources of inspiration : 15 modern religious leaders / Gene
    I. Maeroff, ed.
        p.   cm.
    Includes bibliographical references.
    ISBN 1-55612-602-6
    ISBN 1-55612-556-9 pbk. (alk. paper)
    1. Clergy--United States--Religious life. 2. United States
--Religion--1960- 3. Conversion. I. Maeroff, Gene I.
BL2525.S585 1992
277.3'0829'0922--dc20
[B]   92-27494
                                                        CIP

Published by: Sheed & Ward
               115 E. Armour Blvd. P.O. Box 419492
               Kansas City, MO 64141-6492
To order, call: (800) 333-7373

Contents

Foreword

by Joseph O'Neill

Are the seminarians who are preparing to enter the ranks of the clergy today of the same quality and character as those who were ordained in years past? This was the issue that staff at the Lilly Endowment and at Educational Testing Service (ETS) began to discuss in the summer of 1987. The question was provoked not by nostalgia for some "golden age" but because of rapid change in the type of student applying to seminaries and divinity schools.

In the years following the Vietnam War, the age and gender composition of seminary student bodies changed dramatically. The average age of entering seminarians rose by almost 10 years between 1965 and 1990. And the number of women preparing for ordination increased fivefold during that same period of time. If seminarians had changed, so had American culture and its attitudes toward organized religion. At the level of anecdote, especially when clergy talk among themselves, there was a feeling that priests, ministers and rabbis no longer command the same respect that they had in the past. No longer were the clergy the most educated members of the community. Religion seemed to be retreating from the public forum to exercise its influence only in the realm of the private. And an educated laity seemed free to question what their fathers would have accepted without hesitation.

Have these changes in culture brought a different kind of person to seminaries and divinity schools? Are they as well qualified academically and as well balanced personally as those who have come before them? These were the questions being asked by the leadership of American churches and denominations.

ETS, as the home of such nationally used instruments as the Scholastic Aptitude Test (SAT) and the Graduate Record Examinations (GRE), already had in its databases information about the academic background, levels of achievement and educational indebtedness of a fairly large sample of entering seminarians. In addition, ETS has long played a role in the analysis of occupations, especially those where an examination is used to select or promote personnel. With these assets at our disposal, we at ETS addressed the issue of "quality in ministry" by conducting a broad survey of American clergy—Protestant, Catholic and Jewish—and by compiling databases descriptive of almost 100,000 entering seminarians from 1944 to the present.

As useful as test scores and survey data are, we realized that the qualities of mind and heart that describe the ideal priest, minister or rabbi cannot be captured by quantitative methods alone. To complement our database material we needed in-depth interviews with clergy who are recognized by their peers as outstanding practitioners. Gene Maeroff, senior fellow at the Carnegie Foundation for the Advancement of Teaching, was kind enough to accept the challenge to organize and edit this series of biographical essays. With one exception, all of the clergy interviewed had hands-on responsibility for leading a parish or congregation. Most are not known outside their local communities. Some were chosen through national surveys, others by a vote of their peers. We also identified clergy to interview by polling seminary faculties about their outstanding graduates and denominational officials about those who had made a mark on the life of local congregations.

Whatever the method of selection, each of the persons profiled has been nominated by other clergy for their exemplary pastoral practice. Their religious traditions include Reform and Conservative Judaism, Roman Catholicism and a broad spectrum of Protestant denominations. And we have drawn on the experience of women clergy as well as men to round out our picture of the contemporary minister, priest or rabbi.

These essays follow in the footsteps of such works as H. Richard Niebuhr's and Daniel Day Williams' *The Ministry in Historical Perspective*. But our emphasis is on the contemporary and the individual pastor or teacher. In each cameo portrait a journey of faith shines through: the constant struggle to remain true to traditions that are thousands of years old while adapting daily practice to the needs of today. One of the persistent themes throughout the book is the constant effort to create and maintain a community, a community of faith that sustains a community of life.

This work could not have been undertaken without the generous support of the Lilly Endowment and without the encouragement of Robert Wood Lynn, then vice president for religion at the Endowment, his successor Craig Dykstra, and Fred L. Hofheinz, who nurtured this project from the beginning.

Joseph P. O'Neill
Principal Research Scientist
Educational Testing Service
Princeton, New Jersey
February 14, 1992

Introduction

America is a land in which sometimes it seems that there are few moral heroes, a country lacking men and women who inspire others to walk in righteous paths. Even saying this sounds dated. That is how much has been lost in this country. Where may one turn for moral example? These are times, sad to say, when many Americans bestow their admiration not on the quiet exemplars who labor patiently attending to matters of the soul, but on those who attain material success, those who command the attention of the media. Glitz and glitter are the order of the day.

Once religion could be counted on to produce exemplars whose deeds filled others with hope and inspiration, people who caused the spirits of others to soar and, by example, invited emulation. In some places on earth that still can happen. In South Africa, Archbishop Desmond M. Tutu stood as a tower of strength against apartheid. In East Germany, a few Protestant ministers provided much of the moral resistance in the late 1980s for the revolt that finally led to the collapse of a totalitarian regime. And even in Romania it was ultimately the pastor of a provincial church who became an unlikely hero in the overthrow of a hated dictator.

In America, however, members of the clergy seldom are seen as role models. It appears sometimes that they have become as quaint and peripheral as the blacksmith. It is not simply that the clergy has been sullied by the James Bakkers, the Jimmy Swaggarts, the Meir Kahanes, the occasional priest who takes a mistress or seduces a teen-age boy or even by such a charlatan as Jim Jones, who led hundreds of trusting followers to death in the South American jungle.

Rather, institutional religion itself has been reduced to an irrelevancy for many Americans, regardless of the conduct of the clergy. Talking about God in educated circles is gauche and

1

taking religion seriously can get one labeled as "weird." Tens of millions of evangelical Americans are treated by the media as if they are as invisible as oxygen.

Athletes and entertainers stand above all others in the reflected neon of public acclaim. Michael Jackson and Michael Jordan epitomize the hero incarnate. One poll of 5,000 high school students during the middle-1980s, asking them to list their heroes, produced a list on which the top 10 were Bill Cosby, Sylvester Stallone, Eddie Murphy, Ronald Reagan, Chuck Norris, Clint Eastwood, Molly Ringwald, Rob Lowe, Arnold Schwarzenegger and Don Johnson.[1]

The successful manipulation of money has been a sure route to becoming a role model in today's America. When Donald Trump's star dimmed in the constellation of heroes, it was not because his moral standing had declined, but because his ability to make millions was called into question. So long as Ivan Boesky could balance his arbitrage deals and Michael Milken could peddle his junk bonds they, too, were role models, if only for aspiring yuppies.

By the beginning of the 1990s it took war and CNN to provide America with heroes. Generals Schwarzkopf and Powell surely loomed larger than life during their brief march across the stage of history, but in a world poised on the precipice of nuclear annihilation more pacific sources of moral example must be found in the future. In the wake of Watergate, even government has become an uncertain source of exemplars. Today's elected officials sometimes seem to be little more than full-time fundraisers. The Keating Five in the U.S. Senate, accused of accepting donations that swayed their opinions in the savings and loan scandal, struck some not as aberrations, but as typical. The sad spectacle of the Senate Judicary Committee's confirmation hearing on the nomination of Clarence Thomas to the U.S. Supreme Court was just one more degradation that bemused a public searching for inspiration.

Where may one turn for moral example? There is still the Carnegie Hero Fund Commission and the men and women it honors for such acts of bravery as saving a family from a burning house or rescuing a child who has fallen into an icy lake. Somehow, though, these courageous individuals seem not to inspire very many others by their singular and situational examples.

The emptiness of Americans is an irony in a country that in many ways is among the most religious in the world. Three out of four adults say they often rely on faith for guidance in everyday family matters and almost as many say that attending organized religious services is important in a family's spiritual development.[2]   Among all Americans, 78 percent say they believe in heaven and 60 percent say they believe in hell.[3] Statistics generally show the United States to be one of the most God-fearing lands on earth, with a larger percentage of the population who say they believe in God and attend worship services than almost any other country in the developed world.

There are limitations to these convictions, however. For instance, though the vast majority of schoolchildren profess to believe in God and four out of 10 of them say daily prayers,[4] only 3 percent said in a survey that they would seek out a member of the clergy for help with a moral problem.[5]   What does this mean? How do they perceive the clergy?

The percentage of Americans who said they were members of no faith grew from 2 percent in 1952 to 11 percent in 1991.[6] The *Wall Street Journal* said this about those who opt out of organized religion: "As their numbers have increased, their cultural characteristics have changed: No longer a small marginal group of atheists and social dissidents, non-affiliates today are predominantly young, white, well-educated and socially mobile."[7]   There was even a church in a small Wisconsin town where the pastor was conducting a service each Sunday in 1990 though all of the members had died or moved away. "If no one is here, God is here and he hears prayers," said the frail, old pastor.[8]

How is one to reconcile America's outward show of religion with its failure to look to religion for moral heroes—except perhaps for revering those who have been dead for a couple of millennia? How indeed? It is a question not easily answered. Perhaps Americans are hedging the future by buying spiritual insurance—paying the premiums with no particular commitment to the contract except an expectation that it will reward them eventually by delivering the Big Dividend in the Sky.

In any event, it is clear that organized religion, certainly of the traditional variety, is a diminishing influence in the lives of certain Americans. While faith and grace tend to sustain members of the more conservative denominations, the mainline denominations with their historic interest in more worldly concerns seem to find it ever more difficult to provide inspiration. To appreciate just how far a trend like this may carry a people one can look at England, where the Church of England—despite its marvelous cathedrals—verges on extinction in the big cities. Its communicants comprise just 4 percent of the population over the age of 15. In London, only 1.6 percent of the population are regular church-goers and in Birmingham, 1.5 percent.[9]

These are times, certainly for Americans, when it would be especially valuable to a troubled society to find exemplars within the clergy. Moral example would serve both the affiliated and the unaffiliated. Certainly there are worthy and admirable ministers, priests and rabbis. But their voices are less apt to be heard amid a cacophony of cynicism and their examples are less likely to be noticed.

Balfour Brickner, a rabbi in New York City, captured the sense of the situation when he wrote: "American Jewry is producing the finest aggregation of rabbis it has ever created. They are better trained, more mature, more knowledgeable, more committed to Judaism and the Jewish people, more caring, more familiar with general culture than they have ever been. They are also more unheard, less listened to than any group of rabbis in American history. Fewer and fewer Jews go to where the rabbis are: the synagogue."[10]

Not that those who exhibit moral leadership in a religious sense are found only in the clergy. There are lay exemplars who draw on religious and ethical traditions and there is no wish here to imply that the laity are not as important as the ordained. As a matter of fact, one measure of the health of a congregation may be the extent to which leadership is elicited from the laity. Leadership potential may lie dormant within a person, waiting to be summoned by the inspiration of a leader, by a specific situation or context, or by a notable spiritual experience such as occurred when Jacob wrestled with an angel. Often, the same person who knows how to put together a multimillion-dollar business deal or how to perform root canal surgery must be put in touch with his or her internal gift for lay spiritual leadership.

So, while it is true that congregational leadership is not and need not be limited to the role of those who are ordained, something very precious will be lost if the clergy essentially disappears as a source of inspiration. Americans, after all, are the people who made the pulpit the cockpit of moral imperative. It was during the colonial period, Daniel Boorstin tells us, that the church sermon blossomed into its full glory.[11] The nation's system of higher education is an outgrowth of the attempt by religious denominations to put their moral imprint on America's young.

Of course, those early preachers and purveyors of moral instruction did not always use their influence in ways that all might desire, but their successes have been a sufficient force for good that the muting of this special voice can only serve to diminish America itself.

Admittedly, this is a time of extraordinary change for institutions of religion and for the clergy itself. Where once, according to Peter Berger, the mainline Protestant churches served to legitimate the middle-class culture of America,[12] that culture itself is no longer so secure. And this transformation has been no less unsettling for those who preside over those churches. It hardly needs to be said that being a clergyman is not what it used to be. For starters, being a clergyman might mean being a clergywoman.

But, just as significantly, it is likely to mean that the person in the role—man or woman—has to work harder than ever before to exert influence. Many Americans, including the affiliated, are ready to ignore organized religion and those who represent it, writing them off as relics who, if they have any place in modern society, belong with the other relics—in museums.

Too much is at stake, though, to let careers in the clergy come to be seen as jobs of last resort. If that occurs, able young people may be increasingly less apt to join the ranks of educated ministers, priests and rabbis. Statistics suggest that this is already starting to happen, especially among men. If religion is to be a meaningful force in today's America and if the clergy prepared by the nation's seminaries are to have any moral suasion then more powerful voices will have to be heard and more stark examples will have to be seen.

The problem feeds on itself. As fewer exemplars appear in the pulpits, there are fewer potential role models and it becomes ever more difficult to find people who are inspired to fill these positions in the future. The losses are exponential because as individual congregations are weakened the chances are less that those congregations will produce candidates for the clergy.

Ultimately, the health of religious institutions depends on a synergy of clerical and lay leadership, though, as Garry Wills reminds us, many Americans are uncomfortable with the idea of religious influence penetrating beyond the sanctuary walls and affecting secular behavior.[13] The country in the 1990s is sorely in need of those who can inspire by word and by example and it is difficult to imagine whence this inspiration will come if not from a new breed of clergy. It is a time when it is easier and safer not to don the hero's mantle. Witness Brian Watkins, a tourist from Utah, who died a brutal death on a grimy New York City subway platform when he struggled to protect his parents from muggers.

Yet, the perpetuation of heroism born of moral commitment is essential to restoring the nation and giving hope to a people who are increasingly finding reason for despair. Parents have lost authority and families are in disarray. Almost none of society's institutions retains the prestige and unquestioned authority of former years. The ships of government and industry sometimes seem not to be guided by any sort of moral compass. Many people hardly anguish anymore over decisions that ought to be fraught with ethical implications. Violent criminals have stolen the streets from a cowering public and the criminals murder at the least provocation—or for no provocation at all. The habit of hard work is no longer honored. Prejudices that some thought had been banished are reappearing with fresh virulence. And, worst of all, a generation of urban youth is coming of age under horrible and horrifying circumstances.

Nonetheless, conscience still whispers its plaintive call and many Americans ache for principles. People speak with longing about old-time values and some strive to put greater meaning in their lives. Exemplars from the clergy can be among the heroes of a revivified tomorrow. It should be clear to observers of the contemporary scene that Americans are searching for ways to put more meaning into their lives. Sometimes they seek to be sated by material acquisitions—expensive cars, beach homes, electronic gadgets. Sometimes they turn to New Age nostrums, hoping to find a kind of fulfillment in a blend of astrology and nature.

Others revert to organized religion in their quest for meaning, going back to the denomination of their childhood or to a new one that they have chosen as an adult. This "return to religion" cuts across the faiths and while the adherents are by no means the majority of the population they have infused some congregations with renewed vigor and dedication. There is a yearning to find greater meaning in life. Even children feel it. A theme that Robert Coles develops has to do with the struggle of children to know God and to determine their place in the universe.[14]

The manner in which this new interest in religion plays itself out will in large part be determined by the men and women in the pulpit. Times have changed and the ways in which the clergy relate to congregants must generally be less authoritarian and less pedantic. The challenge is to reach a generation of worshipers who perpetually have one foot out the door.

This book is not about religion so much as it is about ordained men and women, leaders of congregations for whom religion is a meaningful and moving force. No prayers appear on these pages and there are no hidden messages of devotion. The men and women who are profiled are Protestant, Catholic and Jewish; there is no denominational slant. They live throughout the country and they are of various ages, some edging into retirement, others barely embarked on their careers. They are people who have inspired others and are themselves inspired.

Some have wrestled with pressing personal issues, seeking to come to terms with themselves at the same time that they have tried to serve others. Some have had to wage battles in their own congregations to carry out their roles. There have been questions of faith, questions of vocation and questions about relationships with spouses, family, friends and congregants.

The authors of these profiles—all written expressly for this book—are mostly accomplished journalists with extensive experience in writing about religion. All have spent time with the subjects and spoken with those who know them to gain deeper understandings. Kenneth Briggs is a former religion editor of the *New York Times*. Ari Goldman now covers religion for the *Times*. Rosemary Bray oversees the review of books on religion for the *Times Book Review*. Roy Reed and Gene Maeroff are former correspondents for the *Times*. Gustav Niebuhr writes on religion for the *Wall Street Journal*. David Briggs writes on religion for the Associated Press. Pamela Schaeffer is an editor at the Religious News Service. John Dart writes on religion for the *Los Angeles Times*. William MacKaye covered religion for the *Washington Post*. Margaret Poloma is a professor at the University of Akron. David Nichols has written a new book on the Catholic priesthood. John Long is a former religion writer for the *Louisville Courier-Journal*.

There is no attempt here at exposé, but merely to provide a better understanding of the work of a small group of men and women who have decided to make religion their life's work in an era when religion is not even a part of the lives of many of their fellow citizens. Mostly, those who are profiled are of the mainline variety because of the historic context that is provided by pursuing the inquiry in this way. But there are examples of denominations outside the mainline, lending a wider focus so as to allow a comparison of the meaning of inspiration in various American religious traditions.

The Rev. Colbert S. Cartwright, former minister of Pulaski Heights Christian Church of Little Rock, Ark., was an unlikely Moses when he spoke to his white congregation in behalf of school integration more than 30 years ago. He said that white people who tried to keep nine black children out of Central High School were in danger of losing their souls. He could have lost his life for such talk. His was a career that inspired others as he pronounced the simple teachings: turn the other cheek, give to the poor.

The Rev. Jane Shields, pastor of the Evangelical Lutheran Church in Delaware, has taken a keen interest in the seminary education of the next generation of clergymembers, while presiding over her own 600-member congregation. Her nurturing personality has made a family of the congregation and she has provided a marvelous role model for women who have assumed many of the leadership posts.

Rabbi Leonid A. Feldman of Temple Emanu-El in Palm Beach, Fla. is a survivor who has devoted himself to helping Judaism survive. A former Soviet refusenik who grew to adulthood as an atheist and loyal Communist, totally ignorant of his Jewish roots, he entered rabbinical school in his 30s in search of self and now tries to teach American Jews how to be Jewish.

The Rev. Granville A. Seward, for more than 20 years the pastor of Newark's Mt. Zion Baptist Church, has remained at his inner-city post despite distinguished academic credentials that might have opened more prestigious doors. His church is filled with warmth as he energizes a congregation in the midst of one of the poorest of American cities. "In ministry," he said, "so much of the work is done at the point of human suffering."

Father Virgil Elizondo, rector of San Fernando Cathedral in San Antonio, faithful to his Roman Catholic, Mexican-American origin, juggles the roles of pastor and theologian. Hundreds of seminarians from throughout the country have studied Hispanic culture and the unique face of Latin Catholicism at the Mexican American Cultural Center that he founded at San Antonio's Assumption Seminary.

The Rev. Richard L. Manzelmann of New Hartford Presbyterian Church, outside Utica, N.Y., makes no excuses for a career spent in the suburbs—even joining Rotary. He has taken his stands and spoken his mind, though sometimes it meant being regarded as a kind of eccentric uncle. He has tried to keep his congregants from fleeing responsibility. "We've become smaller but stronger," he said of the mainline Church, "because the people who stick with us are going to be here because they want to be here."

The Rev. Paul Duke, caught squarely in the midst of the battles besieging the Southern Baptists, ministers to a congregation of 1,700 in suburban St. Louis. A man who shatters stereotypes in a multitude of ways, he says he is sometimes "exhausted" by the pain of denominational struggle.

Father John Huston Ricard, auxiliary bishop of Baltimore, one of a dozen black bishops in the largely white Roman Catholic Church, is an urban vicar, carefully walking the line that divides the races while trying to bring understanding to difficult situations. "It's worth the struggle," he tells seminarians, speaking from the vantage of a person with a special ability to step back and carefully assess the situation.

The Rev. Carol Anderson of All Saints Episcopal Church in Beverly Hills, Cal. is a pioneer, the first woman priest to be ordained in the Episcopal Diocese of New York and the third in the country. Outspoken and iconoclastic, she is an example for women in a position in which there were no role models less than 20 years ago. "I think there is sexism in the institution, but women should become at ease with the skills they have, and develop them," she said.

The Rev. Jeb Stuart Magruder's ministry at First Presbyterian Church in Lexington, Ky. is a test of atonement and forgiveness—and sincerity. His journey from Watergate felon in the Nixon White House to a pastorate in middle America provides a touchstone against which to measure some of Christianity's most basic teachings. Can he now be an example to others or must he always be a source of embarrassment to those who want to believe that former sinners cannot become models?

The Rev. James Reed in Chicago, after stirring his followers to community involvement and rising to the position of district superintendent in his denomination, the United Methodist Church, has chosen in the closing years of his career to serve two tiny struggling urban churches. He has always tended to avoid the easier, more traveled road and is lauded as "the only minister I know with impeccable integrity" by one of those whom he inspired to enter the ministry.

Pastor E. Eugene Meador of First Assembly of God in Akron, Ohio, strives to retain aspects of the old-time pentecostal tradition while accepting more modern practices that attract charismatics and evangelicals. His is a ministry tempered by the experience of childhood deprivation as he seeks to inspire followers with a straightforward interpretation of the Bible.

Rabbi Rachel Cowan of New York City, convert to Judaism and one of its earliest female rabbis, has emerged as a national spokeswoman for equality of women in her religion. She also has been one of the leaders in helping to reconcile interfaith couples, Jews and gentiles, to their lives together.

The Rev. Adam J. Richardson, following in the footsteps of his forebears as a minister of the African Methodist Episcopal Church, has been a rock and an inspiration for his people in northern Florida. Presiding since the age of 32 over a congregation launched by slaves in 1865, at the dawn of their freedom, Richardson is a preacher of unmistakable authority.

Father Paul Gallatin, pastor of a typical Roman Catholic parish in Oklahoma City, has tried to use his own weaknesses and mistakes to find a foundation for deeper empathy with others. He has sought to reconcile the routinized duties of the parish priest with his abiding interest in the intellectual life.

In their positions these members of the clergy have challenged others to explore the significance of religious faith in an America in which belief has become a fragile commodity. Whether by preaching or by writing, by counseling or by silent example, they have tried to engage people. By and large, this book is about unheralded heroes who have touched others gently, yet profoundly. Few are known beyond their own communities. No claim is made that they are without flaws or that they are paragons. But there are dimensions to their lives that can provide inspiration to a society that needs to heal itself.

Unlike those who sit in Congress and in the nation's corporate executive suites, they have not exerted influence simply by holding visible and powerful positions. Their influence—to the extent that they have any—has been by example, by the invocation of a higher authority than themselves. They have searched inward and have tried to encourage others to do the same. This is the way of those who seek in some way to personify the values they uphold. One study of moral exemplars found that such men and women have a sustained commitment to moral principles, a consistent tendency to act in accord with moral values, a willingness to risk their self-interest for the sake of those values, an ability to inspire others to moral action, a dedicated responsiveness to the lives of others and a sense of humility about their own importance.[15]

Perhaps there will be among the clergy some of the role models that a troubled America needs in an age in which so many Americans are satisfied to find their exemplars amid the glitter of Earth-bound stars, the sort who appear not in the heavens but on the pages of *People* magazine. Being a member of the clergy and trying to serve a congregation at this time in the history of the United States is not an easy job and, in fact, may often be a thankless one. And so it is worth taking a closer look at the men and women who have been trying to carry out that role.

Notes

1. Siegel, Danny. "In Praise of Mitzvah Heroes." *Perspectives,* Sept. 1990.
2. "Religion, Spirituality and American Families." A survey by *Better Homes and Gardens,* 1988.
3. "Hell's Sober Comeback." *U.S. News and World Report,* Mar. 25, 1991.
4. *Girl Scouts Survey on the Beliefs and Moral Values of America's Children.* New York: Girls Scouts of America, 1989.
5. *Girl Scouts Survey.*
6. *Emerging Trends.* Princeton: Princeton Religion Research Center, 1991.
7. Roof, Wade Clark. "The Episcopalian Goes the Way of the Dodo." *The Wall Street Journal,* July 20, 1990.
8. "Empty Pews Don't Silence Midwest Preacher." *Sunday (Newark) Star-Ledger* (Associated Press), Oct. 14, 1990.
9. *Church Statistics.* London: The Church of England, Central Board of Finance, 1990.
10. Brickner, Balfour. "Summoning Our Resources for Renewal." *Sh'ma,* Oct. 19, 1990.
11. Boorstin, Daniel. *The Americans: The Colonial Experience.* New York: Random House, 1964.
12. Berger, Peter L. "Reflections of an Ecclesiastical Expatriate." *Christian Century,* Oct. 24, 1990.
13. Wills, Garry. *Under God: Religion and Politics.* New York: Simon and Schuster, 1990.
14. Coles, Robert. *The Spiritual Life of Children.* Boston: Houghton Mifflin Company, 1990.
15. Colby, Ann and Damon, William. "The Personification of Moral Values Through the Designation of Moral Exemplars." Paper presented at a meeting of the Society for Research in Child Development, April 1987.

Colbert S. Cartwright

God's Stranger

by Roy Reed

*I hear the ancient footsteps like the motion of the
  sea
Sometimes I turn, there's someone there, other
  times it's only me.
I am hanging in the balance of the reality of man
Like every sparrow falling, like every grain of
  sand.*

—Bob Dylan
Every Grain of Sand,

Pulaski Heights Christian Church of Little Rock had long been
one of the more free-thinking congregations of the Disciples of
Christ. The founding pastor had distinguished himself during
World War II by preaching pacifism and going to the aid of
Japanese-Americans interned in the swamps of southern Arkansas. Another pastor had inflamed the state by presuming to
introduce the "communist" Henry Wallace when he brought his
presidential campaign to Little Rock in 1948.

Even Pulaski Heights Christian, however, was not fully
prepared for the freedom of the pulpit exercised by the Rev.
Colbert S. Cartwright on Sunday morning September 8, 1957.

To understand how a single sermon by a shy, owlish little
preacher could threaten the stability of a congregation, it is necessary to remember that in 1957 America was still openly, often
officially, racist. The national government had only just begun
to dismantle the legal artifact of racial segregation in the

Southern states. The problem of de facto segregation and entrenched racism elsewhere was not even recognized in white America outside of a few intellectual redoubts. Little Rock was far from being a hotbed of white supremacy, but any preacher there who espoused racial integration from the pulpit could expect trouble. Integration, it was commonly believed in the American white South of 1957, was a communist plot to destroy the government.

Bert Cartwright was an unlikely Moses. His voice was weak and so were his eyes. His glasses made him look like the bookworm he was. He weighed 110 pounds. The sophomore girls in the church were taller than he. And yet, when he climbed into the pulpit that morning, he spoke words of such power and conviction that members of the congregation remembered the sermon 30 years later as the best they had ever heard.

The sermon was a simple story of one sprite of a girl. Elizabeth Eckford was one of nine black students who had been selected to transfer from an all-black school to Little Rock's most prestigious all-white school, Central High. That transfer was to be the modest beginning of a slow process that would eventually desegregate the entire Little Rock School District.

The plan was sidetracked when Governor Orval E. Faubus called out the Arkansas National Guard and blocked the admission of the nine students. A picture made famous from the news reports of September 3, 1957 was one of a lonely black girl, pretty and seemingly calm, in a gingham and white dress, walking a gantlet of jeering white people as she tried to reach a bus stop to return home. That was Elizabeth Eckford.

Bert Cartwright's sermon the next Sunday was a stark description of Miss Eckford's trial as he watched it unfold in front of Central High School. He quoted the psalms she had read before leaving home to face the hostile crowd. He spoke of her dream of becoming a lawyer. He spoke of visiting in her home and of his shame, that week, at being white.

Then he declared that the nine black students who were trying to go to Central High were human beings, and that white people who lost sight of that were in danger of losing their own souls. Elizabeth Eckford, he said, "has more guts than anyone present here today."

Most of the members seemed to appreciate the boldness of the pastor's words. But a sizable minority were offended. They seized on his last statement. He had questioned their courage, they said.

The trouble boiled for a week. The next Sunday, about 30 members, the entirety of one adult Sunday School class, refused to go into the sanctuary for communion. They asked that it be served to them in their classroom. The request was turned down.

Days later, all of them moved their membership to another church. Pulaski Heights Christian had lost 10 percent of its members overnight, thanks to one sermon.

Cartwright went on to become a leader of Little Rock's brave little band of white integrationists. He spoke up beyond the relative safety of his pulpit and became known throughout the city. The State Police, which kept a close and furtive eye on any person or group that might promote integration, started an investigative file on him. His sermon on Elizabeth Eckford found its way into the file. Plainclothesmen watched the church and at least once recorded the auto license numbers and identities of people parked there after hours. While he became a villain among segregationists, he became a hero to those blacks and whites struggling for racial equality.

Cartwright never quite understood that. He was never a hero in his own eyes. The idea of popularity unsettled him, went against the grain of his theological training as well as his personal inclination. He understood the office of pastor to be appointive, not elective. He believed that his authority came from God. He did not seek popularity inside or outside of the church, like some officeholder looking for votes. That some people considered his efforts on the race issue to be remarkable was slightly puzzling to him. He was simply carrying out his duties as a pastor. That was the main thing he aspired to: being a good pastor.

Years later, he still suffered from knowing that he had caused hurt in the congregation of Pulaski Heights Christian Church. As the pastor, he said, he should have found a way to avoid rending the church's body. If he could not find a way, he felt, then he should at least have figured out how to reach and touch the disaffected members.

He remembered parts of the Eckford sermon with embarrassment. It had been a mistake to say that the girl had had more guts than anyone in his church; that had been unnecessary goading. He recalled poking fun at Governor Faubus's hill-country pronunciation of the word militia—"milishee." That had been contemptuous. Hearing their pastor preach the truth on the race issue was problem enough for some members. They did not deserve to be hurt gratuitously.

The episode reminded him of his first lesson in pastoring. He had just begun his ministry at the First Christian Church of Lynchburg, Va., in 1950, fresh out of Yale Divinity School. Part of his childhood had been spent at Chattanooga, where his father was pastor of the First Christian Church. But Bert was no Southerner. His father had been a leader in an interracial council at Chattanooga, which had set him and his family apart. Young Bert had been teased by playmates because he didn't know how to treat the family's black maid. Cartwright said, "Being under the authority of black maids and yet their being inferior was a subtlety that I had not been able to capture." Later, at Lynchburg, he landed in a brouhaha that reminded him how far he still lived from his adopted culture.

"There were some ministers that had started a kind of Christian youth movement that was designed to be interracial. They asked me to come in and join the young people. And the next thing I knew, they had made me chairman of the group—the newest minister in town.

"So we planned an interracial service at the church I served on Sunday afternoon. We wanted publicity, and we had a planning session where we asked a local reporter to come, and a photographer. On a Monday morning there was this picture of these black and white youths planning a service in the First Christian Church."

There was immediate consternation. He got phone calls from anxious members, so many that he decided to consult the chairman of the board of church officers. As he stood on the porch ready to ring the doorbell, he overheard the chairman saying to someone on the telephone, "Yes, we're going to have to do something about our preacher." Instead of ringing the bell, he left.

The turmoil continued. Finally, at a board meeting a few days later, a deacon asked what the pastor was up to "with all these niggers."

Cartwright had come prepared. He stepped forward carrying his Bible. He turned on a tape recorder, saying he wanted a record of what was said. Then he explained the purpose of the interracial service and said that if his part in it was not in line with the scriptures, he would be happy to have someone point it out. No one took the Bible to challenge him. The meeting ended quickly.

"I did all the things wrong that a minister can do," he said as he looked back on the episode.

First, he said, he should not have lost his nerve on the chairman's doorstep. It would have been better to get the matter into the open at that point. As for the Bible and the tape recorder, he said, that was an attempt to intimidate the board members. "Some of them were not as facile with the language, so that I think I was really cutting off discussion. I was trying to win my points."

Furthermore, he had fallen into the trap of thinking that a pastor can administer the church as he sees fit. The members, believing that the church belonged to them, thought he should have asked permission to use the sanctuary for an outside group. "That had not occurred to me," he confessed.

Whom does the church belong to?

"The church belongs to the members, to the people, under the authority of Christ," he said. "Not to the pastor. And each minister in various kinds of ways learns it. It may be that he decides to move a communion table six inches to the right, and someone will tell him that that is not his privilege."

Bert Cartwright did not become a minister as an automatic consequence of being a minister's son, although he felt drawn to the church early. At the age of six or seven he got into the habit of slipping into the vestry of the church after services to take a private "communion" because he wanted to be part of that fellowship. But his earliest career aspirations ran toward journalism, an interest he never abandoned. He wrote articles for both religious and secular publications until his retirement and beyond.

Both his parents had family connections with the Disciples of Christ in 19th century Ohio and Iowa. The Disciples have long been known for stubborn adherence to Christ's own principles even when they run athwart other ascendant values such as greed, militarism and racism.

Bert's father, Lin D. Cartwright, was the pastor of a church in Coffeyville, Kan., when Bert was born in 1924. The Ku Klux Klan was strong there, and although the elder Cartwright did not denounce the Klan directly (the head of the local Klavern was a Sunday School teacher in his church, and the class he taught included some of the city's most prominent men), he did denounce the things the Klan stood for. That was a bold move at a time when the Klan controlled the politics of numerous local governments in the Middle West. Dinner conversation at the Cartwright house was lively. It undoubtedly was there that the boy first learned the role of a minister in trying to transform society.

He began to seriously consider the ministry at the beginning of World War II. His older brother and sister had become pacifists. Bert became a conscientious objector. From the hard thinking that required, it was an easy step to the clergy.

In later years he could name a number of other people beyond his family who had influenced him in the clergy. There was an older minister named Joseph Hunter, the founder of Pulaski Heights Christian Church—the man who had stirred up Arkansas chauvinism by going to the aid of interned Japanese-Americans. By the time Bert Cartwright became a pastor at Lynchburg, Hunter had moved there to teach at Lynchburg College. The older man was supportive during Cartwright's problem with the race issue. And he helped in another way.

"We had registration cards in the pews for everybody to register their presence on that Sunday, and they'd just leave them in the pews. And he began a practice of just a brief comment on the sermon on the back of his card every week. So I had a critique of my preaching."

Then there was Richard Niebuhr, his favorite teacher at Yale Divinity School. Professor Niebuhr's brother Reinhold, who taught at Union Theological Seminary in New York, was better known to the public. But the greatest influence on Bert Cartwright's theology was Richard Niebuhr, a seminal thinker, a provocative teacher, and, for the young Disciples minister, a personal icon.

During his own crisis of conscience during the Little Rock desegregation tumult, Cartwright would remember the personal tragedy that his mentor had wrestled with. Professor Niebuhr as a young man had taken a Boy Scout troop on an outing and a boy had drowned. Niebuhr had collapsed into mental illness, survived, and come back with a firm religious faith and a strengthened theology.

From Niebuhr, the young minister learned the role of good in order: "That what is, is good in the sense of what has been created is good, and that if there is any order in any system or in life, there is that of good that holds it together and makes it cohere. The absence of good is chaos. So that anything short of chaos is held together by some aspect of good." He also had many occasions to remember Niebuhr's teaching that a person had no right to criticize until he understood what the other person was affirming and trying to communicate.

One thing that he came to appreciate from his Little Rock and Lynchburg experiences was another lesson from Professor Niebuhr: that the church must not be captive to culture, but instead must work to transform culture while it transforms and converts human beings. Bert Cartwright deliberately regarded himself as a stranger each time he moved to a new pastorate.

One advantage in being an outsider was the fresh eye. He was able to look and analyze "and see what is the truth and what is God's and what is to be changed."

Another advantage in remaining a little apart from the culture he lived in was that he was not tempted to court popularity. He felt no need to curry favor with his neighbors. He was often out of step with fellow ministers. Sometimes another clergyman would say, "I can understand glimpses of what you're talking about, Bert. But you don't have a sense of belonging the way I have."

The constant outsider had his problems. "I had to run and falter with the different cultures, not understanding, doing the crazy thing."

He remembered his first mistake after taking the pastorate of the Central Christian Church in Youngstown, Ohio, in

1964. "I went to Youngstown and bought a Volkswagen. You don't do that in Youngstown. It is a steel town."

Through his outsider's eyes, he discovered, earlier than many other observers, that certain evils seemed to be universal in the American culture. Having survived and grappled with the racism of Little Rock, he had looked forward to a respite in Ohio. He was not especially surprised to learn that Youngstown had a strong Mafia. What startled him was that it also had as virulent a strain of racism as any he had seen in the South. The town had once been a Ku Klux Klan stronghold.

His frail body shuddered as he sat in his Fort Worth home 22 years later and recalled something that had happened in Youngstown on April 4, 1968, the day Martin Luther King was assassinated. He had been in the church that evening while the choir was practicing. Someone phoned to tell him the news. He was stunned.

"When the choir came out, there was one of the younger men in the church that I felt drawn to. And I said, 'You know, I just heard that Martin Luther King was shot.' He said, 'Good! Hey, that's great!'"

That turned out to be, if not the dominant sentiment in the congregation, at least an undercurrent. A number of parishioners objected to Cartwright's preaching "sociology." One couple in the choir made a point of leaving conspicuously every Sunday just before the sermon. Suddenly, Bert Cartwright felt more comfortable with the South he had left, where the racism was not concealed.

Coming to terms with racism was part of Cartwright's life-long struggle to maintain his faith. That faith had been challenged severely in 1957 at Little Rock when he had seen the face of evil. He suffered the same crisis of faith in 1957 that others suffered in 1968 when Martin Luther King and Robert Kennedy were assassinated and riots erupted "and it looked like evil was winning and the civil rights movement was going down the tubes."

There were long periods when he had to fall back on another lesson from Yale: that there is a kind of shape to what the church teaches, and that Bert Cartwright's understanding of a particular piece of Biblical doctrine was less important than the whole of the church's traditional teaching. "On a specific Sunday, I was preaching a faith that I hoped that I could take hold of in some aspects."

One consequence of his continuing struggle with faith was a slowly dawning awareness that there was more evil in the world than he had known, and that not all of it would be neatly cleared up through the efforts of well-intentioned people. He told an interviewer in 1963, "I tend toward despair of the church, despair of white persons generally having any effect in the area of racial change. There's a growing sense in me of the irrelevance of what I tend to do."

Coupled with his personal pessimism was a growing pessimism about the role of the church and the ministry in bringing about social change. He saw God more at work in the world and less at work in the church. That was a little shocking to him. He had always believed that Christian ministers should be effective. Then he saw that that was not always possible.

"And so then I began to say that we need to begin to be faithful and—a pathetic way of expressing it—then leave it up to God to see what God makes of it. My whole self-understanding of the church and the world and God was shaken. I don't think I got to the point of no hope, but diminished expectations."

He acknowledged his own sinfulness. "We all fall short before God. Kierkegaard, I think, said there is comfort in knowing that before God we are always wrong."

He never gave up what he called the hard teachings of the church: turning the other cheek, giving to the poor, the social gospel. "But then when I saw the depths of evil and my world falling apart, I began to see that I needed to depend more fully upon God's love and grace and acceptance."

One thing that slightly annoyed him about being a hero of the civil rights movement was the presumption that he spent all his days fighting for racial justice. The truth was that he spent most of his days visiting the sick, counseling people with problems, writing and preaching sermons, encouraging faith, caring for the flock—trying to be a good pastor. On the same day that he went to Central High and saw the mob assail Elizabeth Eckford, he went to the hospital and visited sick members of his congregation.

Jean Woolfolk was a leading member of Pulaski Heights Christian Church during Cartwright's 10-year tenure. She recalled a pastoral visit that he made to her home. Woolfolk's sister Mary had just received a letter from her husband of 28 years saying he had met another woman in a distant state and he wanted a divorce. The distraught sister showed the letter to the pastor.

"Bert read the letter. He handed it back to her, and then he took her hand. He just sat there. He didn't say a word, but after a while tears ran down his face. Finally, he said, 'Mary, I know I ought to say something, but I don't know what to say.' And Mary said, 'Bert, you've already told me all I need to know.' That was all the counseling she needed. That was the finest piece of pastoring I've ever seen."

A number of young ministers through the years have been influenced by Cartwright. One of them, the Rev. Robin Hoover of Fort Worth, recalled being impressed that Cartwright had once gone to bankruptcy court with a family in his church. The pastor thought they needed his support. Hoover said that Cartwright was the kind of minister who could counsel a divorcing couple and remain friends with both.

Another Fort Worth minister, the Rev. Jane McDonald, who entered the ministry at mid-life under Cartwright's tutelage, recalled that when he went to a hospital to visit a parishioner who was going into surgery, he would stay until the surgery was finished—five hours, if necessary. Some ministers would have considered their duty fulfilled by a brief visit before or after. On the day I saw McDonald, she interrupted a hospital visit with a parishioner for our interview. She spent an hour with me, distracted and apologetic, then hurried back to the sick parishioner.

These seemingly simple pastoral duties could take unexpected turns for Cartwright. He was visiting one of his members in the hospital one day when he learned that another member was also there. Unfortunately, the second member had been angry with the pastor for months and had stopped going to church. She had resisted all his attempts at reconciliation.

In his 1987 book *People of the Chalice: Disciples of Christ in Faith and Practice*, he told what happened:

"I told myself that the way she felt about me she certainly did not want to see me. I might even make her more ill. But an inner voice would not leave me alone. I was her pastor. As a pastor I was Christ's representative. I had to go.

"I entered her room and found she was undergoing tests for cancer. She was frightened and poured out her anxieties. Then, unexpectedly, she paused, reached out her hand and said: 'I love you. I'm glad you came.' Her tests proved to be negative. Within a few months her husband died suddenly of a heart attack and I was able to continue Christ's ministry with her.

"I recall this incident in particular when I hear seminary students asserting that ministers should never do anything unless they really feel like it."

The hard choices are not always so serious. Once his board of elders met and agreed that the pastor, not they, should handle the problem of a noisy youngster who had disrupted services several weeks in a row. The boy most recently had leaned out a sanctuary window during the sermon, aimed his cap pistol, and cried "Pow! Pow!" Cartwright got up his nerve to visit the boy's mother. To his surprise, she was also at her wit's end and pleaded for the pastor's advice. He dropped a few hints on childrearing, then suggested that the boy leave the cap pistol at home. The mother was grateful.

His counseling was not always so satisfying. In Youngstown, he spent years dealing with an alcoholic drug addict. She phoned one day with a plea to come at once, that she needed medical attention and her physician would not help. Cartwright phoned the physician and was told, "I have given up on her, and you should, too." He replied, "As a minister, I don't have that choice." He took the woman to a mental hospital and she was treated for delirium tremens. As soon as possible, she checked herself out and continued her addiction. "And I continued to minister to her as best I could."

Cartwright came to understand early that being a good pastor meant more than visiting the sick and counseling the troubled. He encouraged a group of women in the Youngstown Central Christian Church to help children in a nearby school learn to read. One afternoon a week, the women paired off with children who had reading difficulties and coached them. "There was probably as much transformation of the women as there was the children," he said.

He was always nagged by the theological question of what a minister should do about the evils of society beyond the walls of the church. He concluded early that God is in history, that is, that He is involved in the world as well as in the church. It was a happenstance of history that the great evil in America during Cartwright's early ministry was racism. He told a group of churchmen in Little Rock in 1965, on a visit after he had moved to Youngstown, "God is in the midst of all this racial ferment working out his purposes. He is at work in your community and in mine, seeking to redeem and transform, through judgment and grace, our race relations."

He asked the ministers to consider the role of the pastor in changing communities. It is not enough, he said, to take the pietistic view that a clergyman should confine himself to curing the sinsick soul. He noted that converted sinners did not automatically become good citizens, as witness the masses of converts in the Southern Bible Belt who had made no significant contribution to racial justice. The pastor should preach on race, he said. Sermons should show how God tries to integrate and reconcile people. Outside the church, the responsible pastor should serve as a public witness not just for the moral point of view, but for God's justice. He noted that during a recent civil rights demonstration at Youngstown, he had assumed the role of public witness in a speech on the courthouse steps.

His listeners in Little Rock were not surprised. Many remembered that at Pulaski Heights Christian, he had encouraged the congregation to reach beyond the church walls during the school crisis of 1957. When a segregationist-controlled school board fired more than 40 teachers for their suspected integrationist sympathies, dozens of members of Pulaski Heights Christian turned out for a protest rally. Cartwright did not pretend that he had led the parishioners to the rally. But he pointedly had prepared them for what he saw as this work of ministry. Preparing and equipping a congregation to do God's work is part of a pastor's job, he said.

Just how does a pastor go about this preparation? At Little Rock, he had begun the process within weeks after the eruption of the political crisis, as soon as it became obvious that the community was being seriously divided and damaged. What he did looks almost too simple with more than 30 years of hindsight. But in the fall of 1957, any move could have made matters worse. With considerable courage, Cartwright approached a handful of members with a suggestion: "We should get together and talk about our racial problems in Little Rock."

He and the small group set up an eight-week series of Sunday evening "conversations." Those who were interested could come; the rest could stay away.

"We had about 30 persons show up the first night, and we just began listing the questions that each had in mind. There were plenty. Then we began to think how we might best gain the answers. It became clear that answers could only be found by a joint search with some Negroes in the community. So, not sure just what the effects might be, we invited several Negroes to meet with us in our conversations.

"Attendance grew as our white members were for the first time in their lives afforded an opportunity to talk openly and honestly with Negroes. Everyone learned from the experience, but particularly significant was the fact that some cautious members of the congregation attended, and for the first time had their eyes opened to the real issues in the community, and in a Christian perspective."

But talk was not always enough. At Youngstown, the tough steel town where the racism was less acknowledged, he found that government pressure was sometimes necessary. During his six years there, he served on various public bodies aimed at improving conditions for blacks. As part of one inter-racial group, he once spent two fruitless hours listening to the administrators of four hospitals argue that their institutions were not discriminating against blacks, even though they clearly were in violation of the 1964 Civil Rights Act. The only solution was to enlist the help of the federal government to enforce the law. Sometimes, he said, a good pastor may have to call in the feds.

Bert Cartwright was always a reluctant leader. Members of the congregations that he served remembered afterward that his influence had come not from putting himself into the limelight but rather from overcoming his shyness Sunday after

Sunday so that he could stand in the pulpit and preach what he thought was right.

Forrest Rozzell, another longtime member of Pulaski Heights Christian, recalled Mr. Cartwright's quiet insistence. He said the pastor took the view that the members could agree or disagree with his sermons, "but this is what I believe and the way I'm going to act." As a consequence, some listeners left, but others stayed and felt strengthened in their faith. Rozzell was one of the latter. He recalled a time when an anonymous donor provided stained glass windows for the church in appreciation for the pastor's stand on civil rights. Rozzell, while grateful for the splendid windows, was mildly indignant.

"It was puzzling to me that anybody would be surprised that Bert would defend any issue on the basis of what is morally right," he said years later. "My reaction was, 'Well, what did they expect of our minister?'"

Rozzell at that time was executive secretary of the Arkansas Education Association. He was active in state politics. One Sunday after church, he approached Cartwright and told him that he for one wanted the pastor to go on preaching the hard unadulterated truth without compromise. He told the minister that he did not want to attend a church where all the time was spent trying to rationalize or weigh the complications of being a Christian. He said he was too good at rationalizing and compromising in his everyday work, and that on Sunday he wanted his Christianity served up straight.

Evidently, Rozzell was not alone in that sentiment. Cartwright continued to serve it up straight, not only in Little Rock but also in Youngstown and Fort Worth.

As the race issue subsided, the problems of women as ordained ministers began to emerge across the United States. Cartwright had gone to classes with women at Yale Divinity School and he knew what they faced in male-dominated congregations. Within a year after moving to Fort Worth, he was teaching field education courses that included women preparing for the ministry. He encouraged the congregation at South Hills Christian Church to include women as elders, and under his pastorate the church hired a woman student as youth minister. Later, after he became area minister of the Trinity-Brazos Area in 1979, overseeing the common programs and denominational interests of 57 congregations, he made it his policy to supply the names of women along with men to congregations searching for new pastors.

Nevertheless, he encountered criticism from some women. Much of it centered around the traditionally male-oriented language of the Bible. Some felt that passages of Scripture with sexist language should be rewritten for public reading; he felt inadequate to the task. A continuing disagreement between him and some women ministers was over his use of the traditional "Father, Son and Holy Spirit" in referring to the trinity. For one reason or another, some women who had suffered from sexist discrimination saw Cartwright as not sufficiently sensitive to women's issues. A group at South Hills confronted him every Sunday for a period to make clear their displeasure with the sexist aspects of the service, and these women once threatened to walk out in mid-service. Mostly, though, the disagreement was pursued with good humor. "Through their persistence," he recalled years later, "I was to some degree educated, and changed my language and to some degree my style."

Then, one disturbing day, changing his style was not enough. The case of the Rev. Lucy Huff turned him abruptly into an activist.

"I don't think he realized what we are up against until he began to support Lucy Huff in her call to St. Andrew's," McDonald of Fort Worth's First Christian Church said.

Lucy Huff had been married to a physician in Wichita Falls. They had five children. When she and her husband were divorced during the early 1980s, Huff decided to become a minister of the Disciples of Christ. For five strenuous years, she commuted more than 100 miles a day to Fort Worth to study theology and to learn how to be a minister. Finally she was ready for her first pastorate. She and the chosen congregation seemed made for each other.

St. Andrew's was not yet officially recognized as a church. It was a nucleus of a congregation, a group of interested people intent on forming a new church in Arlington, midway between Fort Worth and Dallas. Cartwright, as Area Minister, had led a group of ministers and lay people in studying the demographics of the area and in selecting a site. A retired minister was asked to gather the nucleus of the congregation and begin or-

ganizing the new church. He did a good job, and the congrega-
tion-to-be was ready to call its first full-time minister, a pastor-
developer. A man was contacted, but he turned down the job.
The search committee then turned to affable, outgoing Lucy
Huff.

The first sign of trouble came from the retired man who
had done the basic organizing. It was clear that he was
unhappy at the prospect of having this, perhaps his last project
as a minister, taken over by a woman. He reluctantly went
along with making the committee's call unanimous. But the
next day a telephone campaign suddenly erupted against Huff.
Cartwright, recalling the event, was not sure of the source, but
he suspected that it sprang from people close to the retired
minister.

"There were some very heated moments, some very
embarrassing moments. There was a split, and it looked like
the whole proposition was falling apart."

Cartwright and others tried to build a compromise. The
protesting minister first agreed, then backed off and attacked
Huff's qualifications. He requested another interview with
Huff, and the questions he put to her were described as brutal
and personal.

"It was a very traumatic experience for her," Cartwright
said. "She was directly, personally attacked, even down to her
morality—vicious things. She at one point was about to back
out, and I talked with her, assured her full support if she would
take it. And I told her frankly that it was not just a matter of
supporting women in the ministry, but that I thought the whole
project depended on her, and if she didn't take it the whole
thing would fall apart."

It was then that the canny political instincts of the Area
Minister came into play. The organizing committee went to
him and asked, "What should we do?" Dissolve the nucleus and
start over, he advised.

That seemed draconian. The committee members were
stunned. Nevertheless, they followed his advice. Cartwright
called a meeting of the Trinity-Brazos Area Board and tossed
the issue to it. In retrospect, it is clear that he knew what
would happen, although Lucy Huff and her friends were far
from confident of the outcome. As Cartwright had guessed, the

board voted at once to appoint a pastor-developer to try again at St. Andrew's, and tapped Huff for the job.

She moved to St. Andrew's, picked up the pieces, and never looked back. Three years later the congregation was thriving. She gave Bert Cartwright much credit. His support had been unwavering, she said, not just during the agonizing dispute but later as she organized the new congregation. She met with him at least once a week for advice during that period, and repeatedly she was struck by the creativity of his mind. She also came to appreciate his political savvy.

"You wouldn't know it to look at him," she said. "He'll sit in a meeting and ask questions that sound like he's not understood a thing. Then he will finally begin to comment, and whoa! This man's a fox!"

Cartwright retired in 1989. He might have stayed on longer as Area Minister, but he began to tire of the travel and of being in a different church every Sunday. He and his wife Anne have five children, and most have settled in the Fort Worth area. He wanted to spend more time with his grandchildren. He was also tiring of being a perpetual outsider. "I felt myself yearning for a church home," he said.

His friends remarked on the continuing agility of his mind. He learned to operate a computer. He maintained his long interest in such organizations as the Texas Conference of Churches, the National and World Councils of Churches, the Consultation of Church Union, and the Disciples' Division of Overseas Ministries. The last had once taken him to Zaire.

He also continued to write. For the first time, he could freely indulge a scholarly interest that some of his friends considered bizarre. He had been collecting the lore and songs of Bob Dylan since the 1960s. He had corresponded with other Dylan scholars around the world. He had once written a monograph on biblical references in Dylan's lyrics. By the time of his retirement, he confessed, he had become a full-fledged Dylanologist. With his usual modesty, he said it would be extravagant to call him an authority.

Some friends, mistakenly assuming that he looked at Dylan through the eyes of a minister, continued to ask him how he could condone Dylan's lifestyle, his early use of narcotics, etc. He tried to explain that he studied Dylan as other scholars studied Byron or Keats.

"In terms of literary interest, I do not concern myself with making judgments about his personal life. It is a matter of indifference to me whether or not he is a Christian. It is a matter of indifference to me whether or not I agree with him in his lyrics. He is not a hero to me; he is not a role model. I do not worry about the goodness or badness of rock and roll. It is all a matter of interest in the 'is-ness' of Bob Dylan."

He also thought it was time to go public with a secret in his past. He confessed that when Texas Christian University gave him an honorary Doctor of Divinity degree in 1976, he wore a Dylan T-shirt under his robe during the ceremony. Just to remind himself that while he appreciated the honor, he should not take it too seriously.

Jane Shields

Tending the Garden of Souls

by Kenneth A. Briggs

*"Rejoice in your hope, be patient in tribulation,
be constant in prayer. Contribute to the needs of
the saints, practice hospitality."*
—Romans 12:12

Autumn Brady, barely six months old, was a picture of vitality, her eyes sparkling, her hands waving gleefully, revealing no hint of the critical heart condition that would require surgery again in just a few days. On this bright Sunday morning, in the sanctuary of Hope Lutheran Church, she was on her way to a happier appointment, arrayed in a pure white christening dress for her initiation into the church.

In the midst of the worship service, Autumn was carried forward to the uncovered baptismal font at the foot of the altar by her father, Scott, in the company of her mother, Tammy, and Tammy's parents, the infant's Christian sponsors. Awaiting them with a glowing smile and a quiet greeting was the church's pastor, the Rev. Jane Shields. She began the sacramental rite. At its high point, she expertly cradled the baby in one arm, using her free hand to gather water to pour gently over the top of the child's head, from forehead to crown. She did so once for each member of the Holy Trinity—Father, Son and Holy Spirit.

Propping Autumn up for the whole congregation to see, Pastor Shields proclaimed with delight, "This is our newest little sister, a new little being, a new little Christian." She talked about their new sister's health problems and the need for a second operation to correct a congenital defect. "This is Autumn," she said, "for whom we will pray each day." To complete the welcome, she paraded the baby up one of the church's main aisles and down the other.

Autumn's parents, both reared as Lutherans, were not members of the church, though Tammy had attended services and found the congregation warm and friendly. The Bradys had moved from Cleveland to the vicinity of the church in New Castle, Del., a bedroom community just south of Wilmington. Faced with their baby's second heart operation, the couple approached Shields about conducting the baptism. As was her custom, she scheduled time with them to review the meaning of the sacrament and to get to know the couple. Shields asked further about the baby's health and assured the Bradys that they could count on the church to help them through the ordeal which lay ahead. She made the pledge firmly and with calm assurance. By the end of the meeting, Scott and Tammy were talking about making Hope their church home.

Such attention to people—their talents, thoughts, concerns and needs—is a hallmark of Pastor Shields' ministry. Her example of personal care has become the model for transforming Hope from the bitterly-divided church at which she arrived in 1979 to the vibrant, growing congregation of 600 members, half of whom were born Lutheran, a fourth former Roman Catholics who had become Lutherans through intermarriage, mirroring a national pattern. It is a lively congregation whose enthusiasm about the future translated into a successful $300,000 building and improvements campaign.

That personal touch, without which such a turnabout would have been unthinkable, coexists with a cluster of other qualities which have well served Pastor Shields in this congregation of suburbanites, whose values she exemplifies. In sum, she knows how to manage a church. Efficient, well organized and hard working, she draws people in and involves them with each other as friends and fellow Christians with a shared mission. Hope has the feel of a church with its house in order and on the move. Pastor Shields has knit the congregation into a community of souls who attend to one another's joys and sorrows.

It was with confidence, then, that Pastor Shields could promise Tammy and Scott Brady the support of the church during the trial they were soon to face. Hope had a track record of delivering on such pledges. Dozens of people from a 10-mile radius had discovered this, drawn by the church's reputation for warmth and support, eager to join others with whom they could share both their faith and their everyday cares. In an area without a town center, Hope became a hub, a point of focus and collective identity. From this mix had emerged what Shields referred to as a congregation with a "thirtysomething" character where, as in the television series from which the description was taken, the dilemmas of young professionals balancing home, job and parenthood begged attention.

Coincidentally, the congregation had also entered its 30s, having been founded in 1958 with a handful of people as a mission parish, so, as Pastor Shields explained, the church was going through comparable struggles in its development. At this juncture, Hope was very much a family, open and nurturing to newcomers, dedicated to looking out for those who came into the fold. The rolls were replete with members who had ventured in and stayed, as the Bradys appeared ready to do.

The church itself is a modest building on a nondescript stretch of Highway 273 from New Castle to Newark. The exterior of the church is done in opaque cedarboard. A steel girder running up the front forms the vertical beam of a simple cross. Inside, the cozy sanctuary, with a choir loft to the rear, relies mostly on artificial light. Moveable interlocking chairs allow flexibility. The dominant feature is a vivid painting of the Last Supper done by an artist from the congregation. The painting takes up most of the wall to the congregation's right. Straight ahead, hanging over the altar, was a wooden cross bearing a carved, stylized Jesus. The remainder of the facility consists mostly of a wing housing church offices and a string of classrooms which, during the week, become a full-time child-care center. The building is pleasant and well kept with a pre-fab look that resembles the housing tracts surrounding it.

Shields' age and her multiple involvements with career, family and home place her squarely within the demographic mainstream of her congregants. Like many of them, she is a suburban professional in her early 40s, married with children.

Her husband Tom, a tall, dark, unassuming man with a laid-back disposition, works for an oil refinery. The two met during their undergraduate days at Elizabethtown College, a Church of the Brethren school in Pennsylvania. They have two grade-school age daughters, Caitlin and Meghan, and live in a home built for them in a wooded subdivision nine miles from the church. On most days, she commutes to her job in the couple's red Volvo station wagon and Tom takes the van. The couple share the housework and childrearing as best they can.

Like most of their neighbors, they are kept in constant motion by a ceaseless schedule of dental appointments, school activities, Little League and church events. The calendar is always cluttered, leaving too little time for leisure. Pastor Shields counters these endless demands with discipline. Beginning with prayer first thing in the morning, she sees the children off to school, spends the day in church-related rounds and, if possible, returns about 4:30 in the afternoon, along with Tom, to welcome home the girls and to prepare dinner. Most weekday nights find her back at the church for meetings and appointments, but unless there is some emergency, she takes off half of Saturday and all of Monday for family time and personal renewal.

"Basically I'm a very spontaneous person," she explained one morning as light flooded into her church office through a tall window. It was an unexpected revelation in light of her carefully plotted schedule. "I like surprises—it helps to be that way in the ministry. But in order to continue to be healthy and spontaneous, I have to lead a fairly structured life-style. The ministry is a very hard job. I enjoy it and have lots of fun but it is difficult: demanding and challenging at the same time. I need my mental health." Physical fitness has its place, too. Late in the evening, after returning from her duties and/or helping put the children to bed, Shields pedaled an exercise bike before saying her day's-end prayers. The art of managing herself and the church intrigued her and called forth her creative energies. "I'm a person who actually likes change," she exulted. "It's so much part of the Gospel which is asking us to change constantly. To grow means being open to change."

On a cool spring evening in her home, Shields was talking excitedly about an idea for revamping the basic way the church went about its business. As she spoke, she made salad and kept track of lasagna warming in the oven while Meghan sat quietly at her place at the table. The innovation she had in mind would in her view combat inefficiency by changing the way the church handled its affairs.

"One of the frustrations I live with," she said, "is that I lean toward the visionary side, generating lots of ideas and liking to focus on them. But energizing others to work on them is something else again. How wonderful it must be to be a business executive with all these paid people whose job it is to put an idea or program into practice. There's no reason the church shouldn't have the same resources. In fact we do have these resources with a different motivation—the love of Christ—but the church hasn't begun to tap them like business has." Under her scheme for reform, committees would not be expected to do both the dreaming and the implementing. "You could put two or three visionaries together in charge of an area of ministry," she said. "They'd meet maybe four times a year to pump out ideas. Then you'd have all the tasks assigned to individuals who are the practical doers."

Such imaginative flights into church management schemes, she stressed, made sense only within the larger quest for spiritual guidance and sustenance. Without prayer, visions of smoother organization and all the rest of her pastorate at Hope would be merely going through the motions. Her spiritual nourishment includes talking about her faith—and her doubts—with friends in the clergy and older women in her congregation who have become spiritual confidantes. "I get spiritual strength from these women saints," she said. "They are there for me." In addition to asking God's help for those in special need, she continually goes down through the church roster, starting with the A's, praying for ten or so members each day. It signifies the mutual dependence she feels. "I wouldn't be the pastor I am without the love, prayers and support of my parish," she said. Among the needs she feels most acutely is more space in her week for worship and private spiritual exercises.

Keeping life in balance became more difficult as the church grew and her talents led her to assume wider responsibilities. Shields was elected dean of her conference within the Maryland-Delaware Synod of the Evangelical Lutheran Church in America. It was largely an honorary, ceremonial position which, nonetheless, required significant time and attention. Gettysburg Seminary enlisted her for its board of directors.

She also enrolled in a Doctor of Ministry degree program at Drew University. That meant making time for reading assignments, for trips to the Drew campus in Madison, N.J., and elsewhere to attend concentrated classroom sessions, and for a research thesis. Her topic, "The Pastor as Teacher," explored, as she defined it, "how a pastor's teaching leads other people to understand their ministry of teaching—teaching each other and leading others to take on their own teaching roles." The theme was integral to her basic concept of ministry as a partnership. "I'm a real team player," she said. "I see the ministry as being faithful to the Gospel and that means celebrating other peoples' gifts."

In taking on these new challenges, Shields felt something had to give. So for a period of time, at least, she has relinquished her function as a supervisor to seminarians. Lutheran preparation for the ministry typically includes a year away from the seminary at work full time in a church. Over the seven years that Hope hosted students, the church had become a highly coveted internship, due in large part to Shields' quality of supervision.

Jane O'Hara Shields (O'Hara is her father's surname which she uses proudly to affirm her Irish heritage—her two daughters bear the same middle name) is a trim woman of medium height and brown curly hair with an auburn tint that wreathes an angular-shaped face. Bright green eyes and a broad winsome smile convey exuberance, energy and intelligence. She moves with an understated confidence and an air of ease, two traits that contribute to her ability to remain serene in the midst of inevitable church debates. In her many expressions, both faith and kinship shine through as constants. "She has great inner strength wrapped in a feminine aura," noted Herman G. Stuempfle, Jr., a retired professor at Gettysburg Seminary who served as dean when Jane Shields was a student. "Some people may at first want to reach out to protect her, but they find out right away that she doesn't need it. She has a steely inner fiber."

She describes her childhood as happy and secure. Each work day her father trekked into Manhattan to an upwardly mobile series of jobs at the Federal Reserve. James O'Hara, a disaffected Catholic, encouraged his two daughters to be involved in their mother's Lutheran church, St. Peter's, in Plainfield, N.J. Corinne O'Hara, a Sears employee for many years, was active in the congregation, eventually becoming the first woman elected to the St. Peter's council. Both parents, now retired in New Hampshire, instilled in Jane a deep capacity for joy and celebration of life which she has carried into her ministry. "I love a party," she said with droll resolve. "Our family back then had lots of them."

Jane Shields' desire to become a Lutheran minister was rooted in early childhood. Asked what her ambition was, she would reply flat out, "I want to be a pastor." She had an early role model in the person of the Rev. J. Edward Gonzalez of her own St. Peter's. But reality posed a roadblock. At that point Lutherans, like other mainline denominations, were not ordaining women. By the time that barrier was removed in 1970, during her junior year in college, Shields had put her ministerial goals in abeyance and set her sights on being a school teacher. During a year of teaching fifth grade in New Jersey, however, she felt that call once more, visited Gettysburg and found that "it was a home for me that had been a lifetime in the making." When she broke the news to Tom, whom she planned to marry that summer, he exclaimed with glee, "What took you so long?" Tom saw her as ideally suited to that calling, self-confident and exceptionally organized. "Jane," he says admiringly, "is a natural pastor." With that momentum, she entered seminary with the second class that included women preparing for ordination. That class included two other women, besides herself.

Looking back, Shields expresses surprise that the prohibition against ordaining women didn't seriously trouble her. She reasons that her plentiful supply of native optimism turned aside any tendency toward cynicism and bitterness (given this disposition, she believed there was something providential about being called to be pastor of a church named Hope). "I was disappointed somewhat," she said, "but I was prepared to substitute teach. It didn't make me draw back from the church. I've always lived with the sense of, 'Well now, what's next? There

must be a way to serve as a child of God one way or another.'
There's nothing wrong with being a baptized lay person."

Shields' place in the vanguard of Lutheran women clergy
has inevitably imbued her ministry with issues of feminism. On
these matters she has, in the view of other pastors and church
members, steered a deft course, acknowledging problems in a
comfortable, non-threatening kind of way, pressing certain ones
discreetly. Remembering her own exclusion from many areas of
church life reserved for men, for example, she made sure that
Hope opened all roles to males and females. She recalled vividly
the exclusion to which she was subjected and rejoiced that she
oversaw a church in which her daughters enjoyed full benefits
of being acolytes or crucifers or anything else along the way.

The fact that she took on a church of her own just two
years out of seminary boosted Shields' standing among rank-
and-file pastors, according to her former bishop, Maurice
Zumbrun. He praised her as bright and caring, noting that she
was both biblically and theologically sound. He said Shields
helped the cause of women clergy throughout the Synod.
"Generally, clergy have high regard for women who become parish pastors," Bishop Zumbrun said. "Jane came along and went
immediately into the parish ministry instead of becoming a
chaplain or other kind of specialist. As soon as one person gets
respect, the fears and anxieties of many people [about women in
pastoral situations] are reduced. She's one pastor I never worried about."

For Shields, a more intriguing question is how being a
woman affects her style of ministry. She has gone round and
round trying to analyze her own behavior without reaching
solid conclusions. "I am who I am and what I am is a woman,"
she said. "And that's important because I bring with me some of
those things unique to women and we celebrate that. For years
I have given thought to the question—am I doing this because
I'm a woman?—and I finally came to the point where I know it's
all part of who I am—including my sensitivity to not oppressing
others and looking at every person as equal in God's eyes and
my listening skills, and my being taught to listen to the pain
and hurt of others without judging them too quickly—those
things are important to me no matter where they come from."

More evident is the impact Shields has had on women in the parish. She has drawn some women to the church and, during her tenure, women have assumed leadership posts. Hope's council was two-thirds female, whereas her mother had been a minority of one on the council of St. Peter's. Janice Reissig, the council president, testifies to Shields' influence. As a single woman in her early 30s, she considered herself an unlikely candidate for such a church post. "I'm not the kind of person churches usually choose to head the council," said Reissig, who holds a middle-management position at Du Pont, the chemical giant that is the leading employer of Hope's members. "It's usually someone at least 10 years older than I am, married with kids. I must have come off as being a little flaky, but God told me to say yes when I was told that I'd been selected. I thought, well, the same God that's smart enough to get me to say yes is going to show me how to do it.

"I look at Jane as a pastor friend I can talk to. She's a strong force in our congregation and a major factor why I'm active. She made me realize I could play a stronger role, that I can't just sit passively by. She has such a can-do attitude toward the ministry and Hope. You can tell she really cares about you. I don't know how she does it for the whole congregation, but she does."

Shields' own blending of her public and private selves, as well as her combining of ministry, marriage and motherhood, has struck both women and men at Hope as instructive and refreshing. To the Rev. Sue Luttner, a pastor in north Pittsburgh, who interned at Hope during her seminary days, the lesson from her mentor was a godsend. "She had a good sense of humor and was daring enough to try anything," Pastor Luttner recalled. "She was in her 30s when she got braces on her teeth for a while. She wore dangly earrings. She didn't hide behind her collar but was who she was. Some women in the ministry think they need to be men—with dark clothes, no make-up and short hair, but not Jane. She could be a woman and pastor."

Depending on the occasion, Hope's pastor turns up in a blouse, skirt and clerical collar or in jeans and a T-shirt. "Over the years, I've become much more relaxed about dress," she said. "There's an art to knowing what's appropriate. I would never mix clerical wear with casual dress, never, say, a clerical blouse with jeans." On the informal side, her tastes run to bright colors and motifs of birds, butterflies and fish—playfully funky. Whatever the mode, meticulous planning is evident down to the shade of eyeglass frames. For a counseling session with a couple she has come to know well, she arrived in casual wear, accented by earrings with brilliantly painted tropical birds and a pair of green-framed glasses. The next day, for a meeting with church officials, her more subdued attire included clerical collar and a glasses frame of less conspicuous purple. "I like life, I like color," she said, sitting in her gaily decorated office highlighted by butterfly patterns on a throw rug and cut-glass window hangings. "At the church we had a costume party once where I asked people to come as a religious character. I was greeted at the door by my friend Kathy in a curly-hair wig and a big butterfly on her chest. It was me, of course."

Her example as a clergywoman inspiring other women to utilize their gifts has also had a profound influence. The experience of stretching themselves in challenging situations within the church has spurred some women at Hope to apply their new talents in the job market. The pastor's own story stands as a witness to what women and men can accomplish by investing their talents in vocations that they love.

Peg Legutko was one woman for whom the church became a place of self-discovery. She began as church secretary and eventually became secretary/treasurer of the child-care center. "The pastor exposed me to these new areas and encouraged me to be a leader in roles I wouldn't have put myself into," she said. "I then moved on to a job as a buyer at Du Pont," she said, "using those skills I learned here." Barbara Wasserman, a music teacher, added her tribute to the pastor: "She's provided an excellent role model that says the sky's the limit for what you can be. I've seen many of the girls here really blossom."

If Shields has had a disproportionate influence on females, it was not, she said, by conscious design. Her philosophy of ministry centers on the sacredness of all people and the need to foster their gifts within an egalitarian church. Those who had observed her closely applauded her expertise in orchestrating this design in a congregation of diverse and sometimes clashing interests. What made it work was her adroitness as a talent scout. The Rev. Mark Russell spent his intern year at Hope and is now a pastor in Nescopeck, Pa. "One of the things she does extremely well is finding where people fit in and finding a place for them," he said. "She leads without shoving things down peoples' throats. In fact, she makes people think something is their idea, not hers. The whole congregation feels they can jump in and work. She holds power appropriately, not as something to be guarded or be threatened by. She has power because she earns it and deserves it."

Shields has also been innovative and whimsical. Once, in place of the traditional sermon, she and another woman did a take-off on the film, *My Dinner With Andre*, talking to each other ultimately about the Holy Spirit during a simulated meal at the "Good News Cafe," with the congregation encircling the table. On one Christmas eve, she dressed as an angel to greet people at the door of the church. Her ingenuity was put to the test in grimmer situations, too. When she first arrived at Hope, for example, the congregation was badly split and weakened from years of in-house strife. What should she do to help heal the rift and restore unity? Her announced answer was that everyone would be given an opportunity to air feelings about the conflict during her first round of pastoral visits to their homes but that parishioners would not raise the subject with her after that.

She expected the aftermath of the turmoil to last a year or two. It took five years to dissipate. "I learned how devastating a conflict can be, how hard it is to rebuild trust levels. I had to love the people, show them I cared, lighten things up with humor to help them see that worship has a fun side, model an openness to hearing them. It was also important for me to commit myself to stay with them seven to 10 years so they'd know I'd really come to stay with them."

Her willingness to let differences be voiced contributes to an unusually open climate within the congregation. The openness is coupled with the allowance Shields makes for mistakes by those who tried new things. "Jane's an ambassador," said Barbara Wasserman. "She works well with people who don't agree, showing us that with dialogue we can work it out. Likewise, she sometimes throws out ideas and we know we don't have to accept them."

Ben Ehrets, who was the last student intern at Hope, arrived in September of 1990 very uncertain whether parish ministry was the calling for which he was suited. His work with Pastor Shields convinced him that it was. Among the traits he most admired about her was her ability to sustain a free-flowing forum on church issues. "She lets people know they can say anything," he said. "Dissent and conflict are things they can talk about. Things don't build up. There is always a release." During his time there, for instance, there was discord over the worthiness of some items that were to be acquired in the capital improvement drive. Most of the controversy focused on the proposal to install a $150,000 pipe organ. There was open debate on the proposal. When someone came to Shields with a gripe, she typically replied, "What can you and I do about it?" so as to remind the griper that he or she, not just the pastor, bore responsibility for solving the problem.

In keeping with that dedication to honesty and responsibility, Vicar Ehrets found Shields' candor as his supervisor immensely valuable in helping him assess his strengths and weaknesses. In one of their regular oversight sessions, for instance, she commented that his leadership style tended toward two extremes: Either he did the job all by himself or handed it entirely to others. She advised him to consider a third option, a happy medium whereby he was a participant enabling others to do their part.

Former interns likewise credit Shields with helping them overcome impediments to realizing their full pastoral abilities. For Luttner, who arrived for her year at Hope in the fall of 1986, the need was for greater self-assurance. "I watched the way she conducted herself, especially in situations that were new to her," Luttner said. "She just went into things and did them. I learned self-confidence from her that year. She would let me do anything within the church and if I failed, it was okay." Russell, who succeeded Luttner, said Shields helped him surmount his natural shyness. "One thing I wanted out of the year was to be brought out of my shell because I'm something of an introvert. She encouraged me to do more things to be a leader. In her I saw all the things needed to be a pastor. It helped that the congregation was so warm and loving. You could go there and feel at home. They were down to earth and had fun together—it's the kind of climate Jane sets."

Besides enhancing the growth of individuals, Shields looks for ways to broaden the horizons of the congregation as a whole through regular preaching and church-wide emphases. Under her guidance, the church council began adopting a theme for a major program each year. During the previous year, the focus had been on education. More than 100 congregants had been enlisted in Bible study, exceeding the council's goal. The current theme is evangelism, an emphasis aimed at balancing the more temporal concerns behind the fundraising drive. "My only reservation [about the capital campaign]," she explained, "was that in doing it we not lose sight of other areas of spiritual growth." Thirty people from the congregation were leading the effort to visit lapsed members and potential newcomers.

At the heart of Shields' ministry is consistency. Applying her talents to an ever-shifting array of settings, she displays a singleness of purpose: to bring her full attention to the people to whom she was ministering, rendering the ineffable and transcendent both accessible and personal. Whomever she encounters along her pastoral way, singly or in groups, becomes her exclusive, caring focus.

On one particular Friday evening, her companions were Ernie and Carol, a couple planning their wedding. This was their fifth pre-marital counseling session together (she requires a minimum of three). Pastor Shields picked up where she left off from their last talk, coaxing them anew to examine various aspects of themselves as individuals and as a couple. She devoted her time to matters of psyche and spirit, having, in characteristically methodical fashion, turned over the arrangement of the details—from marching down the aisle to payment of fees and last-minute supplies of hair spray—to a regular wedding coordinator, an unpaid member of the congregation. She gave much thought to what areas of inquiry will best serve couples facing the complex pressures of modern marriage. She asked each matrimonial candidate to sketch a family tree—including the marriages and divorces for, she says, "you are what you were."

Likewise, rather than spending time on the state of their sex lives, a staple item in clergy lists of pre-marital topics to be covered, Pastor Shields asks a deceptively leading question: where do they plan to spend next Christmas?

Ernie and Carol, seated on the couch in the pastor's office, appeared totally at ease, speaking freely and spiritedly about joys and difficulties. Shields, sitting opposite them and, like them, clad in jeans, T-shirt and sneakers, leaned toward them, listening intently, maintaining an accepting smile. From time to time she asked a probing question ("how do you handle disputes?"), brought things down to earth ("we're not making a perfect marriage here—we're making a marriage") or lowered the intensity with a droll remark ("I keep tissues in the left pocket of my robe, smelling salts in the right"). She counseled them to get complete physical exams before the wedding and, since they were writing their own vows, advised them to "keep it simple." Her agenda also included some tutoring in the language of the wedding rite itself. She drew special attention to words in the blessing which exhorted the partners to "find delight in each other" and to "grow in holy love" which, she explained, "is not an emotional love that goes through highs and lows but 'holy love' that comes from Christ and which, unlike human love, knows no limit."

The session was undergirded by a vow by Shields to remain a constant support long after the rings were exchanged and the blessings pronounced. "I'm invested in you," she told a rapt Ernie and Carol. "Farther down the line when you're having problems and struggling with trust, you can call me."

On a typical Sunday morning, by contrast, Pastor Shields's companions, instead of a pair of counselees, numbered in the dozens, gathered as worshiping communities at 8:30 and 11, and she created among them a similar quality of personal intimacy. She wore a simple white robe with matching cincture, a cream-colored stole and a Greek pectoral cross as she entered the sanctuary singing the opening hymn. Standing close to the congregation, in front of the altar rail, she welcomed all, especially visitors, and directed their focus to the newly-painted walls of the choir loft, thanking the work crew (of which she had been a member) for doing the job the day before. Later in the service, she would ask congregants for their intercessory prayers and would offer those of her own, for members in special need. Shields delivered two sermons at each service, one to children who came forward to be around her and another for the adults. She preached in the same voice with which she led the stately Lutheran liturgy, warm and conversational, losing some of the color she conveyed in private as she raised her volume to reach those in the back rows.

The kernel for both sermons was the biblical account of Nicodemus being "born again." She asked the children to imagine what it would be like for them to be babies again, having to learn what they now knew all over again, like saying words. "A man in the Bible named Nicodemus had a question for Jesus," she said. "How could you be born again if you had already grown up? Well, every day it's like you're a baby again for God, who can teach you new things when you wake up again in the morning. Jesus tells Nicodemus—be open to all the wonderful things God wants you to learn this day."

For the adults, this theme became an invitation to take personal stock. The "born again" idea made sense in terms of what God could do for them rather than what they could do for themselves. "We try to shape the world as we think it should be rather than responding to God's action," she declared. "The voice of God speaks. How many of us would be so courageous that we'd be willing to sign a blank piece of paper, leave it on the altar, and let God fill in how it is that you can change your life in response to God?" One way of translating the Greek term for "born again" was to be "born from above," she noted, adding: "Think about what that might mean in your own life, to be receptive to the action of God." As a follow-up exercise, she asked congregants to "walk out of here with a blank stare—with the idea that in that blank, in that emptiness, God will be working already." As they filed out after the eucharist and the final hymn, she shook each hand and looked deeply into each pair of eyes.

With so much emphasis on personal and congregational nourishment and needs, concern for the welfare of larger communities often edges to the periphery of Hope's consciousness. Pastor Shields voices regrets that Hope hadn't made more room for justice and peace issues. "I need to hear the pain of those who are oppressed," she said. "I'm not oppressed. I'm an oppressor. I have to confess that and pray for change." She sometimes wonders if she and the congregation has avoided the Gospel's troublesome prophetic mission. Shields has chosen not to stir conflict by preaching on controversial issues such as the Gulf War, nor, she said, do parishioners seem to want her to. The church ran the child-care center and a food pantry for hungry families and sent money to the denomination's fund for world-wide relief projects, but otherwise the harsh realities of the outside world intruded very little. Hope looks primarily inward.

With the steady increase in membership, Pastor Shields has had to run faster to keep up as the demands on her time, particularly counseling time, have multiplied. "Someone calls and wants to come in and see me in the next couple days," she said, "and I'm already scheduled six weeks to two months ahead. When I say I have nothing open until two months down the road, they ask whether I can squeeze them in, not realizing I've already squeezed someone in. Sometimes I think they think I'm just making excuses or trying to avoid them." She regards herself as a victim of the expectations created by her proficiency and dedication. "I wouldn't call myself a workaholic," she said only half-jokingly about her enormous drive. "I do everything that way."

Driving to Baltimore for a meeting of deans with the bishop, Pastor Shields reflected on the rewards and difficulties in her ministry. Her most fulfilling moments occurred in preaching and officiating at the sacraments of baptism and the Lord's Supper. She profoundly felt the drama of the liturgical year within her life, experiencing the sharply distinct themes of the successive seasons from Advent to Advent. There were profound joys, she said, in being so close to so many people on so many levels, though staying in close touch was becoming harder in a go-go, affluent world. Parish visitation, the pastor's traditional means of keeping those bonds strong, had become less and less possible in an age of complex schedules and varied activity outside the home. The telephone had become a less adequate substitute for face to face visits, she said, but she made the best of it.

With Hope having been revived to the most harmonious and robust condition in its history, she increasingly strives to turn the parish's attention to longer range, more visionary planning. "The congregation's never done it before," Shields said, "and it's still difficult for them to look into the future. Some of it's due to the personality of the parish—it's more crisis oriented, used to moving in and out of quick life and death situations—they never took the time to look too far ahead."

The fundraising campaign represents the boldest strategy for placing the future on the agenda. The drive was partly intended to take advantage of the state's plan to widen Highway 273 on which cars whizzed by the church. A traffic light would be installed at an intersection in front of the church. Hope sees this as a golden opportunity to increase the church's visibility. "At present we have a big sign but nobody sees it as they speed by," Shields said. "With that light, traffic has to stop, and our sign will be in an ideal location. We also want to put up a new, large cross to catch the eye. That visibility is extremely important because we've never had it. I've even had visions of putting some kind of weather-proof banners outside to attract attention."

These ideas reflect the campaign's broader goal of preparing Hope to play a larger role in the community. A new parking lot would accommodate a larger number of cars on Sunday morning. The pipe organ would expand the range of Hope's musical offerings. Repairs to the roof were long overdue, as was replacement of the heating system. Altogether, the project went far beyond maintenance. It is a solid commitment to the future. "Now," Shields had written to the congregation at the start of the campaign, "we are on the threshold of a new adventure as God's people."

Shields' dreams of the future have not diminished her appreciation of the past. Even in her innovations she strives to preserve a tradition she cherished. She seeks new ways to experience the Christian heritage, while holding fast to the legacies. Hers is the mediating role between the customary and the novel.

On a spring weeknight at her home, Shields' family room was filled with Hope congregants. Members of the church council were meeting with "shepherds." In an effort to keep contacts among members close and personal as the congregation became larger and potentially more impersonal, Shields had proposed dividing the church into geographical "flocks," each with a "shepherd." Flocks were left to devise their own agenda within the overall pastoral purpose.

The program had been in effect for about a year and this meeting had been called to evaluate how well the idea had worked. The reviews were decidedly mixed. Four flocks still lacked shepherds. Some shepherds were dismayed because the same members of the flock showed up every time while others had never come. On the other hand, there was much evidence that these small circles had become networks of pastoral care. When someone got sick or in difficulty, fellow members of the flock were responding quickly.

Shields sat on the rug, taking in all the appraisals. Toward the end of the discussion, she summed up her thoughts. Though the program had been largely her idea, she did not defend it in the face of the criticisms, nor was she overly sanguine about its apparent successes. Her reaction was typical of her ability to take stock of reality while gently urging the church to move ahead. Pastor Shields flashed a smile that was full of verve, wonder and good cheer. "I don't think it's hurt anybody," she said buoyantly. "I think we've come a long way in just a year."

Leonid A. Feldman

From Refusenik to Rabbi

by Gene I. Maeroff

I will heal their backsliding,
I will love them freely;
For Mine anger is turned away from them.
—Hosea 14:4

Take thou away from Me the noise of the songs;
And let Me not hear the melody of thy psalteries.
But let justice well up as waters,
And righteousness as a mighty stream.
—Amos 5:23-24

The telephone call came one afternoon while Rabbi Leonid Feldman was sitting in his study at Temple Emanu-El talking with a visitor. The caller was irate. She said she wanted to know why Rabbi Feldman had insulted her nephew, whom he had run into at a community event. "I said something that was offensive?" he asked her. "What I said basically was 'Are you still single and available?' I invited him to temple and said there were lots of single women here. He said he was getting married and so I asked if he was marrying the pretty blonde I had seen with him another time.

"He said he was," the rabbi continued after listening to his caller say something. "I asked if she was Jewish or interested in conversion and when he said 'No,' I said 'I can't congratulate you.' That was it."

The visitor heard only the rabbi's side of the conversation, but it was clear that his caller was not placated by the rabbi's explanation of his attitude toward her nephew's impending marriage to a non-Jew who did not apparently intend to convert to Judaism. "He is stabbing the Jewish people in the back and you think this is harsh on my part?" the rabbi asked after listening to her again. He added: "Intermarriage is one of the worst crimes a Jew can commit after six million Jews marched into the gas chambers saying *Sh'ma Yisrael* [the primal Jewish prayer attesting to God's oneness]."

Finally, after more of the same, the woman told the rabbi that she was going to report his behavior to the president of the congregation. The rabbi was neither intimidated nor apologetic.

Leonid Ariel Feldman is, if anything, passionately devoted to the survival of the Jewish people. He is himself a survivor—a former Soviet refusenik who grew to adulthood as an atheist and loyal Communist, totally ignorant of his Jewish roots. Now, almost 40 years old, in Palm Beach, Florida, he is trying to tell fellow Jews who have spent their lives in freedom how to be Jews. Tall and slender, almost boyish-appearing with his shaggy brown hair, Rabbi Feldman, who speaks with an accent that attests to his foreign upbringing, has turned a quiet backwater of a Conservative synagogue that catered largely to the elderly into a dynamic center of Judaism in a city that a generation ago made Jews feel unwanted.

The size of the congregation has almost doubled to 585 member families and in the process it has grown younger, no longer simply functioning as a winter retreat for those with homes and allegiances in the North. A religious school that served 19 children has expanded to an enrollment of more than 60 that cannot be contained by its two tiny classrooms, forcing teachers to assemble small groups of students in any corner of the building in which they can find space on Sunday mornings. Adult education classes attract as many as 100 men and women every week and services on Friday nights have sometimes been so crowded that congregants have had to stand at the rear of the sanctuary. People who could attend any of a half dozen other synagogues closer to their homes say that they drive more than a half-hour just to go to services at which Feldman presides. "I want to destroy the concept of Rosh Hashonah and

Yom Kippur being the most important days in the Jewish calendar," Feldman said. "I want us to get as many people here for a regular Friday night service as for Kol Nidre [the service ushering in Yom Kippur, the holiest day on the Jewish calendar]. I am trying to destroy the idea that a temple is a place to come to twice a year."

Rabbi Feldman welcomes challenge the way a gambler greets the prospect of a trip to Las Vegas. He was still in the Soviet Union, studying physics at Kishinev State University, when his Jewish identity began stirring within him for the first time. He joined a small group of activist Jews in defying the Soviet government's opposition to Jewish expression. When he was trying to leave the country to immigrate to Israel and was arrested and imprisoned by the KGB, he went on a hunger strike.

Restless and brimming with energy, Feldman acts like a man trying to compensate for what he considers the lost years in his life. He even walks quickly, the long strides of his lanky legs compelling whoever is accompanying him to rush to keep up. He has been a man in a hurry since he emigrated from the Soviet Union to Israel in 1976 and then came to the United States in 1980 because he still felt unfulfilled. He said that he found secular Israelis lacking goals and he objected to the stranglehold that the Orthodox have on Judaism in Israel. "I was searching for something in Israel and I couldn't find it," he said. "In Israel either you're ultra-Orthodox or you're nothing so I became a nothing . . . Suddenly I realized at the age of 28 that I knew physics, literature, this and that, but I didn't know the most important thing—I didn't know who I was." His attempt to learn as much as he could about Judaism led him to courses at the University of Judaism in Los Angeles and eventually to rabbinical school at the Jewish Theological Seminary in New York City.

Because he is so exacting of himself, Feldman apparently believes it entirely proper for him to confront others. The incident over intermarriage that led to the phone call is indicative of his fervor. Feldman says that ultimately his success will be gauged by the extent to which he can get Jews to keep the Sabbath, observe the dietary laws and marry other Jews—including converts. "I expect that every child in our religious school will marry a Jew. That will be the measure of my success. And, if it happens, I will feel that I have done an amazing job."

When Rabbi Feldman was invited to Temple Emanu-El in 1988 to deliver a guest sermon so that the congregation might assess his potential as its rabbi, he quickly dropped the gauntlet. His first sermon, before the job was officially offered to him, was on the importance of keeping kosher. Now, Feldman believes more members observe the dietary laws than did when he arrived. But the transformation was not altogether smooth. One woman in attendance at that first sermon walked up to him afterward and said: "I thought you were a Conservative rabbi," implying that he was acting as if he were Orthodox. She quit the congregation.

When he was taken to dinner during that first trial visit by a small group of movers and shakers, one of the women, Pearl Weinstein, a nonactive member of the congregation, said after his description of how vibrant temple life could be: "You make it sound wonderful, but you'll never see me in temple." She has missed only about four or five Sabbath services since Rabbi Feldman came and, furthermore, is now his mother-in-law. "He is the most interesting, dazzling, passionate man about his religion," she says today of the man who so captivated the Weinstein family that in 1990 he ended up taking as his wife one of the three daughters, Melissa, known as Missy, a former actress who is now pursuing a degree in education.

Feldman's zeal seems to know no bounds and he usually makes no attempt to hide it. For instance, on Simchat Torah, the autumn holiday celebrating the first five books of the Bible, he has helped create a joyous religious frenzy that takes the congregants out of the synagogue and into the streets, dancing with Torahs in their arms. The first year that it happened there were telephone calls from embarrassed members who felt uncomfortable about so unabashed a display of Jewishness in this tony, largely WASP settlement. One board member, who wasn't at the Simchat Torah service but heard about it, invited Rabbi Feldman to lunch at his club for a discussion of the event. "It's a paradise here," Feldman recalls the man saying to him. "We're not going to let you destroy it. Our neighbors won't like it."

Feldman says he peered into the man's eyes and declared: "Let me tell you one thing. Even the KGB allowed Jews to dance in the streets once a year in Moscow." And the rabbi has continued to lead his congregants into the streets of Palm Beach to dance with the Torahs each year on Simchat Torah.

Another kind of celebration has been added at Hanukah, when the congregation holds a large party, replete with potato pancakes, spinning tops and other artifacts of the winter holiday, at a site a half block from a club infamous for its discrimination, where not only can't Jews be members, but they cannot even be entertained for lunch as guests of members.

Feldman's philosophy that Jewish observance should be fun reaches its apex at Purim, the holiday in the spring that marks the rescue of the Jews of Persian antiquity from the hands of the evil Haman, a story described in the *Book of Esther*. Tradition has it that Jews should get joyously drunk on this occasion and Feldman has introduced his congregation to an old Russian custom of drinking vodka and eating pickles and black bread as part of the happy celebration. In the spring of 1991, the synagogue was filled with 400 dancing and singing people who were trying to follow the ritual that the rabbi taught them of inhaling and exhaling in the proper order as they followed each shot of icy vodka with, first, a sliver of pickle and then a slice of pumpernickel. By happy coincidence, in the midst of the Purim party came word that the war against Iraq had ended with an allied victory and the embattled Jews of the Middle East had been spared from the threats of a modern-day Haman and his Scud missiles. The vodka never tasted better.

Rabbi Feldman's candor with the board member who objected to the dancing in the streets at Simchat Torah and with the man who was intermarrying is a hallmark of his approach. When he was asked to meet over dinner with the son of one of the temple's most influential members to discuss the young man's alienation from Judaism, Feldman clung to principles rather than offer conciliatory words. There was a heated confrontation that attracted the attention of those around them in the restaurant.

"He was telling me it is okay to be 20 years old and to march in the streets against your country's involvement in a war with Iraq, to march in the streets when people your age are spilling their blood, when babies in Israel have to be sealed in plastic bubbles," Feldman said of the incident. "It's my job, especially with the young bright people, to make it clear that when it comes to morality there is right and there is wrong. There are issues that are black and white. Fascism is bad, democracy is good . . . I asked him if this were 1943 and Hitler were sitting at the next table and I would give him a gun whether he would shoot him. He said he didn't know. I said, 'That's immoral.' He said, 'That's your opinion.' I said, 'No, it's Western civilization's opinion.'"

Feldman was willing to risk the fury of the young man and even of the young man's well-placed family for the sake of upholding values, but—in the weeks and months that followed— the rabbi did have misgivings about the possibility of being responsible for "losing him permanently from Judaism." As it turned out, the story had a happy ending. Despite his anger at the rabbi, the young man followed through during the summer on a promise he had made to study in Israel and the experience was so moving for him that he said he was reevaluating whether he had been sufficiently committed to Judaism.

Feldman is comfortable defying social convention if he thinks it will strengthen the bonds of Judaism. He deplores the rivalry that Americans take for granted among Reform, Conservative and Orthodox Jews. "We have enough enemies without this. Hitler didn't distinguish among Jews." Perhaps his outspokenness is a result of his unusual journey into Jewish identification, a trip that has led him not to be self-conscious—as many non-Orthodox American Jews are—about stamping himself as different. He is the sort of person who in one instance glared at an audience and declared: "If you don't give 10 percent of your earnings to charity you're a bastard."

His outspokenness may be fortified by his sense of independence. He more or less raised himself after his mother died during his childhood and his father married a woman who Feldman says, as a step-mother, turned out to hate him. He was already in demand as a speaker when he was attending the rabbinical seminary in New York, traveling around the country and receiving substantial fees to give speeches about his transformation from refusenik to rabbinical student. He and a professional writer working with him have shared an advance of about $100,000 from a publisher to write a book based on Feldman's experiences. At this point he is confident that, if he so desired, he could select from among a multitude of pulpits.

"I have proven that religion is anything but boring," Rabbi Feldman said. "Judaism can be exciting, fun and relevant to everyday life. If you can show that, people will respond. I don't believe that a temple should be just for prayer. It should be a social and educational place, too." The thoughts are those with which most rabbis would probably concur, but few seem to be as successful as Feldman in breathing life into the dusty words. Though he learned Russian, Romanian, Yiddish, Hebrew and Italian before English, his accent does not impede his ability to enrapture his listeners.

Nor do his straightforward ways, which may occasionally give offense to Jews who prefer a less muscular religion, seem to be a barrier to his being able to build a relationship with his congregation. Feldman has a warm and engaging side and is so popular that at the reception that follows each service people flock around him like groupies drawn to a rock star. He exudes a kind of innocent charm, a product of his foreign upbringing. It can show itself in the midst of a sermon when he might ask his audience to help him translate a Hebrew word for which his English vocabulary has not yet grown large enough to give him an equivalent or when he pauses during a service to ask if he is pronouncing such a word as "sepulchre" correctly (he was).

His openness and his intellect have won him the approbation of a congregation that some might expect to be more concerned about materialism than about religion. Temple Emanu-El—a place where plaques bearing donors' names are appended to everything from the elevator to the stained glass windows—has many wealthy members whose advantages could easily render them disinclined to be accepting of an immigrant rabbi who is not afraid to point out their transgressions. Merely being at Temple Emanu-El is part of the challenge that seems to excite Feldman. "I believe Judaism can flourish anywhere—in a desert, in the middle of Russia and even in a paradise called Palm Beach," he said.

Missy Feldman praises her husband's outspokenness, recognizing that his candor may sometimes overwhelm. "The one thing I admire so much about Leonid is his honesty," she said.

"It is sometimes brutal, but he believes what he says. He's lived through a lot in his life and his opinions come from that. His words and actions are passionate. He doesn't do anything halfway. It takes a lot more than I have to change his mind. I haven't learned how to sway him to a softer way of saying things. But maybe then he wouldn't be as effective."

The synagogue, a white stucco building in a quiet residential neighborhood with palm trees and pastel-colored houses, is lodged in a community that symbolizes having "made it," American style. A block away is St. Edward's, the red-tiled-roof Roman Catholic church attended by the Kennedy clan. Palm Beach is an island, both figuratively and literally, a place where even the stores are discreet with their almost unnoticeable signs and the gracious splendor of the snooty Breakers Hotel, another neighbor of the synagogue, attests to the glories of old money.

Temple Emanu-El is one of the stations on the national fundraising route traveled regularly by those who want to raise money for Jewish causes. Feldman, who never wore a tuxedo before arriving in Palm Beach, says he now sometimes feels that it has become his uniform. But it is much more than his being in demand to provide invocations at fundraising events that has enamored his congregants. He considers himself, above all, a teacher. It is a role in which he thrives. "Teaching gives me the most satisfaction in my life," Feldman said. "I think it's my main talent and I don't utilize it enough because of all else that I have to do. I talk to people on their level. I came to Judaism late in life and so I don't take anything for granted. I try never to use words that will put them to sleep."

Feldman regards the article he writes each month for the temple newsletter as another way of educating the congregation. He said: "I take it seriously. The newsletter is my only contact with some people. But I do procrastinate. Writing is difficult for me; it's like giving birth. I'll sit down at 11 at night and it'll be four in the morning before I finish the article. I find speaking much easier."

His penchant for teaching takes many forms. When a child is preparing to undergo the rite of bar mitzvah (for boys) or bat mitzvah (for girls) that occurs usually at the age of 13, Feldman meets weekly with the child and his or her parents for the two months leading up to the ritual, which culminates in the youngster chanting a portion in Hebrew from the Torah at the Sabbath service. Rabbi Feldman deplores the widespread lack of Jewish learning among Jews. "The people of the book don't know how to open the book," he said.

The rabbi agreed with the education committee of the synagogue that it was not worth having as members families who joined the congregation immediately before a child's 13th birthday simply for the purpose of having a bar or bat mitzvah. Thus, he concurred when the committee proposed to institute a membership requirement of at least two years before a child would be permitted to undergo the rite. Furthermore, it was made incumbent upon the entire family to attend Sabbath services for a period of time. "The most important thing is that we not be a factory for bar mitzvahs," he said.

Feldman's teaching is firmly rooted in the Bible and in ancient Jewish writings. He largely eschews preaching about current events in isolation from Scripture. "I speak of the Torah and make it relevant to people," he said. It is Judaism and its 4,000-year history that he wants to teach and he says he is glad to leave the news coverage to the anchormen. "Before I was a rabbi, I noticed that some rabbis stood up and talked about whatever they read that morning in the *New York Times*. What they said was just a political commentary. Why should a rabbi think he knows more than the congregants about the homeless or about Supreme Court nominations?" Feldman said he cites current events only to illustrate points made in Scripture.

He also breaks in at various points in the liturgy, not only to translate from Hebrew to English, but, as an etymologist might do, to embellish a word or phrase by explaining the deeper meaning of the Hebrew. "He puts our old Scriptures from thousands of years ago into the moment we live in," said David Feuer, the Argentinian-born cantor of Temple Emanu-El, a man whose rich baritone voice adds beauty and feeling to the service.

So it was that one Sabbath when the portion of the Torah to be read by the congregation was from the 23rd chapter of Genesis, dealing with the death of Sarah at the age of 127 and Abraham's attempt to find a burial place for her, that the rabbi gave the events of the Bible contemporary meaning by linking them to the death that week of a 94-year-old founding member of Temple Emanu-El. Feldman described the intellectually active life that the woman had led until the end, reminding the congregants that being old need not prevent one from enjoying a rewarding life. And when he turned to Abraham's bargaining with the Hittites to obtain land for Sarah's interment, Feldman gracefully segued to the negotions under way that very week in Madrid between Israelis and Arabs, who were still contesting possession of the land. Such are the ways of a rabbi who just a few years earlier could not have imagined himself playing such a role.

"Why did I decide to become a rabbi at a point in life when I didn't even know if I believed in God?" Rabbi Feldman asks rhetorically. "Because I wanted to be a teacher of Judaism, that's what excited me. Instead of teaching people about physics or chess [which he did in the Soviet Union], I could teach this thing that helps people to have a richer life, that helps people to be more moral, that helps to destroy evil in the world. That's basically what turned me on."

Thus it came about that one Wednesday morning at his regularly scheduled adult class, Feldman found himself preparing to speak about the prophet Hosea. "There are 100 people on a Wednesday morning who choose to come to temple," he said to a visitor before striding into the room. "They are very successful people who could be doing many other things other than coming here." It was spring and the last session for the course.

"Do you still remember Amos?" he asked, trying to set a context at the beginning of his talk about Hosea. "By the end of today you will have a clearer picture of these two men than 95 percent of Jews and Christians.

"Chapter 3 has some revolutionary ideas. It begins with a very strange line," he said, referring to the command of the Lord in the Book of Hosea to "Go yet, love a woman beloved of her friend, yet an adulteress. . ."

"What is the traditional interpretation? Can one be commanded about emotions?" he asked.

A white-haired man responded: "If you act lovingly you will come to love."

"You have to work on your feelings through your behavior," the rabbi said in agreement. "If your spouse is getting on your nerves, say something nice. The problem with young people in America today is that they want to wait for the feeling. Judaism says: 'You don't feel romantic? Take flowers to your wife. Then you'll feel romantic.' Don't say, 'I'll start keeping kosher when the feeling comes.' Start keeping kosher and the feeling will come. . .

"I am afraid that Jews sometimes ignore Hosea and stress Amos and Christians ignore Amos and stress Hosea. Hosea doesn't say all you need is love. He says you definitely need justice. But justice isn't enough if you want to be intimate. Don't judge your spouse. Justice is not enough; love is not enough."

Rabbi Feldman elaborated on this theme and then leapt to Chapter 4 of Hosea, taking time to read the first two verses aloud. Like a guide leading his charges down unfamiliar trails, he took the class through portions of the text, pausing here and there to read Hebrew phrases to the class and then delving into individual words that did not readily lend themselves to translation. "It's more than mercy, more than respect. It's *chesed*," he said, pronouncing the Hebrew word with its initial gutteral sound rising from deep in his throat. "Unconditional love. Not just love. The word has lost its meaning in contemporary America. I 'love' New York. I 'love' spaghetti. *Chesed* is more. It's unconditional love. At one extreme people say all you need is love. At the other extreme. . ." He stopped speaking and stood rigid and austere, like a judge, trying to personify the most obdurate interpretation.

In this lecture, as in his sermons from the pulpit, he spoke without benefit of a prepared text, using only a few notes to remind him of what he wanted to cover. "Very often before I dress I have no idea what I'll say. My wife says 'Go take a shower' and my ideas come to me there," he said later, when asked in an interview to reflect on his approach.

This love of teaching, combined with his commitment to spread devotion to Jewish practice, also makes Rabbi Feldman an ardent supporter of conversion. He will spend month after month with an individual who is trying to decide whether to become a Jew, patiently imparting the lessons of Judaism during repeated meetings. One woman he recently converted, a former Methodist, was positively glowing as Feldman and several rabbinical colleagues he had assembled welcomed her into the Jewish fold after quizzing her—as is traditional—for almost an hour about the attitudes, beliefs and knowledge she had developed during almost a year under Feldman's tutelage. "She's going to be a good Jew," Feldman said of the woman who in less than two weeks was to marry a member of the congregation. "I feel confident and comfortable with her. She's sometimes surprised that born Jews take their Judaism less seriously than she does."

The conversion ceremony included a ritual immersion for which the small party walked the two blocks from the synagogue to the ocean. Having changed into a bikini swim suit, the young woman and two female friends who were attending her waded into the roiling waters, where the convert read a declaration of faith as the rabbis, dressed in suits and ties, watched from the sandy shore.

Yet another dimension of Feldman's work stems from his kindred feelings for those Jews who, like him, were born in the republics of the old Soviet Union. Sometimes he's called the "rabbi to the Russians." His involvement with Jews from the Soviet Union began shortly after his arrival in Israel, when, as a layman, he accepted a job working in Italy with Jews from the Soviet Union who were trying to arrange passage to Israel. Requests for help come to him regularly from Soviet Jews. One day, for instance, there was a long-distance phone call from a woman in Kishinev, his hometown, who years earlier had been a schoolmate of his sister's. She wanted to know if he could do anything to help her emigrate to America. Feldman barely knew the woman, having met her for the first time the previous year when he took his new wife to visit Kishinev on their honeymoon. In another case he was beseeched to translate a transcript of university courses for an immigrant, now living in Palm Beach, who wanted to get partial credit for law school.

Given his background and the special role he could play ministering exclusively among the hundreds of thousands of Soviet Jews who have immigrated to the United States and Israel, Feldman feels torn. He calls it the "dilemma of my life," the question of whether to shift his focus to this sole concern for which he is so unusually qualified. Sometimes he thinks that maybe such work is his destiny and that eventually he will end up back in Israel working with Soviet immigrants. Such a move, however, does not seem to be in store anytime soon.

For now, his ministry is based in a disheveled office at Temple Emanu-El, where his desk and even the floor are covered with piles of working papers, the unkempt product of a peripatetic working style that finds the rabbi jumping from one task to another. The wastebasket is filled nearly to overflowing and a shopping bag, crammed with more papers, rests against the wall. Dominating two facing walls are large framed posters in Russian. On one poster, picturing Lenin holding a copy of *Pravda,* appears the slogan: "Soviet power is the way to socialism. This way has been found by the masses of workers and therefore it is the only correct way and unbreakable."

On the other poster, Lenin is saying, "Peace to the Nations" and Brezhnev is replying, "The flag of peace and cooperation among nations was raised by the great Lenin. We will be forever faithful to this flag."

The posters hang as reminders. Feldman said: "There is no doubt in my mind that the only way these people were able to hold half the world in their hands without even giving them butter, without giving them soap, was by giving them religion. Without that passion they wouldn't have been able to hold these people. This is what America does not understand. I was always a believer—I was a real Communist. Communism *is* a religion. That's why I have these posters here. It's not to be cute. This used to be my God; I was a believer. I believed that I was growing up in the best country in the world, that the goal of my life was to destroy capitalism and to establish Communism around the world.

"Then, suddenly, I experienced anti-Semitism. This was supposed to be the greatest system in the world and everyone was supposed to be equal. I knew I was a talented person, but I discovered that a Feldman could not be a journalist, a Feldman could not be a diplomat, a Feldman could not be a principal of a high school. Suddenly I found out there was something wrong with the country and I devoted the next several years of my life to getting out."

His experience has made Leonid Feldman a fervent anti-Communist. He was a big hit as the featured speaker on Jewish Heritage Day at Edwards Air Force Base in California and proudly displays on his office wall the plaque that was bestowed on him on that occasion. "There's just one place in America where people still believe in Communism and that's on college campuses," he said. "Nobody in Poland, nobody in the Ukraine, nobody in Bulgaria believes in Communism."

Feldman has been defined by the particularity of his struggles and realizes that, as a result, he is cut from a cloth somewhat different from that of which many native-born American Jews are fashioned. Sometimes, in fact, those who know and respect him say that one of his deficiencies may be an inadequate appreciation of the distinctiveness of the Jewish experience in the United States. From his vantage, Feldman said: "I have a sense of where I come from, I have a perspective. When I hear of anti-Semitism in America I laugh. It's a joke. So there is a Ku Klux Klan, so there is a Duke running for office, so there are three swastikas somewhere. The fact is that I know that my closest friends and my family will never be able to get a good job in Kishinev. That's anti-Semitism. Americans don't know what anti-Semitism is.

"Separation between church and state is not one of my priorities either. But for most American Jews this is a holy cow. I don't give a damn about it. I'm not threatened by a creche on a lawn somewhere. In fact, I would have no problem with having more religion in America. If suddenly there were prayers in school maybe Jewish children would come home and start asking questions. They might say, 'Hey Ma, how come we don't go to temple? How come all the Christians know prayers and we don't?'"

In his rejection of his former life and his acceptance of things American, Feldman ostensibly has embraced the material aspects of the American dream with enthusiasm. A gold bracelet dangles from his right wrist and he tools around Palm Beach in a bright red Saab 900 Turbo with a retractable sun roof, hardly the baubles of the average young man in Kishinev. Feldman maintains that this is part of his attempt at role modeling. "I want to destroy the old image of a rabbi," Feldman said.

When he negotiated his contract Feldman told the officers of the congregation: "I want to make one thing clear. I want to be a role model for your sons and daughters, granddaughters and grandsons. Therefore, I'm going to drive a nice car; I'm going to wear nice clothes; I'm going to ask for a very nice salary. When some of your brilliant children and grandchildren are sitting in the sanctuary, looking up at me, I want them to think, 'I could be a doctor, I could be a broker, I could be a lawyer, but I want to be a rabbi, just like Rabbi Feldman.' I want you to be able to say you're proud of this decision and to tell them, 'Go for it. It's a beautiful profession and you can also make a living.' I want to destroy the image of the eastern European rabbi who's a poor guy everyone feels sorry for."

Thus, Feldman said that, unlike many rabbis, he accepts no gratuities for officiating at marriages, funerals, bar mitzvahs and other rites. He regards his services as something to which members of the congregation are entitled and says he doesn't officiate at rituals outside the congregation even when money is offered. "I want to destroy this image that a rabbi is always looking for a tip on the side," he said. "If someone wants to send a donation to the synagogue that's fine, but they don't owe me anything. I'm lucky to be doing what I want to do and to be getting paid well for it." His speeches around the country are an entirely different matter and he feels entirely justified to charge fees for those.

Integral to Rabbi Feldman's position as a model for other Jews is the small knitted *yarmulke* (scullcap) that is pinned to the hair at the crown of his head as he goes about town. "It's obviously the most visible symbol I have," he said. "In New York, I only wore it around the seminary or when I went someplace like a kosher restaurant or a Jewish bookstore. But I made a conscious decision not to be seen around here without it. I may be the only person on the island who wears one on the streets. It is part of my role modeling so that everyone knows who I am. A lot of people see it and say, 'You're the rabbi, aren't you?' It also helped me when I was still single and dating. One date said to me, 'Do you have to wear this?' She never saw me again. I take my title and my yarmulke seriously. Wearing the yarmulke is part of that. It means people are watching me. When I return incorrect change I want that

Baptist cashier in Palm Beach to see how honest these Jews are."

An important measure of his success as a role model, according to Feldman, will be whether some of the young people in the congregation eventually enter the rabbinate. He takes pride in the interest that Brian Glusman, a young staff member of Temple Emanu-El, has shown in possibly embarking on a rabbinical career. "Brian is my first success," Rabbi Feldman said of the young man who has enrolled in correspondence courses at a rabbinical seminary. "I worked on him for two years. He was in sales. I've proved to him that Jewish life does not necessarily mean a financial struggle."

Glusman, a genial, Southern-raised redhead with a marvelous command of Hebrew, readily credits Rabbi Feldman for his interest in becoming a rabbi. "He's turned me into something special here," said Glusman, whose job has him performing the functions of program director, youth director, ritual director and Torah reader. "He's gone out of his way to make me shine and he didn't have to do that. An important message that he has communicated to me by his example is that it is possible to be a synagogue professional and to be paid well and respected for it."

It is clear that Feldman seeks to build a future for Judaism by cultivating the young. He even gives time each week to the youngest children in the synagogue's religious school, those in the early elementary grades. And so it was one Sunday morning that the rabbi, one hand on his hip, was pacing across the front of the carpeted sanctuary as the Florida sunshine filtered through the tall stained-glass windows and splashed across the cushioned pews where the youngsters had assembled. "Hanukah has nothing to do with Christmas," he said of the two approaching holidays. "Christmas is a Christian holiday. We don't celebrate it. It's not ours.

"What do Christians celebrate on Christmas?" he asked.

"That's right," he said to a child's tentative response. "They celebrate the birth of Jesus, who they believe is the son of God. Christmas and Hanukah are not the same. They simply happen to be almost at the same time."

He went on to tell the children the story of the Maccabees and asked questions that elicited few responses. "The most important thing about Hanukah," he said, "is that Jewish people wanted to be different. What we are studying here is how to be different, why to be different and how to be proud to be different." After talking a bit about the difficulty of maintaining a commitment to principles and ideas that may not be popularly espoused, Rabbi Feldman left the children with a closing thought: "Christians have a wonderful, beautiful holiday and we have nothing against it. But it's not our holiday. It's too bad some of them don't take their holiday more seriously."

When it comes to identifying his own role models, Rabbi Feldman reaches back to the Bible. He explained: "I'm attracted to King David. He was not perfect and I can identify with him. He had weaknesses and he's not boring. People who are fascinating have a very powerful . . . what we call in Hebrew, *yetzer ha-tov* and, simultaneously, *yetzer ha-rah*, an impulse for good and an impulse for bad—a passion for goodness and an evil inclination. It's what makes people interesting. The internal struggle between the two is what human life is all about. I think King David had it. I can identify with that. I cannot identify with Abraham. I still have a lot of trouble . . . with the offering of Isaac. I have a problem with that. He is too inhuman to me, too superhuman . . . Moses also did not have much passion; he did not have much *yetzer ha-rah*. I can admire him, but I can't identify with him. I'm not attracted to him. You don't see Moses tempted much. But David—he had it all. I guess I would like to be seen that way. Like everybody else, I'm human."

Before he discovered the Bible, Leonid Feldman was propelled on his journey toward Judaism by two other books. The pivotal experience that inspired him to unearth his Jewish roots came in Russia, when he was 20 years old and read Leon Uris's novel *Exodus*, in a Russian-language edition that had been smuggled into the country. This tale of Holocaust survivors and the founding of Israel imbued him for the first time with a sense of Jewishness and inspired him to become a refusenik, seeking emigration to Israel.

What Feldman considers the second great turning point in his restless quest of religious identity came with the reading of another book, *The Eight Questions People Ask About Judaism.* At that juncture, in 1980, he had already reached the United

States and was still searching for purpose in his life. "I swallowed that book in one evening," he recalled. Until then, as the expatriate atheist grasping for something in which he could believe, Feldman had been wrestling with the question of *how* to be Jewish. Suddenly, he was fascinated to find words that he said persuaded him *why* he should be Jewish. Feldman was in Los Angeles then, interviewing for a job as a Hebrew teacher in a synagogue school. He was elated to meet someone who offered to introduce him to the co-authors of the book he had just read, Dennis Prager and Rabbi Joseph Telushkin, who have both written and lectured widely on Jewish issues. A friendship quickly blossomed and the two young authors—now among his closest friends—turned out to exert the greatest influence on Leonid Feldman of anyone he had encountered after leaving the Soviet Union. Less than a year later, partly through their urgings, he decided to become a full-time student of Judaism, embarking on studies that eventually led him into the seminary.

Having found flavor for his brand of Judaism in a cauldron of ferment, Feldman seems to recognize that his particular stew may be too spicy for some. "There are many things I would not do as Leonid Feldman, but because I am *Rabbi* Leonid Feldman I do them," he said. "I don't mind being called a fanatic. That's what Amos was called. I'm not here to please people. Role modeling is a very important part of what I do. Judaism is not just my passion: it's my job." He maintains, however, that his bitter experiences in the Soviet Union and his fervid convictions have not robbed him of compassion. "I am also the rabbi for the afflicted," he said. "So when people have pain my job is not to be a philosopher; my job then is not to be giving lectures. My job is to hold their hands."

And so it was early one midweek afternoon that Rabbi Feldman could be found at a nursing home, trying to comfort a congregant, a wealthy real estate entrepreneur, who had been felled by a stroke that left him speechless and paralyzed in a wheelchair. One could not even be certain that the man, who appeared to be in a sort of suspended animation, knew who the rabbi was or why he was there. But the man's wife, who was also visiting, knew and she seemed grateful for the rabbi's presence.

"I wish I could do more of this," Feldman said afterward of the portion of his role that involves ministering to the ill and the isolated. He explained: "There are many bored, lonely people with nothing to do. It changes their lives if someone comes to see them. You don't have to say much when you come to see someone in pain."

Performing this sedentary function, however, seems to take extra effort by Feldman. More often, he is a whirlwind, hardly able to remain in one spot. He acknowledges this: "I'm obsessed with the idea that there is so much to do in the world that I don't want to waste any time. There are multimillion-aires sitting at home, waiting to be asked for their money. Raising money should be a priority of mine, but I just don't have enough time. There is no reason we shouldn't have a $100,000 scholarship to send every child who wants to Jewish summer camp or to Israel. These people need to be groomed. You don't go to people who barely know you and ask them for money. We have only two windowless classrooms for our kids. We're sending them a message. Come after school, at four in the afternoon, and sit in a little room with no windows."

Rabbi Feldman worries that he is an idler unless he is performing a task that he considers productive. He has even embarked on a Ph.D. program in international studies at the University of Miami, spending a day and a half a week on campus as a student, preparing for the day when he hopes to write a dissertation on Soviet Jewry. He has constructed for himself a schedule that allows no time for athletic pursuits in a place where the climate attracts people simply because they lust after the chance to play golf and tennis and swim year round. "I couldn't justify spending five hours a day pushing a little ball around a golf course," said Feldman, who has no tan though the synagogue and his nearby apartment are minutes from the ocean and its lush beaches. "I've even given up chess because I was playing so seldom that I was not as good as I used to be," said this man who was a tournament competitor in the Soviet Union. He said:

"I see things that most Americans don't see. I see that Palm Beach is not the norm, that even America is not the norm. Most of humanity is not worried about developing cholesterol. They don't worry about cheesecake. Most of humanity is not on a diet. This is the least of their problems. The rest of the world is worried about where they will get a piece of bread tomorrow. Americans are worried about 'How do I avoid the cheesecake?' It's ridiculous. It's unreal.

"Palm Beach is the capital of relaxation and fun. I don't allow myself to relax. I've seen too much pain in life. I say 'How can I play golf when there is so much to do in the world? Who can afford to spend time with tennis lessons and bicycling all day?' I get angry. As a result, I get restless. I am driven. I constantly have to be productive. I say to my wife: 'Did you have a productive day today?' Even on a Sunday. I cannot just have a quiet afternoon on the beach. I have to finish a book. I have to finish three articles. We go on a vacation and I have a full briefcase."

All in all, even with a personal dynamism that a small community like Palm Beach seems hardly able to contain, Feldman has found ways to be an effective spiritual leader, winning the respect not only of his congregation but of his peers, as well. "He's a remarkable young guy," said Rabbi Steven R. Westman, president of the Board of Rabbis of Palm Beach County. "It's interesting that this is his first congregation and yet he already has an international reputation. He's full of boyish enthusiasm and charm. There is an aura about his presence that is unusual for his age and he is able to carry people along with him."

Perhaps Feldman's unusual route to the pulpit has done much to enhance his success with a congregation decidedly older than that found at the average synagogue. "Part of his charm to people my age," said Sybil Sanders, a congregant who has already taken two adult courses with Feldman, "is that he wasn't born in the United States. He is a new American and his approach is different. We respect him for his tremendous intelligence and his ability to learn so much so fast and to pass it on."

As a person who came late to religion without a background in it, Feldman built traditions for himself as he went along. He has done much the same for his congregation, stitching a sense of community into the once-frayed fabric of Temple Emanu-El so that active congregants have come to rely on certain regularities that now bind them together. There are, of course, the celebrations Feldman has instituted at Purim and

Hanukah and the other holidays, but there is more. For example, young children under 13 are called forward to gather around the rabbi and the cantor—where they are given sweets—several times during the Sabbath services, imbuing the youngsters with a sense of belonging. Congregants are invited to stand individually at the Friday night service and share their experiences of the week with the congregation. These and other practices initiated by Feldman have lent fresh vigor to a congregation that seems to revel in the excitement generated by its rabbi. It may well be, as the rabbi contends, that his ability to help Judaism flourish in Palm Beach could be the most important lesson he might teach about the resilience and relevance of the ancient faith.

Granville A. Seward

Divine Chemistry

by Rosemary L. Bray

> *Be watchful, stand firm in your faith, be coura-*
> *geous, be strong. Let all that you do be done in*
> *love.*
> —1 Corinthians 16:13

The 11 a.m. service at Mt. Zion Baptist Church promised to be especially glorious on this February morning. Hundreds of men and women filled the pews on either side of the great sanctuary. A winter sun lit the freshly painted walls and warmed the wooden beams that arched across the ceiling. All the usual signs of Sunday morning in a traditional black church were there: the hugs and laughter among members of the congregation; the low rumblings of spirituals played as an organ prelude; the exclamations of delight as one long-time member returned to church after an illness of some months; the gracious efficiency of the ushers, dressed crisply in navy blue suits or dresses as they handed out the thick program to members and visitors and led people to their favorite seats.

Out in the vestibule, there was the rustling of choir robes and the scurrying feet of children as the Youth Choir assembled before the processional. And finally, there was an energy-filled silence, as an elegantly dressed young woman, Lisa Brown, stepped to the pulpit to greet the congregation and begin the celebration.

"What is today?" she asked.

And in one voice, they answered her:

"This is the day that the Lord has made; let us rejoice and be glad."

The members of the downtown Newark church were especially glad this day. It was February 24, the 23rd anniversary of the Rev. Dr. Granville A. Seward's arrival at Mt. Zion, and its 1,200 members were prepared to honor their pastor as well as their Lord. After the choir processed and sang "All Hail the Power," Mrs. Eva Powell, one of Mt. Zion's deacons, led the invocation, thanking God for the day, for their safe arrival, for the celebration itself and the gift of being alive to see it.

Later in the service, two of the deacons carried from the altar to the floor directly at the front of the sanctuary an enormous oak chair with red upholstery that is, in the traditional African-American church, the literal seat of power. One of the deacons, Julius Cooper, asked Dr. Seward to sit, then asked those of the congregation who would to join them in a group pastoral prayer.

Nearly as one, the congregation rose and pressed toward the front of the church. Those closest to Seward joined the deacons in the ancient ritual of the laying on of hands, the metaphor for the vesting of authority in a servant of God. For those unable to reach the pastor, they laid hands on their neighbors instead and built a chain to the sanctuary where, for several minutes, there could be heard only the fervent prayer of Deacon Cooper and the answering affirmations of the congregation as they called on the Lord to bless and strengthen the man who both led and served them.

There were dozens of songs and tributes to Seward on this day: poems from young children in the Sunday School; reminiscences from old friends now on the deacon board, two glorious solos from a long-time church supporter, Robert Madwood.

One of Mt. Zion's members, Sondra Boulware, asked listeners to concentrate on why they were gathered on this winter morning:

"Let us focus on this man called by God," she asked the congregation. "For God had not given him the spirit of fear but of power, and of love of a sound mind. I'm speaking of a man who had committed life to a cause. The cause is Christ Jesus. I'm speaking of a man who has very strong convictions about his faith in God. I'm speaking of a man who radiates love and happiness, who shows compassion and who is a source of strength.

"I'm speaking of a man who has a burning desire to be ever closer to God," she went on. "I'm speaking of a man who has led Mt. Zion to grow from a cold to a warm community, through his spirit. I'm speaking of a man who is a man for all seasons, who has a delivery to make that is in season all year long."

There were stories of thanksgiving from those whose lives had been touched by Dr. Seward, tales that were part religious testimony and part biography; in fact, the biography was as much Dr. Seward's as the speakers'. For it seemed that there was little about him that this congregation did not know, few things about his life that he had not shared with them freely. Much of his life, many of the challenges he faced, had become part of the lore of Mt. Zion Baptist Church. And with each year and each new revelation, he had gathered to the church a more connected and committed following.

One moving commentary about his life came from Minister Patricia Richburg, a deacon who had decided to answer the call to ministry—this, in a denomination more often noted for its desire that women keep silent in the churches. It was Minister Richburg who reminded the congregation of Dr. Seward's life-long love of science, his youthful dream of becoming a chemist. And it was Minister Richburg who told all those assembled that he had, in the end, not really forsaken that dream.

"Reverend Seward, you are a scientist for God," she said from the pulpit. "You study the word of God; you teach us the theories of salvation, faith and grace; we are taught the natural phenomena of those who trust in the Lord. We learn of the universal mercy and grace that Jesus brings. We are all equal in God's eyes—and you allow us to live it."

Throughout the morning and well into the afternoon, the celebration continued, right down to the festive supper in the church hall at the back of the sanctuary. There were selections from the adult choir at the meal, as well as the acknowledgement of honored guests. And the entire hall was decorated with enough red and white balloons and napkins and tablecloths to be mistaken for a Valentine's Day party. But that is fitting; the most compelling story of Granville A. Seward's powerful life is one about a love triangle: the relationships among a man, his church and his God.

Joy is a hard thing to talk about in a cynical world. But there is no other word for what you see on Granville Seward's face, in his walk, in his warm and teasing affection for the members of the congregation, behind the pulpit in the heat of a Sunday sermon. No matter how filled the church on Sunday, how large or small the Friday night Bible study class, no matter how stirring the music or the message at the Thursday night fellowship, there is no one at Mt. Zion who is having a better time than Dr. Seward.

In the sanctuary, behind the pulpit, at the altar or the mourner's bench, he is literally bouncing on the soles of his feet as he walks. In the pulpit, he jumps, as though bouncing doesn't expend enough energy. His voice booms, and there is often laughter in it; he sings beautifully, projects his voice enough to be heard at the back of the church as he leads the congregation in song.

He is a small man in stature, but it's impossible to think about that after a few minutes around him. He laughs so much, talks so much, touches people so much that his height is plainly irrelevant; here is a man who takes up a lot of room.

"The joyful, warm side of me I take from Mother," Dr. Seward says thoughtfully. "I think of my father as more stern. Of course, I only knew him on Sunday; he worked every other day [as a barber]. He'd leave the house at eight and come home at eight, so I only saw the tired, weary side of him. I've always regretted—I always wish I'd known him a different way."

Seward was born in Greenup, Kentucky in 1934, the third of six children. Early in his childhood, the family moved to Columbus, Ohio, but kept in contact with the extended family. It was within that close-knit family circle, in fact, that Seward made his first public appearance as a preacher, at the age of 6.

"I must have been six or seven down in Greenup at a family reunion. I remember all the men were on this big porch. My grandfather said, 'I want my grandson to come up and say the 23rd Psalm for me.' Now our neighbor was a Pentecostal minister, and he would take time out with me and tell me about the Bible when I was six or seven, so I had memorized the 23rd Psalm and I got up and said it."

Seward begins to chuckle at the memory of it. "I don't know if there's a psychological character to this, but after I got through with the psalm, they clapped. And my grandfather got his hat and he said, 'Now, let's give the preacher an offering,' and he passed his hat. They were throwing their nickels and dimes in there. And you know how old timers would take their money and wrap it in a handkerchief? Well, I had this handkerchief with my coins in there. For a little poor kid, here I was, coming back from the family reunion rich!"

His family was religious, but not churchgoing, so young Granville Seward went along to church with his neighbors. Something about it appealed to him. He credits a Loretta Young movie, *Come to the Stable*, about two nuns intent on building a hospital, with his decision to become more deeply involved in the church. "The night I saw that movie, I decided I was going to get into the church."

He began by reading the Bible. He planned to join the Catholic Church, "but something didn't seem to be right." And the varieties of religious experience began to confuse him: "I had friends who were in different churches," he remembered. As a kind of last resort he decided to go to a Sunday service at Shiloh Baptist Church, just two blocks from his home. He'd attended Sunday School there as a child, but had heard that going to service was a different matter. "It was rumored that you had to have a change of suit every Sunday to go to Shiloh, because it was THE church; poor raggedy folks like me—that was not the church that we could go to."

But he did go, and he felt good there, good enough to return for evening service that same night. In a few months, he had joined the church, and was using his after school earnings from a drugstore job to tithe at Shiloh. It was a commitment that caused a serious run-in with his father, who had quite negative attitudes about the clergy.

"Daddy was a lodge man, and he knew a lot of deacons and people of the church; he thought ministers were a bunch of fakes. I remember one night in the kitchen he said, 'Your pastor's living better than you are. We don't have a car; we don't have all the things your pastor has. You just give your money to him.'

"I said, 'Daddy, I'm not giving money to the pastor, I'm giving my money to God because the Bible teaches tithing and I think it's right. I'm going to do it anyway.' And he said, 'Well, you'll just go on naked.' I said okay, and from that day to now, I've bought my own clothes."

But it was another conversation with his father, about a different matter, that Seward says shaped him psychologically. "One Sunday afternoon, [his father] took me upstairs to where he kept his papers—his insurance papers. He said, 'I want you to know about these things, because if anything happens, I'm counting on you to see the family through. I can't count on your older brother.'

"I was proud because I was singled out, you know, that my dad thought I was better than my older brother to just kind of step in if anything happened. Well, it happened sooner than expected—about six months later he died and I took the ball.

"So, I was the man [of the house]. Mother would sometimes be crying and I would say, 'Mother, you have to trust in the Lord, he will see us through.' So, I would take those Social Security checks and pay the bills and my sister next to me, we would walk to the A&P and do the marketing."

It was this early experience, Seward believes, that introduced what he thinks of as a fault and a burden: a reluctance to relinquish control. "I had to make things go. I had to see a thing through and if it didn't work, I had to see that it worked. I have been that way ever since (my father's death) because I had a responsibility; I've run the church like that."

If the young Granville Seward was an adolescent of uncommon responsibility, he was also a young man with a lively mind and varied interests. He was an active churchgoer, true enough, but he was still vulnerable to the lure of a less ordered life. In junior high school, for a time, he flirted with cutting classes and hanging around on the streets of Columbus in imitation of his brother. It took the timely intervention of a science teacher to guide Seward away from the fast lane.

"I really was a predelinquent," he says with more laughter. "I was about 13 then. I'll never forget that science teacher; his name was George DeLoach. He pulled me aside and called me a knucklehead; told me I had a good mind but I wasn't doing anything with it. And he didn't just give me a lecture; he made me his little assistant.

"That meant standing up in front of the class with the teacher. And he'd say, 'Bring me these chemicals, or a beaker,' and I'd go to the back with my set of keys—I was a big shot! He was my idol. And by him bringing me around the lab and working with me—that started my interest in science."

It was with Mr. DeLoach's encouragement that Seward entered the local science fair, sponsored by the Ohio Academy of Science; it was the first time in memory that a black student had entered the fair. Seward won a superior rating and became eligible to compete in the statewide contest. He didn't win the top prize, but all the recognition was enough to whet his appetite for chemistry, especially when, by the time he was a junior at the predominantly white East High School, he won the Collins Memorial Prize in chemistry, the first black student to win the school's highest science honor. That honor, in turn, led to a major disappointment.

"I always remember that the winners of the Collins Prize got ten dollars, and their names were engraved on a bronze plaque in the hallway of the school," Dr. Seward said. "I got the 10 dollars, and I saw that plaque come down, and all my senior year I waited for it to go back up again with my name on it, and it never did.

"I worked as an assistant in the lab my senior year, and one time I was looking for something in a closet, and I found the plaque there; it never did go back up. It hurt me, it really did. I've not yet seen my name on that plaque."

All the while Seward was charting a possible course for himself in the world of chemistry, he remained an active participant at Shiloh Baptist Church. By this time, he had become a sought-after teen revivalist, and even formed a singing group with two friends; the group, The Three Psalmists, were a popular draw throughout Ohio during the summer months. By graduation from high school, he was feeling torn between the desire to study science more deeply and the desire to give his entire life to God. It was a struggle that ended one July morning.

"I got up that morning and there was peace in my mind. I had no dreams, I heard no voices. It's just that on that day, there was no more struggle, only a sense of confidence about my life's direction. I was 17 years old. And I called my pastor and told him I needed to see him.

"He always appeared very stern, and he had these glasses, and he used to look over them at you. I can remember climbing the stairs to his study and sitting down to tell him that I believed I had been called to the ministry. And he began to examine me—how did I know I had been called; what WAS the ministry. I thought it was a real grilling. I thought to myself, "He doesn't believe me. I felt really shaken by it."

After some minutes of interrogation, however, the minister leaned back in his chair and smiled at Seward. " 'I've always known that you were called,' he told me. 'I just wanted you to know. I never told you, because I didn't want people to call you to this ministry.' "

But it was to be an uneven road to his heart's desire. After a little more than a year at Otterbein College, a Baptist-run college in Westerville, Ohio, Seward dropped out for lack of money. In the meantime, he had fallen in love and married Carole Moorehead, a young woman he had met during an appearance during a revival meeting in Zanesville, Ohio.

He would not return to college for five years. During that time, he worked in the salvage department of Westinghouse Electric Corporation to support his wife and family. Seward also commuted 70 miles each way to pastor the First Baptist Church of Rendville, Ohio—a small church most noted as the site of the conversion of Adam Clayton Powell, Sr., a prominent New York minister and father of the noted congressman.

By the time he had earned enough money to continue his studies at Ohio State University, he was the father of two children. He completed his degree in sociology in 1962, and took a job working for the Franklin County Welfare Department as a caseworker. His warmth and affinity for people convinced superiors to move him to the position of intensive caseworker, where he handled the cases of approximately 30 families in an effort to move them into the workforce.

Throughout this period, Seward continued to pastor at the Rendville church, but he had never given up his dream of formal theological training; he had determined that he wanted to attend Colgate Rochester Seminary. But Dr. Seward confesses that because of his youthful attitudes, Carol was at first reluctant to repeat their experience of his undergraduate years.

"Because I didn't do right. She was with the children all day and I always had to go back to the library. I was down in the [student] union having coffee or in one of those little cafes, you know, around the university, talking all this revolutionary stuff. And so she said she wasn't going through another degree with me. I didn't know how we were going to work it out. But the old folks say 'The Lord will make a way.'

"She and I were going to take a vacation and leave the children with the grandparents. We were going to Cape Cod. So I planned the trip so that somehow we were going through Rochester on the way to Cape Cod."

While they were there, the Sewards toured the campus and met Dr. James Bartlett, at that time the president of the seminary. "He was so gracious," Dr. Seward recalled. "A marvelous, beautiful man. He received us so graciously that Carol said, 'Well, if you can get accepted, we'll see if we can't come.'"

In 1964, he was accepted into the master of divinity program at Colgate-Rochester. He resigned his pastoral position with the Rendville church; he and Carole, by now the parents of three children, packed up their belongings and relocated to Rochester. "It was one of the greatest moves of my life," Seward believes. "It was out of the experience of going there that so much of me was shaped."

The intellectual rigor of a formal theological education was precisely what Granville Seward had hungered for, and he reveled in the opportunity to immerse his mind as well as his soul in the search for God. "I have a great thirst for literacy and learning; learning is special because, to me, truth is all one," Seward explains. "It manifests itself in various disciplines, but ultimately, truth is all one. I'm always after the quest for ultimate meaning. And it is religion that lends itself to the expression of what is the ultimate experience of us all."

Seward speaks with great affection about one of his favorite characters in literature, Don Quixote de la Mancha. "I find Don Quixote facinating. I can remember when they created the musical [based on the book], I could really relate to the song, "To Dream the Impossible Dream." Seward leans back in his chair, humming a few bars, then goes on.

"I value the tradition; I can stand in it. And so I buy into the tradition for those things I can use today. But I also like people and things on the cutting edge, those who aren't satisfied with the present proposed solutions. I always say there must be a way to get it to work."

Seward's questing intellect, combined with his personal warmth and his practical experience in the ministry to a small congregation made him a popular student on the Colgate-Rochester campus. By 1967, when he received his Master's Degree in Divinity, he had also won a doctoral fellowship in Theology at Harvard. But he turned it down, choosing instead to accept the call to Mt. Zion Baptist Church in Newark, long regarded as one of the most prominent congregations among African-American Baptists.

Seward was only 33 years old when he came to pastor the Newark church in 1968. Although that doesn't seem especially young at first glance, the median age of African-American ministers is about 52, according to the sociologist and theologian C. Eric Lincoln, coauthor of *The Black Church in the African American Experience*. And it was important for the young pastor to establish his position with the congregation. "When I first came here, you know, the old guard—they had everything under control," Seward recalls. "Here I was, 33 years old, coming to this historic, established congregation. So, I had to wrestle the controls away."

But there was more to be done than a simple divestment of authority from a handful of long-time members. In many senses, Mt. Zion was very much a church set in its ways. "When I first came to serve Mt. Zion, I found a cold, formal church by black church standards," Seward says. "Only one deacon would dare audibly to respond with an 'Amen.' Gospel singing was not a part of worship; in fact, it was frowned upon." What was missing in his new pastorate, Seward believed, was a vibrant sense of spirituality. What he most wanted for his membership was the knowledge that he has possessed, in some form or another, since junior high school: "God can take every situation and recycle it, and bring out of it some positive value. That constant awareness of the way God operates has been the joy of my life."

Seward's work at Mt. Zion Baptist Church for the past two decades has been an experiment of sorts. Can an old and established church change its character? Can a formally educated, even cerebral minister make contact with those whose education has been limited, and still remain in touch with the deep spirituality that is the strength and the hallmark of the traditional African-American church? As with most things, Seward answers with an enthusiastic yes.

It was only natural that his attraction to what he calls "the quest" led him to examine scripture, especially the New Testament, in an effort to formulate a theological basis for the synthesis he was after. Always fascinated by the story of Paul's conversion, he focused on the image advanced in 2 Corinthians 5:17: "If anyone is in Christ, he is a new creation. The old has passed away, behold, the new has come."

Most conservative branches of the Protestant faith regard this as evidence of the need simply to be "born again." But Seward is not a fundamentalist; his years of study and prayer have led him to believe that the contemporary Christian life may find support in many places. "I had to examine as carefully as I could the basic materials, the primary scriptural sources, while remaining open to the voices which speak to us in our own time and situation," he says.

He heard and found support in the work of Paul Tillich and his notions of sin and estrangement; in the work of liberation theologians such as James Cone; in the theories of individuation and self-actualization advanced by psychologists Jung and Maslow. These seemingly disparate voices helped Seward form what he calls the "theology of the New Humanity." It is a theology marked by reconciliation and fundamental change, and rooted in a conversion experience that is uniquely African-American—i.e, a personal and powerful encounter with God Himself. Those who embrace this new identity in Christ come away with "a new sense of the possible, a new sense of freedom and a new sense of responsibility."

Seward lives his life and approaches all the aspects of his ministry at Mt. Zion on the premise that "being in Christ can and does give to life a capacity for wholeness which cannot be found elsewhere. . . . Being in Christ shifts the responsibility for self-actualization from one's will power and determination to faith, which expresses itself in activity. . . . God is our hope and help."

Much of this formal statement of Seward's functional theology comes from his doctoral thesis in ministry, "The New Creation and the Emergence of the New Humanity," written in 1982 while on sabbatical from Mt. Zion. Even though Seward had gladly turned away from doctoral study more than a decade earlier, he had felt the need to be "retooled a bit" as the day-to-day work of ministry went on. At first he thought of only a course or two, but the president of Colgate-Rochester suggested that he ask his congregation for a sabbatical to earn the Doctorate in Ministry. Seward designed a way to schedule his classwork, then met with the deacons.

"To my amazement they said, 'Yes, you don't ask for much.' And they recommended it to the church and the church accepted it unanimously and gave me a sabbatical and paid every dime. And they provided money in the budget that any weekend I wanted to fly home, I could. This congregation has always been very supportive of me."

Members of Mt. Zion are only returning in kind the support and the love they feel from their pastor, reflecting back to him his buoyant belief that all things are possible. There is no clearer example of this new sense of the possible than the number of Mt. Zion members who have determined that they themselves will answer the call to ministry—at least five in the past two years. Two members of Mt. Zion are currently full-time students at Colgate-Rochester Divinity School; one woman is awaiting news of admission to theological school; one man has an additional year of work before completing his undergraduate studies, and one has recently begun college to earn her degree before continuing on to divinity school.

Theodore James, 43, is a senior at Colgate Rochester Seminary. A music teacher for nearly 20 years and the father of a grown son, he had always dreamed of becoming a classical pianist, but that was a dream that evolved over time to encompass his love for the church. "As a child people used to tell me that I would be a preacher, and I would get angry with them," James says. "I didn't want to be a preacher. There were times, though, as I was growing up, that I felt different than other guys my age. Later on, I came to accept that I would have some connection with the church."

For 18 years he lived out that connection as Minister of Music at St. John's Baptist Church in Newark. It was the church of his childhood; his relatives attended the services, he even met his wife there. After so many years, however, James found he was doing occasional sermons, and members of the congregation were once again expressing their belief that he was meant for the pulpit. "I found myself having some encounters with the Lord, but I didn't want to acknowledge what was happening," James says. "I just didn't want to preach. I was angry with God. He had disturbed my comfortable life, I didn't know anything other than music, and I thought about all the sacrifices I would have to make."

Some of James's agitation also came from his changing relationship with St. John's; after a lifetime at one church, he felt it was time to move on. One of the young men who had been a part of the youth choir at St. John's was now the assistant minister at Mt. Zion. It was this young man who told Teddy James about an opening at Mt. Zion for the position of minister of music, a job that would ultimately lead him to a preaching ministry. "I came to Mt. Zion as a troubled musician," he remembers. "I started to attend the Thursday night fellowship; that's where I started talking about some of these issues."

The Thursday night fellowship at Mt. Zion is a key ingredient for Dr. Seward's vision of the new humanity. Originally known as the weekly prayer service, which, under the old order, was attended only by what Dr. Seward referred to as "the faithful few," the format was changed to reflect Seward's idea of what his congregation might really need.

"The format was changed from traditonal Bible study to the study of life as we were living it, with all of its conflicts, both inner and outer," Seward says. "It was almost like group therapy, but in the context of prayer, singing, Bible study and fellowship. . . . We sing, we shout, we pray, we discuss ourselves, we experience God." Here was a prayer meeting as conversant with contemporary theologians as with the prophets, as relevant as the stresses of urban life or the strains of a career change.

After talking for a few weeks in these fellowships, Teddy James went to see Seward privately. "He gave me some scriptures to read and study; we talked about it a lot. And he suggested that I come to the Colgate-Rochester conference on ministry that they hold every semester, along with the conference on black ministry."

James accepted his call and began what he calls "the longest walk I'd ever taken in my life," with the help of Dr. Seward. "He's been a good friend and a mentor to me. I'm a very creative person, and he's allowed me to do some things other pastors would not allow me to do. We've had African drums here, drum majors and batons. We even had a Bible rap." James worked out a part-time arrangement with the church where he continues to serve as minister of music on the two weekends each month that he commutes home from Rochester to see his wife.

At first, he says, Colgate-Rochester was simply his pastor's alma mater. But one evening, while sitting in chapel, it all changed for him. "There's a big stained-glass window with Jesus in it. And on this particular day, the face of Jesus was just alive for me. I could hear him saying, 'This is where I want you to be.' I just cried and cried. And I knew I belonged here. Being here did create some hardships for me, but I'm going to leave everything up to God."

Patricia Richburg, 40, is what is known as a "licensed preacher" in the Baptist faith. A preliminary level in the ordination process, a prospective minister preaches a trial sermon and is "licensed" to preach by the congregation, pending the satisfaction of other requirements. These requirements vary among different churches—Baptists have congregational polity and are not subject to overwhelming denominational authority. But for Mt. Zion members, college and divinity school is mandatory, a reflection of Dr. Seward's own passion for learning.

For Richburg, this means starting over again. "I wasn't really a student," she says. "I just wanted to get through high school." She enrolled in a local community college to take an introduction to psychology course, but had to drop out; the work was too difficult. She has begun again, this time with remedial classes.

Although she is sometimes anxious, she is not deterred. She knows that she has been called; she knows her pastor is with her; that is enough. "He's so wonderful because he's himself; I appreciate that.

"He's not one to take the Bible and interpret it the way so many men do," she says softly. He allows us [as women] to step out and do the things we're able to do. When I realized I had a calling, he didn't knock it. He preached toward me."

Richburg had grown up in Mt. Zion, but left as an adolescent, as so many young people do. For a time, the church was one of the few constant things in her world. Born in North Carolina to a teenage mother, she was given to a paternal uncle and his wife to raise. The couple moved to New York with young Patricia when she was six. Their lives were not happy; her uncle left shortly after their arrival.

One day when Patricia was eight, her aunt—the only mother she had ever known—left for work and didn't come home. "The other tenants let me stay for a month. They fed me and helped me get ready for school. Eventually they took me to the police."

Patricia told the police about the only other kin she knew—the aunt of the woman who had abandoned her. It was this woman who took her in, adopted her, and ultimately raised her. She eventually finished high school and went to work for New Jersey Bell, where she started out as an operator and eventually became a personnel specialist. Along the way, she had a son and a daughter, now 12 and eight, respectively.

"I was a grown woman, at my job for 10 years. [Having children] was planned; that was my way of getting the love I thought I needed. What I did wasn't the right thing to do."

She had returned to Mt. Zion by that time, in need of spiritual support; "I personally asked God for my forgiveness, to help me to sustain myself and to make it." But in encountering Dr. Seward, she found even more.

"I'll never forget the day the deacons called and asked me to become one of them. I remember it was Marie McRae called. And I said, 'Do you know about me?' And they still wanted me; I thought that was the most beautiful thing in the world. Even my pastor approved of me the way I am."

It was that acceptance that cleared the way for Richburg to view herself as more worthy, her story as important and valuable. Now she believes a large part of her ministry will be to bring her difficult story to others. "I just want to be able to tell people there is hope. If you just keep your faith in God, he will direct your path, he will give you the ability to live through things you didn't think you could live through."

And she relies heavily on the affirmation she's received at Mt. Zion, through the fellowship of its members and the commitment of Dr. Seward.

"He's bringing the Holy Spirit into the church. He's trying to bring us to where we claim we're at. We're not as spiritual as he'd like us to be. Many pastors drive a Mercedes and wear gold. He's mostly into getting an education and edifying God."

Seward's congregation want him to write a book. They think he has plenty to tell the world about Jesus, about the love of God, about the new humanity. He thinks about it, but can't imagine when there would be time. "I feel that my best ministry is to individuals, that where my strength may lie is in the personal dimension of the Gospel."

His strength is there because he, with God's help, has earned it. "The basis for all my joy is the crises that faith has brought me through," he says. "In ministry, so much of the work is done at the point of human suffering. The death of others, counseling, relating constantly to people who have AIDS and the other human tragedies that are part of life. My approach has always been not to go around it, or deny it, but to go right through it."

Dr. Seward would be the first to admit that, as wonderful a life as ministry is, it can be draining, exhausting. But it is never debilitating. Granville Seward knows that God is with him always. "I feel I have a very personal relationship with God. I know God through Jesus in a relationship that allows for anger; I challenge Him.

"I think we even chuckle at times, especially when we're dealing with me. I'll say, 'God, ain't I a mess?' And he'll say, 'Yes, but you're mine.'"

Virgil Elizondo

A Particular Man

*To do theology from the standpoint of the poor-
est and most disdained sectors of humanity is
not to jump on a bandwagon.*
—Gustavo Guitiérrez

When Virgil Elizondo was growing up on the near-west
side of San Antonio, during the late 1930s and early 1940s, his
father, Virgilio, ran a mom-and-pop grocery store on the corner
of Perez and Minter. Virgilio was accustomed to working long
hours, not only in the store but on the streets of the barrio as
well. A neighborhood grocer operates on a thin margin in the
best of times, but these were tough times, and income from the
store wasn't enough.

To support his extended family—his wife, daughter, son,
mother-in-law, and father—Virgilio took to selling candy wholesale by day to other small grocery and drugstores in the barrio
while his wife tended to customers at their own store. By evening Virgilio was tired. Still his day's work was not done. There
was his own store to tend—shelves to stock, floors to sweep,
accounting to be done, and orders to be placed. By late evening
Virgilio was exhausted. Yet there was still one last matter to
attend to. And while he regarded it an obligation, he approached it more in the spirit of pleasure than duty.

A religious man—though not, by his son's account, a
"churchy" man—Virgilio would end his day in prayer. He
would settle into a living-room chair, facing a picture of the
Sacred Heart of Jesus on the wall opposite, and talk to God.

But he didn't spill out his troubles to the Almighty. He didn't ask the Lord for favors. Rather, he tried to make God laugh.

God, Virgilio reasoned, must feel awfully burdened hearing all mankind's woes, all the heartbreak, all the daily disappointments. What God could use was a bit of comic relief, a little lightening up. So, from Virgilio, God heard jokes, the funniest jokes the exhausted grocer had heard that day, in the store and on the streets, from his friends and from his customers. Virgilio would laugh as he spoke to God. And while there's no record of any response from God, Virgilio felt better after communing with his maker and generally went to bed refreshed in spirit, relaxed in body, and better disposed toward the rest of the human race.

What does Virgil Elizondo, who grew up to be a Roman Catholic priest, make of his father's simple, if somewhat unconventional, piety? "It makes a lot of sense to me," he says. "Humor is one of the great gifts of grace. The God-imagery of my father is still some of the most profound I have to this day. He could have run circles around most theologians."

It's rare for an American diocesan priest to be perceived as a visionary. Even so, there are those who insist that a hopeful future for harmonious coexistence among the peoples of the Americas is best envisioned and best articulated in the writings and teachings of Virgil Elizondo, a cathedral rector in his middle fifties who lives and works not more than a hundred feet from the exact cartographic center of San Antonio. For several reasons, Elizondo's priestly life has been anything but commonplace among American diocesan clergy, those priests who work directly with that 27 percent of the United States population which calls itself Catholic.

Elizondo is a diocesan priest who also happens to be a theologian, an unlikely combination in the United States. Ordination to the priesthood as a member of a religious order—the Jesuits, say, or the Franciscans—often means opportunities for advanced education, travel, and, something dear to the American heart, specialization. But becoming a diocesan priest in this country generally spells a lifetime of working in parishes, with little hope of earning further theology degrees or finding a change of scene outside the boundaries of the diocese.

As a theologian, Elizondo enjoys the status of the special-ist. From all over the world come requests for his consultation, his speeches, his enthusiastic and inspiring presence. Elizondo travels tens of thousands of miles every year. During his al-most 30 years of priesthood, he has had ample time for study and reflection. He holds one earned doctorate—from the In-stitut Catholique in Paris—and two honorary degrees, including one from the Jesuit School of Theology at Berkeley. He got his master's in pastoral studies at Ateneo University in the Philip-pines. He is the founder of the Mexican American Cultural Center, a leading institution in the United States for the train-ing of Catholic ministers to the Hispanic community, and the Incarnate Word Pastoral Institute, both of San Antonio.

Elizondo has served as the director of religious education for the Archdiocese of San Antonio and as academic dean of Assumption Seminary, also in San Antonio. He is the author of nine books and the editor of many others. He speaks seven languages, which is useful because Elizondo's work is of inter-national scope. Elizondo, in fact, is one of 43 Catholic theolo-gians worldwide who edit *Concilium*, a prestigious international theological journal published in seven languages. In short, he is an energetic scholar whose curriculum vitae is eight dense pages long, more than half of it devoted to keynote addresses delivered and articles published.

Impressive as all this is—and Elizondo's vita would be the envy of many a full-time academician—he is a working pastor as well, a man rooted in place and time who incorporates into his writing and teaching the particulars of his concrete, pastoral experience, both the sublime and the prosaic. When he theolo-gizes, Elizondo does so having recently presided at daily Mass, heard his parishioners' confessions, baptized their babies, wit-nessed their marriages, anointed their sick and dying, and bur-ied their dead—also after having looked into the latest in a se-ries of plumbing problems and met with the parish bookkeeper. And, conversely, when he tends to his pastoral duties, especially when he preaches, which he does exceptionally well, he brings a world of exposure to what he has to say.

While most pastors exercise substantial spiritual authority in the lives of their parishioners, their influence rarely extends beyond the walls of their respective churches. It's different with Elizondo. Figuratively, anyway, Elizondo's church, San Fernando Cathedral, in downtown San Antonio, is home to a sort of international parish of millions: its 9 a.m. Sunday Mass is beamed by the local Spanish-language Univision station to a satellite and appears on cable television in many places in the United States, Canada, Guam, Mexico, Puerto Rico, and the Virgin Islands. Although Elizondo is not always the presiding celebrant for the televised Mass, "Nuestra Santa Misa de las Americas," he is its executive producer and the guiding energy behind the program.

There is something else that makes Virgil Elizondo unusual among parish priests in the United States. He is Hispanic. And Hispanic priests are not plentiful among the American diocesan clergy, even in a Southwestern state like Texas, which has a large and growing Hispanic population. Why a traditionally Catholic group like the Mexican-American yields so few religious vocations is a much-debated question in the American Church. Many bishops are quick to contend there are few qualified Hispanic candidates. But Hispanic priests, Elizondo included, point to a none-too-subtle discrimination, past and present, on the part of bishops, vocation directors, and seminary administrators that has discouraged Hispanics from seeking a life of service to the Church.

This tension could account in part for the defection in recent years of thousands of American Hispanics to evangelical and fundamentalist Protestant denominations, where Hispanic clergy are more plentiful and congregations smaller. Having a Hispanic pastor like Elizondo—one who relishes the faith practices of his people's past and has unapologetically revived them for his parishioners—is rare and cause for outright celebration.

San Fernando Cathedral is just across Main Street from the pleasantly shaded Plaza de las Islas, in a downtown neighborhood of government buildings, small pawn shops, check-cashing establishments, and stores that sell guns. The cathedral's exterior walls are a muddy tan, flecked with cream and streaked with black, particularly around the arched central doorway. The sanctuary of San Fernando—where the altar, lectern, and tabernacle rest—is approaching its three hundredth anniversary and is the oldest cathedral sanctuary in the United

States. The rest of the building has stood about a century and a quarter. The original church was constructed when Texas was still part of Mexico, and the so-called addition, which is in fact the vast majority of the structure, was begun in 1868, 23 years after Texas had become part of the United States. The sense a first-time visitor gets of the building's interior is that of an even weatheredness: everything—the floors, the pews, the doors—is worn smooth by the touch of human hands or feet.

On this bright, warm Sunday morning, about two dozen 15-year-old girls in beautiful dresses were celebrating their *quinceanera*, the colorful Hispanic equivalent of the traditional Anglo coming-out, after which, as Elizondo has written, a girl begins her "social development outside the home." In the Hispanic community, all such rites of passage typically have a strong religious component. San Fernando was unusually crowded this morning, which made it all the harder for the TV camera people to make their way around.

Elizondo entered the church from the back, in a procession composed of three altar boys and two associate pastors, shaking hands and greeting people seated along the center aisle. From the sanctuary he greeted those present in the church and those watching the Mass on television. He also welcomed, by name and city, out-of-town visitors who had traveled to San Antonio to participate in the Mass they'd seen so often on TV.

Elizondo's appearance is that of an unreconstructed if gently aging Boy Scout. He's short, about five-foot-six, and thickly built, with short, well-muscled arms and small, strong hands. He is fair-complected, his black hair bearing only traces of gray. A little crescent of mid-life, mid-section paunch that shows beneath shirt or his Mass vestments belies his active life. He wears glasses that are just slightly too big for his round face, and they ride down the ridge of his nose in a hopelessly unfashionable way. He's an affable man, with a boyish laugh and a boyish grin, and there's a hint of youthful shyness in his demeanor. But his voice undoes this.

When Elizondo opens his mouth and out comes that deep, rich, authoritative voice, so heavily yet pleasantly accented, a listener's attention unreflectively shifts to whatever he is saying, all the more so when he is preaching. During his sermon this morning he shared some thoughts with the girls and their families about love. As he spoke, he stood just a few feet from a circle on the floor of the old sanctuary that marks the exact center of his native city.

"Love," Elizondo said, "is not cheap, not merely a response to an attraction. Love is a lifetime discipline of learning, an education of the heart. What love means for you as young women—for all of us—is that there is nothing more life-giving than to be a life-giver to another. But, unfortunately, we humans are too often life-*taking*, because we immediately think the worst of somebody else, or become so impatient with them. So often we love another person when the other person is, humanly speaking, lovable. But when they start showing faults or become diseased, we're through with them, disgusted."

After Mass, Elizondo greeted parishioners and visitors on the sidewalk in front of the church, alternating between Spanish and English with great ease and sometimes lapsing into "Spanglish," a creative combination of the two. Elizondo is more apt to hug people than to shake hands, and he gave and received countless hugs and pats on the back. He posed for photographs with the girls and their families at a reception on the front lawn of the cathedral rectory, on the top floor of which are his living quarters. He was awash in a fiesta-like atmosphere that went on until it was time for the next Mass to begin. Elizondo's parishioners don't just come to church and leave at the first opportunity; they stick around. What happens outside the church is, in its own way, as important as what happens inside.

A parishioner, an old woman, was dying of cancer at Baptist Hospital, where Elizondo visited her on Sunday afternoon. He wore a black, short-sleeved clerical shirt with a Roman collar, and he carried with him a vial of holy oil, the kind priests use to anoint the sick and dying. He stopped at the nursing station in the intensive-care unit, introduced himself, and asked if the woman's family was with her. Experience told him that critically ill patients are often difficult to understand, and that a close relative can be both a reassuring presence for the patient and a translator for the priest.

"They just stepped out for lunch, Father," the nurse on duty told him. "They'll be back a little later."

"How is she?" he asked.

"She's waiting to die, Father. It could be anytime now." The nurse looked at her watch. "Actually, we expect she'll go yet this afternoon."

Elizondo walked down the hall, searching for the room number the nurse had given him. Scanning the numbers to the side of the doors, he said, "I'm surprised the family all left at once. Often people's greatest fear is of dying alone." He found the room and looked in.

The dying woman lay on her side, with her back to the door. She was emaciated, her neck unbearably thin and her arms the diameter of broom handles. Intravenous lines ran into her body from bags attached to poles on either side of the bed. A larger tube carried fluids away, to another bag, also fastened to the bedstead. In this larger tube there was a momentary rush of blood. Elizondo walked into the room and around to the other side of the bed. He bent over the woman and spoke her name in his deep voice—tender now, and soothing—while he gently touched her hand.

Suddenly, and with startling force, the woman raised her torso from the mattress a foot or so and tried to speak. Her voice was excited and her speech garbled. Elizondo couldn't understand what she was saying. In reassuring tones he told her who he was, that he was here to bless her, that God loved her and was with her—that God was ready to take her home. He wanted to anoint her, he said. But the woman continued to speak, excitedly and unintelligibly. Was she frightened of him, terrified of death? Or was she ecstatic, happy to see him, to be near the end of her pain, to be going home?

Elizondo was confused. *If only the family were here*, he seemed to be thinking.

The dying woman fell silent and slowly eased back onto the bed. Elizondo put his hand on her forehead and made the sign of the cross. He touched her hand again. He prayed aloud, softly. The woman was calm and quiet. Again there was blood in the large tube, a spasm of red mixing with some other liquid. Then the tube was clear again. "God loves you," Elizondo said. "God is with you." He gave her a blessing. Gently, he patted her bony shoulder and walked out of the room.

In the hall he said, softly, "She may have been fighting me off, and she may have been trying to hug me. I couldn't tell." He stopped at the nursing station and asked the nurse to tell the woman's family that he'd stopped by. Visiting the dying is never routine, he said as he stepped into the elevator, but sometimes it's worse with an older person. What is now called the Sacrament of the Sick used to go by the foreboding name of Extreme Unction. Before the Second Vatican Council, the sacrament was administered only to the dying; so a priest's arrival meant death was imminent, or so the sick person had every cause to infer. Although today's Sacrament of the Sick is for those seriously ill as well as the dying, some older people still associate anointing solely with death and react in panic to the priest's presence.

Later, driving back to San Fernando, Elizondo reflected on his personal view of death and the afterlife, which are at the center of any priest's ministry and, presumably, uppermost in his mind. "If the Lord is merciful, I think he'll take me quickly," he said, giving a short laugh. He fell silent after that. "But, then," he said, "it's not for me to decide." Elizondo was quiet for a few more moments. Then he spoke again, quietly and deliberately.

"I think," he said, "I think death is going to sleep and waking up in eternity." He paused again. "I have no death wish," he said, "but I've had a pretty packed life, and if the Lord wanted to take me today I'd be thankful. I'm looking forward to it, that eternal feast, a place of succulent foods, and the best of good drink, and the best of friends." His voice was even softer now and his speech slower. "I think heaven is an unending fiesta with all our ancestors and relatives and friends, when we come to accept each other as we *are*. I think we're going to have a lot to talk about. I think we'll look back and laugh at the stupidity of some of the molehills we allowed to become mountains. There'll be a lot of joke-telling." He smiled. "I think of heaven as the ultimate acceptance of being accepted by God as I am," he said. "God is merciful and God is just, and God combines mercy and justice in a way that none of us can even begin to suspect. And thanks be to God it's only God who makes the ultimate judgment, and not one of us."

Elizondo founded the Mexican American Cultural Center—
"MACC," as it's known—on the campus of San Antonio's Assumption Seminary in 1972, shortly after the Chicano movement began gathering momentum in the United States, seeking
the political, social, and economic betterment of the Hispanic
peoples. "The hidden anger of a sleepy and festive people was
erupting violently all over the United States," Elizondo has
written. So great was the need for an institution like the Mexican American Cultural Center, and so intense the demand for
its services, that "MACC was born an adult," Elizondo says. It
is his most enduring accomplishment, with hundreds of seminarians and priests from all over the country studying Hispanic
culture and the unique face of Latin Catholicism there every
year.

"A lot of our own have been alienated from their culture,"
Elizondo says of Hispanic clergy and seminarians. "They've lost
touch with what makes the Hispanic Church unique and vibrant. Many Anglos have had little or no exposure to Hispanic
Catholicism, and without some introduction to it they are entirely lost ministering to Hispanics. When you look at Latin
Catholicism from the categories of European Catholicism, you
get a rather macabre understanding of it, especially when you
see the way we deal with death and with the dead who've come
before us. Our celebration of the dead on November second is a
very festive thing: we make skeletons, we bring up pictures of
the dead, we make altars to the dead. Because for us the dead
are *alive*. And by our keeping them alive in our hearts and
minds, we give them life. A lot of Anglos don't understand it,
but when you understand it from within you get a totally different notion of it."

MACC's founding showed Elizondo to be capable of seeing
a need and meeting it well, but it also revealed a broad prophetic streak in his intellectual makeup. Demographers expect
that by the turn of the century Hispanics will be the largest
minority in the United States and will constitute a substantial
portion, some say half or more, of the American Catholic population. Given the generally dreary history of American
Catholicism's insensitivity and sometime hostility toward its
Spanish-speaking members, MACC and Elizondo's writing and

teaching have been nothing short of gifts to the Hispanic faithful, gifts that will be even more appreciated in years to come.

Elizondo's drive to explain his people and their religious faith derived from three sources: his upbringing, his own seminary experience, and his early years as a priest shortly after the close of the Second Vatican Council, in the mid-1960s.

His parents were Mexican immigrants who fared well enough financially with their grocery business, but many of their neighbors struggled to survive and did so only with the help of merchants like the Elizondos, who extended credit. The comfortable insularity of the barrio, with friends and neighbors constantly stopping by the grocery store and the extended family living in the same house, which adjoined the store, was a source of comfort and pleasure to young Virgil, who thought of himself and his family and friends as *Mejicanos* residing in the United States. Slowly, however, reality intruded. Elizondo began to notice that he was perceived as different. He recalls seeing a sign on a downtown San Antonio restaurant door: "NO DOGS, NIGGERS, OR MEXICANS ALLOWED." Spanish was the language of the barrio. He struggled to learn English in the early grades and to avoid speaking his native tongue at school, where the nuns looked askance at the use of a "foreign" language. The comfort of home became a haven in a sometimes-ugly Anglo world.

Deep religious faith marked his home life, part of it home devotions, such as his father's telling jokes to God, and part of it church-related. The family store and home were just across the street from Christ the King church. "One distinct thing I learned very early in my life, way back, was that many of our families here were very, very religious, but they were parish-centered, not so concerned with dogmas or Church politics or Rome," Elizondo says. "So you learned to love the Church, but at the same time not to be that hung up about it," a point of view he holds to this day.

Many religious priests from Spain worked as pastors in San Antonio at the time, and they had a reputation for acting as if they'd been sentenced to serve time among a lesser people. Elizondo was fortunate to have Father Vincent Andres for his pastor. Andres was a Spaniard who had a penchant for getting things done. "He never let law get in the way of doing what he wanted to do," Elizondo recalls. "He always said it was better to ask for forgiveness than to ask for permission."

As a college student at St. Mary's University, in San Antonio, majoring in chemistry, Elizondo considered applying to medical school. But priesthood exerted the greater draw. At the time he wasn't aware of the distinction between the diocesan and religious priesthood. He applied to study at Assumption Seminary, in San Antonio, solely because he didn't want to attend an out-of-town school. The idea of priesthood did not please his parents, particularly his father. "The only difficult thing about seminary was how to tell my parents I was going," he says. "It was even more difficult than I thought it was going to be. All my family is very anticlerical, for all good historical reasons. The Church in Mexico, unfortunately, had a very poor record; it betrayed the people in many ways. So even though the culture is deeply rooted in Catholicism, it doesn't trust the officialdom within the Church."

Seminary was not one of the high points of Elizondo's life. In retrospect, he believes the studies were meager, the instruction poor, and the pastoral content virtually nil. Though he won't discuss any of this in detail, part of Elizondo's distaste derives from his having witnessed ugly official discrimination against black and Mexican-American seminarians. While it never affected him personally—he was a gifted student—he saw what it did to others, and that made a lasting impression. "I can remember many fine men—God, the way they humiliated them, asking them to repeat things in class, purposely mispronouncing their names in horrible ways! It was bad news."

Elizondo was ordained a priest of the Archdiocese of San Antonio on May 25, 1963, about eight months after the opening, in Rome, of the Second Vatican Council, whose shock waves are still felt. Vatican II is the context of Elizondo's theological and pastoral work. Among many other things, the council emphasized the need for religious and cultural pluralism in the Church. Where Vatican I had emphasized matters pertaining to the Church universal, Vatican II stressed the Church *particular,* the indigenous Church, place- and culture-specific and pastored by the local bishop and his priests. The council fathers reiterated those beliefs and practices that are of universal importance to all Catholics, while at the same time reminding the Church of its long-standing practice of building upon the indigenous culture wherever possible. This notion was to be of signal importance to Elizondo's priesthood.

As a seminarian in his last year of theology school, and later as a new priest, Elizondo followed the council proceedings with great interest. Like most young diocesan priests, upon ordination he worked as an associate pastor in parishes. His vocation took a dramatic turn in 1965, however, when then-Archbishop Robert Lucey appointed him archdiocesan Director of Religious Education just months after the close of Vatican II. While his friends tended to the mechanics of parochial life, Elizondo worked as an educator during an exciting yet profoundly confusing time in Church history. Great chaos inevitably attends great movement, and post-conciliar euphoria was larded with ambivalence and tumult. Religious educators all over the world struggled to interpret the council's directives and sentiments.

The difference between Catholicism as practiced by Mexican-Americans and that of their non-Hispanic counterparts in the United States was always significant, but the disparity was heightened after Vatican II, when Catholicism in the United States became (as Elizondo puts it) "Protestantized"—less devotional, less solicitous of the saints and the Virgin Mary and more centered on Jesus and the *word* of God. All over the United States, Hispanics were angered by priests who, afire with what they saw as the "spirit" of Vatican II and smitten with what Elizondo describes as a "Protestant fear and distrust of images," sought to rid churches of their statues, shrines, and votive lights and to usher in a bright new era of "Christocentric" Catholicism. These priests often belittled those who objected to this summary housecleaning, made them feel foolish or vulgar for their cherished beliefs and devotions, and urged them to grow up and get with the progressive program.

Elizondo himself delighted in some Vatican II-inspired liturgical changes—celebrating Mass in the vernacular and facing the people as he did so, for example—and he briefly acquired a taste for the lean new look churches were taking on. "There was a new church here in San Antonio where I helped out on weekends, St. Timothy's, built very beautifully in the round, just wonderful for the new liturgy," he recalls. "But the people weren't at all happy with their new church. It wasn't friendly. There was an abstract Christ up there by the altar, but no statues. I remember talking to these people, trying to explain to them why they shouldn't have all those saints' statues cluttering things up. After all, we were supposed to be *Christo*centric, right? Oh, yes, I had *all* the right terminology.

"They listened patiently. Then in all their wisdom they said, in essence, 'Yes, Father, you're absolutely right, we've got to be Christocentric, but to be Christocentric doesn't mean to be Christo*exclusivist*. If you're at the center, you have to be the center of something. You're not alone or you wouldn't be the *center*. In the New Testament, Christ was always with people, he loved having people around, so why don't you want Jesus' friends around? The saints are his friends, and they're *our* friends.' It made sense. So, in came the saints! They could have all the statues they wanted."

This incident was humbling for a young priest much taken with incarnational theology, which stressed God's having taken an enfleshed existence, Jesus' humanity as dignifying human life, and God's redeeming sinful humanity through a selfless act of both divine and human love. The incarnational approach was hardly new, but Vatican II had given it a boost, and it came to great popularity in the years following the council. Latin Catholicism had always had a strong incarnational flavor, particularly in its emphasis on the communion of saints, the connectedness of the living faithful with those who had gone before them, especially the saints, the Virgin Mary, and ancestors. Now Elizondo came to see that a rich incarnational understanding of the faith was his all along, the legacy of his upbringing in the barrio. And he underwent a "gradual reconversion to the profound faith and its expressions of a people who for many, many generations did not have priests or nuns around and yet maintained the faith"—people like his parents and grandparents.

Two years into his assignment as religious-education director, Elizondo acted as a translator and personal aide for Archbishop Lucey during a 1968 meeting of Latin American bishops at Medellin, Columbia. The meeting's objective was to study and interpret the documents of the Second Vatican Council as they pertained to a mostly Catholic region, terribly poor and desperately short of priests. Medellin was the beginning of Elizondo's broad exposure to Latin American theologians and to a growing regional movement known as liberation theology.

During the Medellin conference Elizondo met two men who would exert a particularly significant influence on him in the years to come: Monsignor Francisco Aguilera, then national director of catechesis in Mexico and now an auxiliary bishop of Mexico City, and Jacques Audinet, a professor at the Institut Catholique in Paris, where many Latin American theologians and bishops had studied.

Later that year, Elizondo went to Anteneo University in Manila to study for a master's degree at the East Asian Pastoral Institute, headed by a friend of his, a Spanish Jesuit named Nebreda. From Nebreda, who echoed the fathers of Vatican II, "I learned much about the beauty of cultural diversity. . . . I also came to understand better, with his help, the deeply personal and personalizing nature of Christian revelation and faith," Elizondo has written. "I came to realize better that, in the light of the *personal* character of the incarnation, the cultural conditioning of the individual was not to be thought of as just an aid to proclaim the gospel, but as the medium through which God chose to reveal himself." Elizondo's time in Manila was his first extended period away from San Antonio. "I could begin to see things about us here that I had never suspected," he says.

Aguilera began inviting him to teach in Mexico City several times a year and pushed him to write about his people. "I remember having phenomenal anthropological, philosophical discussions with Augilera about who the Mexican in the U.S. really was," Elizondo says. "We had roots here, we had history here, we had memories Mexicans didn't have and yet we shared a memory, but we were different, *very* different, from the Anglo-American. Who were we, exactly?" The answer was far from clear. But Elizondo took Aguilera's advice and began to write about his people. When he did so, he kept another mentor's lessons in mind, too—those of Nebreda, of Manila.

Back home in San Antonio, Elizondo continued to mull over and write about the questions he'd discussed with Aguilera and Nebreda. When MACC came into being, in 1972, it provided both a forum for Elizondo's teaching and writing and many invaluable sources of insight, plus additional exposure to Latin American theologians. During his early years at MACC Elizondo focused upon reclamation: reclaiming for himself and his people those elements of Hispanic culture and worship that had been lost to acculturation or suppressed after Vatican II. Suitable textbooks for MACC students were hard to find, so Elizondo wrote them himself. No question he posed was more significant than that he'd begged with Aguilera in Mexico City: *Who are we, exactly?* The brown Virgin of Guadalupe held some answers.

During her several appearances, in 1531, to an Indian peasant, Juan Diego, on the outskirts of Mexico City, the Virgin urged the pre-Columbian Indians suffering under the Spanish to mix with their conquerors, accept the Spaniards' religious faith, and live—as opposed to dying in great numbers, broken in body and spirit, which was their present plight. The Indians accepted the Virgin's maternal solution to their grievous problem, and the Mexican race is the result of the fusion. Thus two important words found permanent places in Elizondo's anthropological vocabulary: *mestizo* ("mixed," "hybrid") and *mestizaje*, which he defines as "the origination of a new people from two ethnically disparate parent peoples." Celebrated by Mexicans as the maternal face of God and the mother of their race, the Virgin of Guadalupe was of great significance to Mexican-Americans, too, Elizondo concluded—a perfect symbol for another mutuality, another *mestizaje*, this one north of the Mexican border.

During his years at MACC, Elizondo further articulated the differences between Anglo and Hispanic culture, bearing in mind that Mexican-Americans are products of both. "I realized we were looking at two different anthropologies, two different views of life," he recalls. "The Anglo considers life a problem to be solved or an obstacle to be overcome, whereas the Mexican considers life a mystery to be lived and celebrated. Sure life's a problem, so let's *enjoy* it." He came to see that Hispanic Catholicism is as different from Anglo-American Catholicism as the latter is from mainline Protestantism.

"Mexican Catholicism is very personal, very prophetic, very festive," he says. "U.S. Catholicism is very *obligation*-oriented. For Mexican Catholics, the image of Christ being whipped is appealing because life *is* hard. But there's resurrection. God triumphs through death itself. In the U.S., however, we can't tolerate the unpleasant, so one of the problems with U.S. Catholicism is that we love Easter Sunday but don't want to take Good Friday too seriously. The Mexican, on the other hand, sees life as an ongoing Good Friday and Easter Sunday. Now, admittedly, the Hispanic side too easily accepts problems: 'That's life,' we say. Whereas the U.S. side picks up the challenge and does everything it can do. But there are some things we *can't* do.

"You see, the Anglo wants to *understand* everything, wants to get into categories and definitions and dogmas. The Latino is far more comfortable with personal relationships—with God, with Mary, with the saints. 'Dogmas are fine,' we say, 'but the Pope will take care of those. Whatever the Pope wants, fine, we'll believe it, but meanwhile I really like St. Anthony. He's one of my good friends.' I think Christianity is at root a personal relationship which was later codified into doctrine. But doctrine and dogma cannot substitute for the personal relationship."

During the mid-1970s, Jacques Audinet, with whom Elizondo had become friends after their meeting at Medellin in 1968, suggested that Elizondo further the work he'd done at MACC and earn a doctorate at the Institut Catholique. Elizondo accepted the invitation and went to Paris. There, with the help of Vatican II documents and the direction of Audinet, Elizondo came to see that "every concrete Christian community had the privilege and obligation to reflect on the meaning of its faith. No matter how many excellent christologies there might be in the world, it was no excuse for the local community"—the local, place-specific Catholic Church—"not to work out its own expression of who Christ is and what he is doing in their midst," he has written.

Early in his time in Paris, "some unidentified inner drive kept pushing me to discover a connection between Jesus and our own situation," Elizondo has written of this period. "Intuitively I felt it was there." Elizondo's repeated reading of the gospels caused him to conclude that Jesus' origins bore many striking similarities to those of Mexican-Americans, who, often rejected by both Mexico and Anglo America, occupy a physical, psychological, and spiritual borderland not unlike Galilee in Jesus' time—from which, popular wisdom had it, nothing good had ever come.

"In his continued identification with the poor and rejected of society, Jesus entered and left human society as a reject," Elizondo wrote in his thesis, subsequently published as *Galilean Journey*. Elizondo made the point that the incarnation, God's enfleshment, was God's entrance into human history, and that, God being God, he could have entered human history at any time or place he chose. He could have become part of any cultural milieu, occupied any station in life. And yet he chose to enter human history as a poor Jew in the borderland country of Galilee. *That*, Elizondo believed, was significant, because it neatly confounded human expectations about how God operates and aptly reinforced Jesus' message, which is for all places and all times.

The God of history who entered history, whose death and resurrection placed him beyond history, is still at work in the world, revealing himself anew every day, and nowhere more so, Elizondo concluded, than among those at the margin of human affairs, the poor and the suffering and the outcast. Those who generally don't amount to much in the world's eyes are thereby called to a prophetic role in society, just as Jesus was. Elizondo came to see that Mexican-Americans exercise this prophetic role during their many fiestas, in which their joy, despite their suffering, speaks of their inner realization that they are, in flesh and spirit, the beginning of something new. The poor "are the privileged of God. God lives with them and among them. It is in the face and person of Jesus the poor Galilean that the face of God is manifested," Elizondo wrote. Mexican-Americans' "*mestizaje* is their Galilean identity and challenge," he said in his thesis. "The world's rejection of *mestizaje* is not unrelated to God's choice of it. What the world rejects, God chooses—to advance the historical working out of the *eschaton*, the final age, one step further."

Elizondo came to see that the Mexican-American is at the center of yet another *mestizaje*, as northern Mexicans blend, biologically and culturally, with Anglo-Americans in the Southwestern United States. Marginalized, but exuding many human traits North American culture is losing or lacks altogether, the Mexican-American is a likely agent for a more harmonious coexistence between two widely differing ethics. In his very being, the Mexican-American *is* the merger of the two. It was in Paris that Elizondo came to see the strength of the differences. "My thesis of mutuality is that each—the Mexican, the Anglo—has a great deal to offer the other, both in terms of religious expression and in terms of society in general," he says.

Just as Jesus refused to be the temporal revolutionary who forcibly, violently, liberates his people from an oppressive regime, Elizondo does not entertain violence against those whose prejudice keeps Hispanics from realizing their potential. Nor is he blind to his people's deficiencies. "We have the tragic sense of history," he says. "We know we've been stepped on. But we're not saying we want to get rid of those who've done us injustice. On the contrary, we'd like to join with them and have them join with us, and together we can create something new that's better for both. We're crazy enough to believe that both can be winners."

Unlike many today who advance notions of "liberation" from "oppressive structures," Elizondo does not proceed by way of bashing all things Western. Both the man and his ideas are moderate, their measuredness deriving from their solid grounding in Scripture and Catholic doctrine and practice. Elizondo believes too much in original sin, in good and evil, to succumb to the heady wine of utopianism.

His interest in liberation theology continues, however. One of its chief proponents, Gustavo Guitiérrez, a parish priest in the slums of Lima, Peru, and author of the seminal *A Theology of Liberation*, is one of Elizondo's heroes. As with any popular movement, Elizondo says, liberation theology has had its occasional excesses, but mostly it has been misunderstood by a European-thinking Vatican establishment. "It's a tragedy, a disaster, that Rome doesn't recognize its friends and allies," he says. "The institutional church has failed to recognize the incredible fidelity of people who are interested in liberation theology and basic Christian communities, the two great fears of Rome. These are the two sources of new energy that will give the Church incredible new life in Latin America—and great credibility. And these people are far more faithful to the Church than a lot of our contemporary progressive theologies of the

Western world. In fact, some of the progressive theologies of the West consider liberation theology to be neo-conservative, because it speaks of 'sin' and 'grace.' Liberation theology takes up all the classical themes and reinterprets them from the perspective of the poor and the suffering"—which is precisely what Elizondo has done.

Elizondo was appointed rector of San Fernando cathedral in 1983. It was his first pastorate and an unusually big challenge. San Fernando was a depleted parish, the church badly in need of repair. "Some of Virgil's detractors said that he had been an intellectual, an academic, a philosopher, but not a pastor of men and women, not a shepherd," said his friend Henry Cisneros, a former mayor of San Antonio. "Some predicted he would be incapable of reaching down in the way one must to be a pastor. But he proved them wrong. He took a church and made it *the* best: the best liturgically, the most active, the most energetic, the most involved, the most colorful, the most community-oriented, and the most family-centered. And he projected it internationally, on television." So popular is San Fernando today, with both Hispanic and Anglo Catholics, that parishioners who arrive at the cathedral fewer than 10 minutes before some Sunday Masses find themselves standing for an hour in the back of the congested church, if not on the front steps looking in the open doors.

Many who watch the televised Mass write or call the Cathedral to praise the very things San Fernando parishioners relish. These include Elizondo's pungent blend of pre-Second Vatican Council liturgical splendor—processions, incense, bells at the elevation of the Eucharistic bread and wine—with the best of the post-conciliar reforms, including the use of the vernacular (generally Spanish) in the Mass, lay people as scripture readers, energetic, upbeat music (often interlaced with traditional hymns, some sung in Latin), and compelling preaching. What also pleases many viewers is San Fernando's unabashedly "old-style" decor: plenty of statues of the saints and the Virgin Mary, large stations of the cross, flickering votive lights, and vivid stained-glass windows—the very sacramentals that traditionally gave Catholicism its human face, but which contemporary Catholic liturgists have been bent on purging with unholy zeal. There is also the matter of how what happens on the television screen strikes those at home—or in the hospital, or in prison. A great many Hispanics watch the Mass, of course, but so do a lot of Anglos, of all ages. And from their many enthusiastic letters to Elizondo one can infer a hunger for rich liturgical expression unavailable in their local churches. A great deal of joy and harmony and mystery come through in San Fernando's Masses, a deep spirituality that fully acknowledges life's pain and confusion and joyfully celebrates its redemption.

Janie Dillard, Elizondo's assistant—mother of eight and grandmother of 11—is a pleasant, expressive woman in her middle fifties who is herself the daughter of Mexican immigrants. She was working in her congested office in the cathedral rectory one afternoon when Elizondo stopped by, a young man in tow.

"If one of the parents was a U.S. citizen, is the child a U.S. citizen?" Elizondo asked.

Dillard answered immediately: "If they were born *here*—yes, automatically."

"Born in *Mexico*—of *one* U.S. parent?"

"No," Dillard said.

"His mother was Mexican and his father U.S. Does that qualify for citizenship?"

Dillard said, "For dual citizenship, maybe."

"But only up to a certain age, no?"

"Yes," Dillard said.

"See, he's already 21, is the problem," Elizondo explained.

"And he lived in *Mexico* all these years?"

"Yes."

"Tell him to go talk to Susie at the congressman's office," Dillard said.

"His father was a doctor and left him when he was six years old," Elizondo said. "All he has is this picture." He showed Dillard a wrinkled black-and-white photograph. "Ah," Dillard said maternally. The picture was of a little boy seated upon the knee of a man in his late twenties or early thirties.

The man looked rather somber, but the boy seemed happy. "The father's somewhere in the States," Elizondo said. "If he's a doctor and he's alive, he could probably be traced through the Medical Society, no?"

"Sure," Dillard said. Then, "Father! You know what?—tell him to go to Catholic Families, to the Immigration Office. Tell him to talk to Victor. They would immediately be able to trace something."

Elizondo and the young man departed.

The exchange was one of several weekly reminders at San Fernando Cathedral that San Antonio is only a hundred miles from the Mexican border, and that a lot of people on the southern side of that border want to move north. Why do newcomers, legal and illegal, come to San Fernando for help?

"Because we try to find some way to help them, or refer them to someone we know who can help them," Dillard said. "But mostly, I think, simply because they're *listened to*."

Elizondo later told Dillard that he had located the doctor through the American Medical Association and had passed a phone number along to the young man. The young man called Elizondo a day later to report that he had called his physician father, but that his father had tried to disclaim him. The young man was hurt, he told Elizondo, but he still wanted to claim his United States citizenship, even without his father's help.

Elizondo speaking: "I come out of the very particular. What has been fascinating to me, and certainly very affirming, is that someone who is historically and spacially thoroughly situated has incredible universal appeal. The more specific you are, the more particular, the more *universal* you are—not the other way around.

"What's motivating me in my work is that I more and more appreciate the incredible treasures of faith that our Mexican tradition has and which, unfortunately, clergy and other well-intentioned people are throwing out because they don't understand or appreciate them. I realize, too, what enrichment these treasures could offer to the total Church of the Americas. I say this with great certainty: the Mexican expression of the faith could be the salvation of U.S. Catholicism. My people have a lot of things to learn, but what we have to offer is a rich personal and collective expression of faith.

"When others—Anglos, Protestants, whatever—take part in our Christmas procession or our Good Friday Way of the Cross, they all have a common feeling: they're a *people* at that moment, a people on a pilgrimage of faith. You should hear their comments—phenomenal! In the United States, Catholics have been somewhat afraid of public expressions of the faith, but the Mexican has the ability to express the faith publicly. My experience tells me people are hungry for that.

"I'm very Vatican II-based. What Vatican II said was beautiful and powerful. I loved it. When I think of how far we've come in the last 20 years, I think it's miraculous. When I see how far we have to go, it's scary and depressing and painful.

"So we need to keep on the pilgrimage, knowing we're never going to get there. That's part of the tension of being in the Church—you're in a movement that has started but is not yet complete. It started with the resurrection and Pentecost, but it won't be fully achieved until the final coming of Christ in his glory. I'll only come to the fullness of life the moment God calls me. Meanwhile, I'm in the tension of what has been started but is not fully here. And I don't feel *we* have to finish it. But I do hope somebody at least *continues* it."

Richard L. Manzelmann

In Search of the Suburban Soul

by David Briggs

*Do not be conformed to this world but be trans-
formed by the renewing of your mind so that you
may discern what is the will of God.*
—Romans 12:2

The New Hartford Presbyterian Church dominates the center of
the upstate New York community, outside of Utica, for which it
is named. Founded in 1791 by Jonathan Edwards, Jr., the large
white church has retained the New England colonial style
passed on by the Puritan ancestors of the original congregation.
The imposing building would be perfect on a traditional New
England village green. Here, amid the gas stations, movie the-
aters and stores that surround it, the church is an oasis of ar-
chitectural integrity and pastoral relief.

Inside the church kitchen one December morning, two
women were preparing tuna fish sandwiches for a tree-trimming ceremony to be held after Sunday worship service. As the
minister made small talk, the women dutifully followed the rec-
ipes set before them. If it seemed a bit odd that directions were
needed to mix tuna fish and mayonnaise, neither the women
nor the minister seemed to notice. There is a routine for nearly
every activity at the church.

The only discordant notes at New Hartford Presbyterian
come during the congregational singing, and even those follow a
pattern. The hymnbook is designed for people who can read
music, but the voices raised even for folk selections appear to be
transformed by a hidden synthesizer until all the songs come

out sounding like "Faith of Our Fathers." The organist treats the small sanctuary as if it were the cavernous confines of Shea Stadium on a day when jets from nearby La Guardia Airport fly steadily overhead. The cacophony is expected by the members of New Hartford Presbyterian, where well-dressed members fill the pews, and worship in the formal manner that befits New Hartford Presbyterian's status as the community's upper-class church. It's the kind of place where a minister dumping a bag of garbage in the chancel, as once happened, is a cataclysmic event.

It was the first Earth Day when the Rev. Richard L. Manzelmann, who was still new in town, spread garbage before church members to make a point about how human beings have despoiled the world that God created. "You could hear the gasps in the congregation," recalled Bob Jones, a longtime church member. "Dick turned and looked them straight in the eye and said, 'I bet some of you are thinking he went one step too far this time.'"

That Manzelmann has stuck around for more than two decades since that day, still getting the congregation's attention with sermons that challenge them to take seriously the social and spiritual aspects of the Gospel, is cause for reflection in an age of religious individualism.

Nobody left that week. Twenty years later, the story is commonly recounted by church members with a smile and the explanation: "That's Dick." In nearly 40 years of ministry, Manzelmann has walked the line between pastor and prophet, from gently encouraging a conservative congregation in an affluent suburb to examine McCarthyism to helping establish a Head Start program for impoverished youth in the church where he had his first pastorate. The boundaries of propriety were stretched but never broken, and his flock profited even as he preserved and strengthened his own soul. Janna Roche, a student assistant to Manzelmann in 1989 and 1990, says such actions are a mark of his integrity. "To me, there's something that motivates him that must be a divine being," she said.

Many sociologists of religion today warn of a tendency for churches to be co-opted from their divine calling by the societal trend toward individualism. Instead of upholding the transcendent message of Christianity, they say, many churches tailor themselves to the personal desires of their members, whether it's a liberal Protestant church that emphasizes social activism or a conservative church offering a set of moral guidelines. "At a certain level, finally it mistakes the order of creation," said the Rev. Michael Haggin, another Presbyterian minister in upstate New York. "It imagines the individual is given and the God then is tried on, and it fits or it doesn't fit. If it doesn't fit, it's discarded."

These are the elements in the battle Manzelmann has fought throughout his ministry. Even though at times he is treated like an eccentric uncle for his views, he has resisted the temptation to reinforce the preferences of his flock, and has instead slowly transformed the lives of the people he has served in small churches in upstate New York.

Harry Love wasn't so sure Manzelmann was right for the church at first. A respected surgeon, he didn't mind a liberal sermon urging greater care for the environment, but a minister dumping trash in the church, well, that act probably would be taken on the road soon. "My background is Presbyterian and quite conservative, and I had never seen that kind of activity in a sanctuary," Love said. "It was an eye-opener."

What Manzelmann did for Love is noticeable each time he talks to a patient at critical points in their lives. With Manzelmann's encouragement, Love was able to talk about his own faith with patients before surgery, "to draw them out, let them be able to use their faith when they needed more support than a human being could give them." He remembers in particular the conversation he had with an elderly woman who was dying of cancer, and afraid of what was coming. "As we got to talking, that anxiety disappeared as she brought up the faith that she did have."

The Rev. Thomas Troeger, an author and professor at Colgate-Rochester Divinity School who served as an assistant to Manzelmann in the early 1970s, said Manzelmann represents the ideal of what Protestant ministry should be: intellectually rigorous and passionate in its convictions. "To me, he gives WASPism and Protestantism the best possible name."

Standing at the window of the church study looking outside, speaking in a low tone as if he were addressing generations of critics who equated assimilation with selling out, Manzelmann said it is no coincidence his ministry is to the upper classes. "I'm kind of particular. I'm not a flaming liberal. I'm snooty in a way. I belong to them."

Like an Irishman telling Gaelic jokes, Manzelmann can comfortably say that the best place to store ice cream in the summer is a Presbyterian church. One year when Christmas fell on a Sunday, Manzelmann invited the congregation to show their affection in ways beyond the stiff formality of handshakes. "It was a little unnerving," he said. "One man refused to hug another man." The subjects of the *New Yorker* cartoons that are tacked up on one side of his office and often provide fodder for sermons resemble members of his flock: individuals subservient to a routine. One cartoon in particular seems to strike a chord in his ministry: Someone is saying, "Well, we're trying on religion to see if it fits, and it does." When the cartoon is mentioned to Manzelmann, he says, "Isn't that exactly where we're at today. That's exactly it."

This is the tendency Manzelmann is fighting, whether it is by dumping garbage in the sanctuary or refusing a couple's request that their wedding vows be changed from "as long as we both shall live" to "as long as we both love each other." He thinks that Americans are good at running away, and his task is to help people not run away.

His services include both visual and verbal images to get people to think about issues such as the environment, world hunger and United States policy in Central America. Underneath his reserve is a passionate commitment that church should never be boring. Luther's advice that people should put their eyes in their ears does not play well in a video age, according to Manzelmann. A recurring threat in Manzelmann's sermons on morality is that he may one day emulate the prophet Isaiah and walk naked through the sanctuary to make his point. "I always try to make it in some way interesting," he said. "I think the church is dull." For a Shaker Christmas service, to get across the idea that the best gifts are the gifts of self, little girls in costumes gave simple gifts to one another such as the gift of laughter, the gift of love and the gift of hope.

One time, Manzelmann and Troeger rode a tandem bicycle around the sanctuary on Troeger's last day to symbolize how well they worked together. Troeger still marvels at the cheering and weeping that went on that day in the conservative Protestant church: "The people just cheered when we rode that bicycle. They cheered at the top of their lungs." The next day, when he went to Colgate-Rochester, "I broke down and sobbed uncontrollably for several hours. . . . I do not believe there is a greater pastor than Dick."

Even as Manzelmann challenged the congregation with uncomfortable social teachings, compassion for the individual congregant has always held primacy. Troeger said what may have been Manzelmann's lowest point came following a service that recreated a 19th century revival led by the flamboyant Charles Finney, who was not shy about employing emotional techniques to exhort sinners on the "anxious bench" to the point of conversion. Although the intent was to honor the church's evangelical heritage, two couples with Pentecostal backgrounds left and never returned because they thought their style of worship was being mocked. "Dick was devastated. He went into a deep depression," Troeger said.

Two years ago, Manzelmann had planned to show the film *The Last Temptation of Christ*. One of the parishioners vigorously opposed it, however, even threatening to quit the congregation if the film which had been criticized for portraying Jesus as tormented by sexual fantasies, was shown. "To Dick, it really wasn't an issue," Roche recalled. "He ended up not doing it." Manzelmann kept a copy available at the church for members to borrow, and a couple of months later it was shown without incident to the youth group. "He wasn't giving in to pressure, but he was sensitive to the way other people felt about it," Roche said.

When Troeger, caught up in the anti-Vietnam War sentiment of the early 1970s, caused an uproar in the community for refusing to salute the flag at a public meeting to reduce tension between the community's youth and police, Manzelmann stood behind him in public, and privately gave him advice he had first picked up working in Greenwich during the McCarthy era. "I didn't salute the flag and I said something about it in my remarks. Holy shit was about to break out in the church," Troeger said. "Dick stood by me through it and at the same time he chastised me." The lesson is not forgotten nearly 20 years later: "He told me we've got to work with these people. We are planting grace and a sense of justice in a conservative WASP parish."

Seven days a week, 24 hours a day, Manzelmann has been available to his congregation. He has kept up a phenomenal schedule throughout his ministry, setting a goal of making one pastoral visit a day, excluding hospital calls. When congregants faced a personal crisis, "I've tried to be there, not noisily, not with cliches, just be there, let them know that we care."

The Rev. Paul Drobin, a local Catholic priest, remembers being struck by Manzelmann's pastoral presence one day while on his hospital rounds when he observed the Presbyterian minister praying with a patient. "He did it very softly and prayerfully, and I thought, 'Oh, this is wonderful.' If you pardon the pun, he's not preying on people, he's praying with them."

Nothing in the church escapes the attention of Manzelmann, who includes designing the church bulletin and arranging the flowers for services among his duties. Troeger recalls his plan to remove longtime window decorations—"Victorian bric-a-brac," according to Manzelmann—from the church as revealing not a fussy aestheticism on Manzelmann's part, but a belief in Puritan values that an over-ornate design disrupts individuals' struggles to bring clarity into their lives. "In working on the church, he was working on the design of the suburban soul," Troeger said.

Manzelmann said he had several chances to move to larger congregations, but turned them down. "I've never wanted to be a big deal in that sense of the word. It distances you from your people. You tend to be more of an administrator than a pastor." His mind drifts off as he thinks about his decision to spend 22 years in a small church in upstate New York. "In the old days, they talked about settling the ministry. That's a nice word: You settle in a place. You live in a place," Manzelmann said. "After being in a parish for 22 years, you know everybody's story. In everybody's story, there are moments of pain. And there's a lot of pain. One of the things of the ministry is to try to deal with that pain."

Even the deepest spiritual anxieties of a minister and his flock are not off limits in his sermons. When he was shocked into a painful self-appraisal by the comments of a fellow minister, Manzelmann shared his response to the gut-wrenching question: "Dick, do you think your congregation believes?"

"Let me risk being honest with you and tell what my answer was that night last year," he said in the spring of 1987 to a congregation he had ministered to for more than 17 years. "My answer that night was, 'No, and that makes me very sad.' That is exactly what I said and if my wife remembers, she can verify it. But both that question and my answer have haunted me ever since." It was a harsh answer, and one he would qualify later in the sermon to say some Presbyterians believe and some don't but no Presbyterian believes deeply enough, fervently enough.

But it is not a criticism he rejects. The longer he continues in his ministry, the deeper Manzelmann says his faith has grown. From the young man who decided to become a minister for largely professional reasons to the minister who could spin dazzling sermons with admirable literary references amid social activism to the one who is contemplating retirement after experiencing four decades of the personal pain of individuals, Manzelmann has been on his own spiritual journey.

In the end, despite what he learned from such giants as Paul Tillich and Reinhold Niebuhr about the great struggle in Protestant consciousness to make sense of God, he could no longer deal with the issue on simply an abstract, intellectual level. "My God, the man has suffered with so many human beings," Troeger said. "There comes a point when you say, 'Jesus, help me.'" The revelation that he doesn't think he really became a Christian until recently indicates how seriously Manzelmann has taken his spiritual journey: "I think in the early days, one tried to separate oneself from being too pietistic and maybe one was almost embarrassed about Jesus. I'm not embarrassed about Jesus anymore. I think he is at the center of our faith."

In an emotional sermon about Niebuhr, Manzelmann talked about how it took a stroke to make the great theologian realize the depth of his reliance upon God. Nearing his own retirement, Manzelmann said at age 61, "I think I understand now what it means to follow Him more than I ever have before, even though we stumble along the way.'"

Growing up in Plainfield, N.J., then an affluent suburb of New York City, Manzelmann did not show a particular interest in religion. He went to Sunday school but not to worship services at the Dutch Reformed Church to which his mother belonged. "My father was not religious in any sense of the word," he recalled. "He was an engineer." The ties to a Protestant heritage were largely cultural: a formulaic grace at mealtime and an avoidance of movies on Sunday—"Catholics did that." He joined Trinity Reformed Church at age 15, but only after his younger sister shamed him into it by doing it first. "I don't remember any theological emphasis. I just know that it was dull."

During World War II, with his father often away from home on business, the church became his mother's social group. But the young Manzelmann found solace in books. "I had a lot of illnesses as a kid. I was treated as fairly fragile." In his first year of high school, fighting bronchitis and measles before antibiotics were widely available, he missed half the school days. (He later came down with mononucleosis the day he was ordained.) In high school, Walter Edmonds, Ernest Hemingway and Kenneth Roberts were among the writers who fired up his imagination.

It was a conversation with a clerk at a small bookstore that led Manzelmann to the local Presbyterian church. "I used to chitchat with her in my loneliness. She encouraged me to go to Crescent Avenue." Back at his old church, they thought he was social climbing. "The two snobby churches in town were the Episcopal Church and the Crescent Avenue Presbyterian Church," he said. "That was the only Presbyterian Church in the world that ever looked down upon Episcopalians. The people who were somebody went to Crescent Avenue Presbyterian Church."

What excited him was the new minister and a style of preaching—"relevant, creative, imaginative, very rational"—that would later characterize his own ministry. Having a preacher debate whether God exists struck him as gutsy. "He had something to say, and that was important." His own sense of religious conviction was still nascent, but Manzelmann started to develop a creative side during his high school years.

A quiet person made even more so by having grown a foot his first year of high school—"I was shy and awkward and tall"—he discovered he could express himself with marionettes. He would put on puppet shows throughout the community, providing his own dialogue. "I was able to articulate and express myself behind a screen." Even today, it is behind the pulpit that Manzelmann opens himself up most to other people. "I think it's really hard for him to be real human with people," Roche said. "When he's in the pulpit, he's able to be most feeling, most connected with people."

His particular gift as a preacher remains his ability as a storyteller. His sermon topics come from sources ranging from Kafka and Wittgenstein to the *New York Times* and "Masterpiece Theatre." One Christmas sermon on the social and spiritual dimensions of the birth of Christ recalled the scene from John Mortimer's *Paradise Postponed* where the English rector Simeon Simcox replies to a son who criticized him for talking of low-cost housing for the poor on Christmas Eve: "I thought Christmas was a story about the lack of adequate housing." In a recent sermon about the need for individuals to discover God's grace, Manzelmann told the story of his meeting with a "very sweet" elderly couple's only son, a man who had gone to work right out of high school and had become vice president of his company. After both of his parents had died, the son came to Manzelmann with a paltry contribution to the church memorial fund and a great deal of boasting about how he was a self-made man. Manzelmann contrasted the arrogance of the son with the experience of his seminary professor, Niebuhr, who wrote numerous books about the grace of God but only discovered it after he was crippled. "Pity that we can only discover that grace when we are struck down. But we are called as Christians not to wait for that, but to realize it now," Manzelmann pleaded.

By the time he entered Muilenberg College, Manzelmann's intention, formed by a lifetime disproportionately spent in sickness, was to become a doctor. That plan changed when a chemistry professor told him he would pass only if Manzelmann vowed never to take another chemistry course. But he did well in English and in required courses on the Old and New Testament and theology. He also became involved in social concerns, and was chairman of the Christian Association's Social Action Committee and a member of Americans for a Democratic Society. He disassociated himself from the more pious students. "I certainly was not pious. I deliberately smoked—I still smoke, shameful—because I did not want to identify with the Lutheran priests who were to my way of thinking, well, spooky."

With advice from a Presbyterian pastor, he decided to enter the ministry, mostly for what he says were career reasons, rather than religious ones. His sense of the eternal was not as well developed as his appreciation of the upward social mobility that being a Presbyterian pastor offered. "I don't think there was that much religious conviction there to sustain me," he said. "I would certainly talk about it, but I don't think that it was very real. . . . When I look back on it now, I feel, how did I have the nerve to become a minister?"

His grandmother tried to discourage him. "You'll never make any money," she said when he announced his decision to his family at the dinner table one evening. But becoming a Presbyterian minister seemed a prestigious choice to his parents. "They saw it more as a comfortable thing for me to do, certainly respectable, more as a career choice than as a faith commitment," Manzelmann said. "It was respectable. Eisenhower became a Presbyterian. Adlai Stevenson became a Presbyterian. We were in the center."

A conversation with Manzelmann can be a peripatetic event. During one lengthy interview, he moved throughout the church study, settling his 6-foot, 4-inch frame for brief periods in one chair after another, alternately standing and even moving the conversation into the church kitchen so he could reflect more comfortably atop the sink counter. He ponders questions and makes little eye contact. At no time does he appear more deeply lost in his own world than when he discusses his personal spiritual journey. A surprising revelation—"I just have some feelings that I didn't become a Christian until recently"— is delivered almost parenthetically as he discusses his own path to the ministry in the self-critical style with which he challenges his congregation.

"I look back and wonder what was there and pressed me into that and think about how thin it was compared to where I am now," Manzelman said, stamping his foot as he stared out the window of the church study. "I'm kind of embarrassed about that, except the '50s were rather thin."

Union Seminary in the 1950s was not the place to go for lessons in civil religion, or to muster up support for a ticker-tape parade to celebrate Gen. MacArthur's successes in the Korean War. It was a time and place for theological giants in American Protestantism. In theology and politics, everything was up for grabs. Paul Tillich and James Muilenburg. Athens versus Jerusalem, philosophical theology pitted against biblical theology. Students teased each other about tenets such as double predestination that had been fiercely held within the Presbyterian Church for centuries as they struggled with new ways to understand the responsibility of Christians in society.

For Manzelmann, it was a new arena entirely. It was so overwhelming, he admits now, that he even cast a protest vote for Dwight Eisenhower in the 1952 election because he objected to the deification of Adlai Stevenson by seminary students and faculty. "It was a reactionary decision that I regret," he says. "I think Adlai Stevenson is one of my heroes." To atone, Manzelmann, who places his honorariums from weddings and funerals in the church memorial fund, dedicates hymnbooks to such figures as Stevenson or Eleanor Roosevelt. "That's part of the game I play around here, too. They think I'm much too liberal."

But it was not a doctrinaire liberal gospel that Manzelmann says he picked up at Union: "You developed a critical mentality. You evaluated and analyzed."

Perhaps the most influential presence on campus was that of Niebuhr, who taught that contemporary culture must be addressed from a faith perspective. Niebuhr forced people to look at things in their lives they would rather not deal with, Manzelmann said. "We must deal with the real issues in our lives and not dodge them," was Niebuhr's legacy to Manzelmann. "That has stayed with me: to help people deal realistically with the world around them, as well as the issues around them."

What Niebuhr also taught Union students in the early 1950s was that humility and modesty reveal, rather than detract from an individual's moral stature. In a speech to Manzelmann's Class of '53, Niebuhr apologized to the students for having suffered a stroke and not being able to teach his regular classes. "His modesty was overwhelming," Manzelmann recalled. "This towering figure in American theology apologizing to us for not having shared with us in class. He began to cry. Of course, we all cried, too."

Manzelmann has always found that Christian realism comes with a price. "Everything is under examination. That doesn't lead to a lot of comfort. That doesn't make you very popular, either. I've never been a very popular pastor." In a criticism that was taken as a compliment, his current assistant has told Manzelmann: "Sometimes, people don't think you're with them."

In truth, he has never been away from them. Despite a widely held view around Union at the time that "God was only in East Harlem," Manzelmann cast his lot with the upper middle class early on. A summer spent working as an assistant to Jim Robinson at a church in Harlem reinforced his later conviction that each group in society is in need of special attention. Robinson, a black minister who grew up in poverty in the South and later went on to found Crossroads Africa, which became a model for the Peace Corps, struggled to make sure members of his congregation had adequate heat and food and housing. But he told Manzelmann that in some ways he would have the more difficult pastoral job in ministering to materially self-assured flocks that would have greater difficulty turning to God in their times of need. "What you need to worry about is their inner life, their stress, their alcoholism," Manzelmann remembers being told by Robinson.

Even as he assumed the trappings of a Presbyterian minister, Manzelmann never let go of the lessons of humility and integrity taught to him by Niebuhr and Robinson, a hands-on minister who often could be seen sweeping the sidewalk in front of the Church of the Master. Though his assistant berates him for doing work that is beneath the pastor's dignity, Manzelmann still makes the coffee before church on Sunday morning and does such tasks as unplugging the toilets and sweeping the sidewalk when they need to be done. The pastor and the church are one. "It's a whole lifestyle for him," Roche said. "It's God's church, but it's his church."

Manzelmann's first job as an assistant at a Presbyterian church in Greenwich, Conn., gave him a valuable introduction to the tensions of ministry to the affluent. In the civil religion days of the 1950s, attracting Presbyterians in an affluent New York suburb was like finding Southern Baptists for a Billy Graham crusade in North Carolina: Open up shop, they'll be there. "It was one of the things everybody did," Manzelmann recalled. "We took in 75 members one Sunday morning."

But as the maids and gardeners from Scotland who originally made up the bulk of the membership were being given minority status by the chief executives moving into the community and choosing the most prestigious church, the tensions placed on ministers who felt called to speak out against Sen. Joseph McCarthy's "witch hunt" of Communists and to support the United Nations were high. Session members publicly complained of liberals in the church, and the senior pastor and Manzelmann "were very careful in what we said because we didn't want to alienate the congregation." Even coming straight out of Union, Manzelmann said, "I was very naive, and I was concerned about my own safety, too."

It was there Manzelmann met the Rev. John Bates, a fatherly figure who taught him how to minister sensitively to the congregation and retain his integrity. "The way I learned from John Bates was to discuss issues, to try to be informed, to deal with them patiently and gently," Manzelmann said. "You give other people room, too." Knowing where to draw the line between confronting people with the demands of Christianity without alienating them with a confrontational style has been the challenge Manzelmann has accepted throughout his ministry.

Troeger said he asked around about Manzelmann before he accepted the job at the New Hartford church. "The word that was used in every single case without exception: He's a man of tremendous integrity."

As Manzelmann approaches retirement, he acknowledges being haunted by self-doubt. "One always lives with the tension: Am I being too chicken, or playing it too safe?" Nothing seems to sadden Manzelmann more about the Presbyterian Church than its tendency to be preoccupied with administrative matters such as where to locate its new headquarters. "It's become bureaucratic," he says with disdain. "We're now people of the book—not the Bible, but the Book of Order."

In spite of what Manzelmann considers a certain arrogance and abuse of power in the church of his youth, the Presbyterian Church in the 1950s and 1960s was right in the middle of a number of social issues. Leaders such as Eugene Carson Blake took what Manzelmann calls "prophetic and very responsible" stands for social change amid a church rooted in a ministry that respected the intellect of its members. "I was proud of that: to be a Presbyterian. I always felt my calling was to serve middle class, upper middle-class people." Presbyterianism at its best, according to Manzelmann, offers churchgoers an intelligent, prophetic, informed ministry that is relevant to the issues of the day. It was this mission that he carried to his first pastorate at North Presbyterian Church in Geneva, N.Y.

He stayed there throughout the 1960s, leading his parishioners through the days of the civil rights movement, the Vietnam War, the sexual revolution and the era of assassinations with a pastoral sensitivity that enabled him to be as much at home in the Rotary Club as with small groups of social activists planning to desegregate the schools and provide low-income housing.

That the Head Start program—an effort to provide impoverished youths at an early age with the skills and self-esteem that would enable them to be successful later on in school—found a home in his church may have been Manzelmann's greatest pastoral triumph. The large church had the space for the program, but he found that racial barriers immediately went up when the idea was proposed. "The facilities would depreciate faster. Valuable furniture would be broken. The Oriental rugs would never make it."

The objection that generated the most emotional power was that lower-class blacks would be handling the same toys as the church's Sunday School children. Manzelmann's wife, Joan, was so furious at one point that she offered to have Head Start in their house. What was obvious to her was obvious to her husband: "The conflict was racist, yes, and a class issue."

Manzelmann used his influence to slowly win the congregation over with arguments both practical and moral. At the same time that he met with the local newspaper publisher to have a reporter who was perceived to be hostile to Head Start switched to another beat, he gently worked to convince his own congregation that it was possible to perform a community service without changing the character of the church. Manzelmann, who had been switching chairs and swinging his legs in an agitated fashion as he discussed the controversy, smiled as he recalled its denouement. "It brought in a little income. That was the selling point."

By the time Joan Manzelmann was able to observe the "beautiful" sight of her youngest son and a Head Start child each cutting their fingers to see if their blood was the same color, the congregation was patting itself on the back for its progressive stance. "Head Start became a respectable way of dealing with the poverty issue. Then, they became proud they were the place Head Start took place," Manzelmann said. That it became their triumph and not Manzelmann's is a testimony to his pastoral style. "I like to come in the back door on most issues," he said. "I think I have a way of convincing people not by argument. but by just quietly leading them beyond their prejudices to some kind of faithful understanding."

During his 10 years in Geneva, N.Y., the most public stand he took was to read the names of the Vietnam War dead at a downtown prayer service. He never marched in protest or took part in demonstrations, and would not throughout his pastoral career. "It's not that I didn't want to. I just felt responsible to my congregation. I felt it would have wounded my ministry with them." By the time he left Geneva, in addition to finding a home for Head Start, he played a major role in establishing a low-income housing program and a pastoral counseling center, and was among a small group of people that joined together to integrate the public schools. Manzelmann helped elect an activist on desegregation to the school board, and was part of a coalition that won approval of a school redistricting plan that spread black and Hispanic students—who had been all placed in one school—among all four of the city's elementary schools. The church he served, which once fought having poor 4- and 5-year-olds in its midst, now includes a soup kitchen in its ministry despite having since merged with a church with an even more conservative reputation.

Manzelmann, who calls himself "a liberal with a conservative style," says he objected to the possibility of seeking social progress through confrontation: "Because I've always been in middle- and upper-middle class congregations, I've always wanted to give them a lot of room to discuss and dialogue on these issues. I've never wanted to alienate them with my convictions."

It didn't hurt that the man once accused of being uppity for gravitating away from the Dutch Reformed Church of his childhood was comfortable in the outward role of a Presbyterian pastor, easily hobnobbing in the community's elite circles of political and economic power. "He had the ability to be a good friend of the power structure. He didn't alienate them," said Elizabeth Heaton, the director of Head Start. She recalled how city officials and leading corporate figures appeared flattered to be invited to meetings where social issues were raised because of the way Manzelmann treated them.

He was a member of the Rotary Club, and a strong supporter of art and musical events in the community. His proficiency as an art historian was such that he lectured on Chagall at the local museum. "I took leadership in other areas of the community," Manzelmann said. "When you put concern for the poor and concern for good music together in the community, one lifts the other up to respectability." Nor was it an act. With his black, horn-rimmed glasses and reserved demeanor, Manzelmann is not going to be the first guy on the dance floor, nor the last to leave the neighborhood pub. He still is nervous about waiting in the bar of the nearby Italian restaurant to pick up a pizza for the youth group. Joan Manzelmann said it took her husband six weeks to ask for a second date because he thought her dress was too "tight-fitting" on their first outing, when he took her to the Metropolitan Opera.

His is a curious combination of conceit and modesty. He can matter-of-factly state that "I was a mythological figure in Geneva," but in a room full of invited guests in his own house he will take a seat toward the back, almost shyly allowing others to dominate the conversation. Many of his pleasures are simple ones, such as giving wood carvings and toys he makes himself as Christmas presents to his friends.

On what he expects will be his last church Christmas party as pastor, Manzelmann stands next to the tree, grinning with the self-satisfied look one imagines he might have had as an adolescent after putting on a successful puppet show.

Around him, members of the congregation are singing Christmas carols and building ornaments out of scraps of paper and other odds and ends. During the singing of "The Twelve Days of Christmas," one group with children in it pounds the tables after their part, and Jim Marsh unabashedly sings loudly and off-key the conspicuous lines of "two turtle doves" that have been assigned to him and his wife. In a church where propriety dies hard, inhibitions have been broken down in a simple tree-trimming following a Sunday service.

If he had some regrets as he approached retirement, other than the time he failed to spend with his own family, it was not that he chose the ministry: "It was the right thing for me to do. Over the years, I have developed a deep sense of calling and commitment to this task." His regret is only that he could not do it again. "I wish I could start it all over again, knowing what I know now. I feel it and I believe it and know it much more deeply than I did before."

In an age of religious individualism, his advice to young ministers is: "Let the church be the church. The church has a unique, special, particular thing to contribute." And that special thing is not offering a variety of secular self-help groups to pack the house. "The whole point of the church is self-help is not what we're into. We're into the help God can give us."

Manzelmann's chief criticism of the church is that grace is cheap, "without obedience, without any real sense of discipleship."

But he has not given up hope. Having begun his ministry in the glory days in terms of membership, he sees a new opportunity to replace what he calls "the Protestant scowl" of recent years with the more familiar "Protestant smile." Only this time, Manzelmann said, it will not be a triumphal mainline church that abuses its authority, but one that appreciates the benefits of retaining its integrity in the face of secular culture by operating from the margins of power. "We've become smaller but stronger because the people who stick with us are going to be here because they want to be here."

Jeremiah has replaced Hemingway as the sustaining force in Manzelmann's life. "I like Jeremiah. He's my prophet. He feels things so deeply, so passionately, so painfully," Manzelmann said. "At the end of Jeremiah, there is hope." On the day he confessed to his congregation that his first response to his fellow minister was that his congregation did not believe, Manzelmann concluded it is "nonsense" to resign oneself to the idea people don't believe anything anymore.

"We believe all sorts of things. We believe in love and we also believe in hate. We believe in peace. but we also believe in war. We believe that terrorism is terrible, but we support terrorism and supply arms to terrorists in Central America. We believe in democracy and we support undemocratic governments in South Africa and Chile. We believe that the best things in life are free and we believe in money, especially plastic money. . . . We believe in salvation by exercise and diet and we believe in salvation by faith. And some of us even believe in Jesus. It's all mixed up and not much of it makes sense when we put it all together.

"So when the father says, 'I believe, help my unbelief,' we know exactly what he means and we know exactly where most of us are. I believe, but not enough, so help my unbelief, move it, nourish it. It's a no and yes answer. And I think that is fair, for me, for you. The issue for us is to let our belief grow. And then maybe our God can do something with us and with our world."

Paul Duke

Nights Of Darkness Prove Thy Grace

by Pamela Schaeffer

He drew me out of the pit of destruction . . .
And he put a new song in my mouth, a hymn to
our God.

—Psalm 40:3

On a Saturday afternoon in mid-August, a bride and groom listened attentively to a clergyman's words of counsel as they waited to exchange their vows. Although the ceremony was typical for the setting—a Southern Baptist church in suburban St. Louis—the minister's charge to this couple was not.

"Regard each other as mysteries," the Rev. Dr. Paul Duke challenged the couple. "Hold each other, but know that each of you is beyond the other's holding," and be assured that "God, who has met each of you, will meet you in marriage in ways you have never been met." The language was surprising because Southern Baptists, overwhelmingly conservative in their approach to theology, are more inclined to speak of certainties than of mysteries. The words said more about the minister than about the denomination he represented.

Duke has been pastor since 1986 of Kirkwood Baptist Church, home for a congregation of about 1,700 Southern Baptists, mostly of a moderate to liberal bent. The congregation is noted for its active laity who oversee much of the administrative side of running a church and value Duke for his spiritual and intellectual acumen, his preaching skills and his deep sen-

sitivity to personal and social pain. They gratefully acknowledge that their pastor is quite different from the stereotype of
the moralistic, revival-minded Southern Baptist pastor who
compensates for lack of formal theological training by dispens-
ing pious discourse. By virtually every measure, from Duke's
extensive theological training and affinity for mystics to his
Woody Allenish looks and his droll sense of humor, he is set
apart. Helpless to explain what he calls "this sort of Mediter-
ranean face," which contrasts sharply with the lighter coloring
and features of other family members, he says with a boyish
grin, "We used to joke a lot about the Jewish milkman."

Duke readily concedes that, if the externals are wrong for
the stereotype, his temperament, as well, often seems alien to
his role. "There are ways in which this kind of work calls for a
public kind of person, an extrovert by nature," who is energized
by being with people, he said. He is, by contrast, buoyed up by
solitude and reflection. "In order to speak every week of sacred
mysteries, I have to draw from silence," he said. "The constant
battle to protect for myself what is necessary for me personally
and at the same time to respond to legitimate claims of a congregation on a pastor's love and time; this is a conflict on which
I am impaled. I call myself an introvert in drag."

In recent years, certain aspects of the public side of Duke's
work have been especially draining. His attention has been
diverted from pastoral duties to wrenching political battles in
his denomination, the 14-million member Southern Baptist
Convention. A rancorous fundamentalist-led fight over Biblical
interpretation pushed the denomination, the nation's largest
Protestant body, sharply to the right in the 1980s. Many highly-
educated pastors like Duke, who refused to force the Bible into
a straitjacket of literal interpretation, are viewed by those in
control as the enemy, a threat to Southern Baptist identity as a
"Bible-believing" body. Ironically, Duke and other progressives
agree that Baptist identity is at stake—its heritage of the autonomy of the individual believer before God. This, as well as
the fuller truth of the Bible as both history and myth, is being
contested by those who lately have gained control of Baptist
institutions and forced out persons who value intellectual
foundations for faith.

In the battles, Duke emerged as a leader of the Cooperative Baptist Fellowship, a dissident organization formed by moderates in 1990 as an escape from fundamentalism. He is co-chair of the fellowship's committee on theological education, a group charged with finding alternatives for students unwilling to attend the six seminaries affiliated with the Southern Baptist Convention now that they have become spoils in a denominational war. Many Southern Baptists contend the fellowship is leading the denomination inexorably toward schism. Duke hopes that if a break comes, the organization will not remain a separate religious body. "To form another denomination would be a sin," given the 20th-century ecumenical achievements, he believes. He would prefer that the fellowship become a catalyst for merger of several Baptist groups.

But Duke, who describes himself as having an uncomfortably strong need to please, has come cautiously and reluctantly to his part in the Baptist drama. He finds the role of dissident to be difficult, in part because of his personality. As the middle child, he says, he was "the Switzerland" of the family, the one committed to keeping peace, or at least assuming neutral ground. The tensions have torn at Duke's own family, troubling perhaps most of all the person who was his earliest model for ministry. That person is his father, the Rev. G. Nelson Duke, who helped to build the Southern Baptist structures that Duke is leaving behind.

Paul Duke, the second of three sons of the Rev. G. Nelson Duke and Wilma Awbrey Duke, was born in Montgomery, Ala., on July 18, 1953. His brothers are David and John. David heads the religion department at William Jewell College, a Baptist school in Liberty, Mo., and has dropped "Southern" from his description of his own religious affiliation, calling himself simply "a Baptist." John is minister of Christian education at Hillsboro Heights Baptist Church in Huntsville, Ala.

The family provided an informal case study for Nancy T. Ammerman, director of Baptist studies at Emory University's Candler School of Theology in Decatur, Ga., who has written a book about the Baptist controversy entitled *Baptist Battles: Social Change and Religious Conflict in the Southern Baptist Convention*. According to sociological surveys Ammerman has done, Paul Duke fits the model of a progressive—highly educated, pastor of an urban church, supportive of women in ministry. But the book also describes varying cultural and political perspectives at work in the controversy, in part the result of generational gaps. "My father, my brothers and I are all in that book, though not by name," Duke said.

Jeanie McGowan, a longtime friend of the Duke family, describes the elder Dukes as "very conservative" but "wonderful people" with enviable parenting skills. She recalls being inspired as a young woman by Wilma Duke, teacher of her Sunday school class. Wilma Duke told the class that she often prayed to become so enamored of the Bible that she would actually *prefer* it for leisure-time reading over other books. "That was a neat role model for me at that age," McGowan said.

"We're not as conservative as mom and dad are," said David Duke of himself and his brothers. Yet, he said, family ties had remained strong and his parents had grown to respect their sons' choices. His parents managed to nurture religious vocations in their children and gradually come to see that the path of faith can lead beyond parental horizons, he said. While he does not regard his parents as strong beacons for his intellectual journey, he recalls some "open territory" for it to take place. Despite his mother's prayer, David Duke recalls that there were always other books around. "They read, and they gave permission for the pursuit of truth," he said. "At least if you have books around, you have a fighting chance."

Paul Duke's interest in following his father's vocational path came "embarrassingly early." He struggled as early as eighth grade with conflicting certainties. He attributed his aspirations to a need to please his father, yet he felt that "something larger" was involved. "At our house faith was in the air and we breathed it," Duke said. "We bathed in it at night, and when we'd put on our pajamas, faith tucked us in. To me as a child, prayer smelled like toothpaste and felt like my father's arms."

The boys attended public schools, where Paul was always uncomfortably conscious of the stereotype of Baptists as "Bible-thumping, narrow-minded people who never have any fun." Then, Paul followed David to Samford University in Birmingham, Ala., a Baptist school and the alma mater of their parents. David, a senior during Paul's freshman year, served as Paul's mentor, suggesting books. Tillich, Camus, Kierkegaard and Bonhoeffer are among the authors that Paul remembers as influential. He graduated in 1975 with a double major in history and religion and a wife, the former Cathy Chandler, whom he had married in 1974. He followed David again, to Southern Baptist Seminary at Louisville, the oldest and most prestigious of the nation's six Southern Baptist seminaries, where each earned a master's degree. David went on to earn a Ph.D. at Emory University, but Paul, perhaps responding to what he remembers as initial parental displeasure over David's decision, ignored advice to branch out beyond Southern Baptist schools and remained at Southern Baptist Seminary to take a doctorate with an emphasis in New Testament.

Paul said he sometimes wondered if he took the right path, but realizes that David "was always more independent, I think more brave in some ways, more willing to be defiant. I think I just admired the heck out of him and still do." To illustrate the relationship, he began flipping through a wheel of snapshots on his desk. He presented for inspection a picture of two young boys dressed as cowboys—8-year-old David, looking cocky and in charge, his boot-clad feet spread wide apart and his hand resting on a holster at his hip; 4-year-old Paul, looking tentatively toward his brother. "It's a parable," Duke said. "It captures a lot of who I was and who I continue to be."

Nancy Ammerman has fond memories of her friendship with Paul and Cathy Duke and other students at the seminary in Louisville, a "wild and wonderful bunch," who were part of a Sunday school class at Crescent Hill Baptist Church. For her, as for Duke, the class was an exciting "Big Chill" experience of intellectual inquiry and deep friendships. "I remember it as a place to explore what it meant to be church, to be a believer. It was a true, open space for people to be vulnerable" and to question cherished truths, she said. "We looked at passages of Scripture and really struggled with what they were trying to say." She remembers the class as the place where she found the courage to say that she thought Paul, the author of the New Testament epistles, was wrong to limit participation of women in the church.

"My guess is that most of us had an image in our heads of our home churches and were testing the limits of our traditions.

We had a very clear sense that we were doing things that weren't normal for Southern Baptists to do, but also that we were on the cutting edge of where the denomination was going. I think in a lot of ways this is the kind of experience you find yourself trying to create in new forms in order to make it possible for other groups to function in open, creative, egalitarian ways."

Several of the people in the group, like Paul, went on to carve out significant niches in progressive Baptist life, becoming pastors of congregations or, in recent years, leaders in dissident organizations. Duke acknowledges that the magic of the group derived in part from intellectual energy. The rethinking of patriotism and "new political agendas" of the late 1960s undoubtedly had much to do with the spiritual formation of many in the group, he said. But for Duke, it wasn't so much the raising of new questions that stands out in that period ("I'd already done that in college," he said) but the deep bonds, the "blood ties" that gave him a new sense as a young adult "of what it means to have friendships and link them to faith." Beyond the electricity of complementary personalities, members of the group were, in his perspective, "living an experience of the Gospel" by their deep commitment to one another. They shared meals and projects; "had incredible parties and retreats," he said.

Except for Cathy, Duke's wife, the key relationship for him in the group was with Grady Nutt, a Baptist minister who led the class with his wife, Eleanor. Grady and Eleanor functioned less as teachers than as a "center of hospitality," Duke said. They provided "encouragement and care" that played a crucial role in his spiritual formation. He reached again for a snapshot, this one in his wallet. "See, pictures of my family," he said, flipping past pictures of Cathy and the couple's two children, Stephanie and Chris. "And Grady."

In the snapshot, Grady has his arm around Duke's shoulder. He stands a head above Duke, who is five feet seven inches tall. "Grady was "big, big in every way," Duke said. He recalls big hugs, a big laugh, strong convictions and an outrageous sense of humor. Grady was captivated by Duke's preaching skills, and he became what Duke describes as "one of my balcony people"— someone who "stands up there and looks at you and cheers you on. Duke still feels that support, but in memory only, for Grady was killed in a plane crash in 1983.

Duke's gift for public speaking had not gone unnoticed before Grady entered the scene. An eighth-grade teacher had encouraged Duke to enter a speech competition and he had won the top award for his state. But Grady brought something new.

"I've always had a sense of humor and a sense of mischief," said Duke, "but I think I also have had a tendency when speaking of being inordinately heavy. He showed me how to be less ponderous and to let humor have its play. G. K. Chesterton said the reason angels can fly is that they take themselves so lightly. Grady helped me take myself more lightly."

Another source of inspiration was the Rev. Dr. George Buttrick, who taught a course in homiletics during Duke's first semester at seminary. Buttrick, longtime pastor at Madison Avenue Presbyterian Church in New York City and, after his retirement, chaplain at Harvard University, died in 1980, leaving Duke another important legacy: the model of a "muscular style of preaching, by which I mean that it really grappled with the mind, with the world, with God." Buttrick was also remarkable as a great preacher whose integrity matched his words, "one of those people who carry a profound contagion in who they are," Duke said. "You couldn't be around him without being changed."

Fundamentalists were pointing fingers at Southern Baptist Seminary, citing its "liberal" leanings, even as Duke was enjoying what he describes as an "incredible freedom" there. Academic inquiry, not doctrinal barriers, set the tone and all the tools of historical and literary criticism of the Bible were brought into play. To such leaders as the eloquent W.A. Criswell, longtime pastor of First Baptist Church in Dallas, such teaching methods were a sign of "the curse, the rot, the virus" eating away the very core of Southern Baptist faith. Thundering against "higher criticism" in 1985, he warned pastors attending a Southern Baptist convention in his home city of a "massacre of Christian orthodoxy."

By the time Criswell delivered that sermon, Duke recognized it as part of an organized campaign by conservatives to gain control of Baptist institutions and seminaries by electing officers opposed to progressives. For a time, Duke became involved in what he now regards as a misguided attempt to counter the conservative onslaught by using the same tactics: organizing on a political model. But earlier, in the late 1970s and early 1980s, Duke said he had scoffed at public warnings from the Rev. Paige Patterson, president of the Criswell Center for Biblical Studies in Dallas, and Paul Pressler, a Houston judge, that a campaign was underway to make Biblical "inerrancy" the password for true Southern Baptist believers. Duke had grown accustomed to a "crisis" erupting periodically in "our big, weird family" over biblical interpretation. Fundamentalists "had been hollering for a while, so we just got used to them hollering," he said.

Something else was occurring in Duke's life in the early 1980s that may have diverted his attention from the larger scene. He was experiencing a severe emotional crisis. In his mid-20s, Duke was completing requirements for his doctorate and serving in his first assignment, part-time pastor of a small church in a rural area about 45 minutes from Louisville, when he became clinically depressed. "I was having difficulty functioning. I could not read or concentrate. I was very fragile." He had a pervasive feeling of sadness and "would fall into tears at the strangest times."

"There was no one thing that led to my sickness," he said. "It had to do in part with the fact that I had grown up externally and lagged behind internally, in part with the fact that I was preaching things I had not personally experienced. When you make a commitment as early as I did, you are set for a crisis later on. There was a widening distance between my external world and internal world, and I was getting angrier and colder."

He turned for help to the Rev. Dr. Edward Thornton, a psychotherapist and Baptist minister who headed the pastoral care department at the Louisville seminary and had the marks of a potential "soulmate." Duke talked weekly for about eight months with Thornton, who used a Jungian approach to help him confront his past and present and analyze his dreams. Thornton "granted the presence of God to our conversations and he permitted these long, terrible stretches of silence," Duke said.

With some trepidation, Duke recently shared memories of this period with his congregation in a sermon in which he discussed the atmosphere of his childhood home. Duke said he generally opposed rehearsing personal material from the pulpit ("Some in the congregation will invariably attach themselves in new ways to the preacher as opposed to the Gospel"), but had departed from his rule in order to set the tone for a series of evening services in which members of his congregation would talk about their own experiences of faith. Duke said he had reached bottom during his counseling, and then, as he described it, one evening "something happened." He was alone, trying to study, but very tired, and for a moment he closed his eyes. "When I opened them I had the most unmistakable sense of a Presence in the room. It was a more powerful sense of being with someone than had a human being walked in and stood in front of my face. I heard no voice, but words were given to me, words of acceptance and assurance and promise. I have thought of other explanations for what happened to me that night, but my heart was persuaded then and has never stopped being persuaded that I had been visited by the risen Christ."

The experience transformed Duke, who says he remains acutely aware of the possibility of a potential split in a minister's life between word and life. "I think the pastorate is a dangerous profession, because all you do for God you are expected to do, paid to do, and you are doing it publicly. If the door to your heart is always open, and warmth is always escaping, your fire goes out. There's an enormous and very subtle danger of speaking more about God's word than hearing it and acting upon it."

Nevertheless, his experience of "presence" was more than a turning point in his depression. He said it led to his discovery that faith is not always comfortable or certain. An avid reader of both fiction and non-fiction, he began to enlarge his knowledge of the works of Christian mystics. Some of these, as well as writers on the mystical life, have been influential in his spiritual growth. He has been impressed by Meister Eckhart, a 14th-century German priest of the Dominican order who wrote of a divine spark within each human being and was censured by the church as a pantheist; Thomas à Kempis, the 15th-century ascetic who wrote *Imitation of Christ*; Julian of Norwich, the 14th-century English anchoress whose visions included an image of Jesus as "mother"; Thomas Merton, the 20th-century intellectual-turned-Trappist monk who wrote prolifically on mysticism and social justice.

Above all, he said, he enlarged his understanding of "the character of Christ," a knowledge that he regards as "risky" but essential to interpreting Scripture. "By the clear words of the Gospel, by one's own personal experience and by the example of the saints, one comes to know Christ, who teaches us to read Scripture. In my faith system, Christ stands over Scripture, and every particular text we are to read in light of who we know him to be." By contrast, fundamentalists assume "that every part of Scripture speaks with the same authority," he said.

As Duke's depression was waning, he and Grady Nutt wrote a hymn together that has become the official anthem at Crescent Hill Church. Although Duke said the experience was such a meeting of minds that it was hard to know which words were Grady's and which were his, two lines suggest the mystical dimensions of Duke's interior conflict: "Fierce and gleaming is Thy mystery," and "Nights of darkness prove Thy grace." The depression, Duke now feels, "was a wonderful experience in many ways."

It was mid-afternoon on a Saturday. On Duke's calendar that evening was a wedding reception for the couple he had spoken to of mysteries. He was also anticipating spending two days with his brother David at a resort area near St. Louis. The Duke brothers, who had recently collaborated on a book called *Anguish and the Word: Preaching that Touches Pain*, would be using the time to prepare a two-week course on the German theologian Dietrich Bonhoeffer that they planned to teach together at William Jewell College. But for the moment, Duke was worried about Sunday morning.

"I have a sermon threatening to be stillborn," he said, borrowing from imagery he had developed in an article on preaching. Comparing sermon preparation to stages of gestation, Duke had written of "an interior stirring and kicking, a feeding and growing. . . . To be pregnant with some sermons is to glow; with others it is to feel mostly sick. In the actual birthing, some arrive rather easily while others require considerable pushing; some are breech, some don't want to come forth at all by Sunday but must be seized by force, arriving at the pulpit like Paul at his apostleship, 'untimely born.' Most good sermons take the preacher down to the gates of pain." Each of the pastor's children will "bear the most notable—sometimes the most ludicrous—resemblance to the preacher." Yet each of the sermons, like children, will be different, and "by some wonder . . . will often not only live and breathe, but cry out with a sound that is eerily or beautifully the voice of another."

The next day Duke said he had worked late into the night refining his sermon on Job, the first of a series of four on the hiddenness of God amid suffering and loss. Duke works 12 to 20 hours a week on his sermons, carefully refining his words, while trying to anticipate the reactions of his congregation. That effort builds on the foundation laid during a three- to four-day retreat. Each year, Duke piles books, articles and notes into his car and heads for solitude, often at the Archabbey of the Order of St. Benedict in St. Meinrad, Ind. He spends several days planning his preaching topics for the year and sharing intimate celebrations of Catholic Mass with the monks. It is an "annual fix" that he relies on for distance from his daily routine.

Duke's appreciation for structured worship is shared by many members of his congregation, although some, he said, would prefer that services be more in the free-wheeling "revivalist" mode. Southern Baptists have no rubrics for worship, but tradition is divided into two streams: the so-called "Sandy Creek" style, in which sermon, prayers and music appeal to emotions, and the more formal "Charleston" style, most prominent in North Carolina, which Duke learned to appreciate during his college and seminary days. Taste in music at Kirkwood Baptist Church runs to the classical. On the Sunday Duke preached about Job, a visiting pianist played Chopin in morning services, Mozart in the evening. About once a month, and for special Christian celebrations, such as Easter, he "robes" for services, he said.

A few members have left Duke's congregation since he arrived because they considered his theology too liberal or his worship style too formal, but others have joined for the same reasons. Those who remain say he is immensely popular. Duke said he discovered "lingering tensions" over worship style after he was appointed pastor and decided to get conflicts out in the open in a "Geraldo Rivera-type meeting" where various points of view, including his own, could be aired. "I told them that every person has a range in which he or she can personally worship God with integrity," he said. "It's shaped by experience, by personality and by personal needs. Some were asking me for a less formal style of worship, and I gave them the reasons for my preferences, including theological reasons. A lot of Baptist worship is sort of chitchatty. Worship leaders stand in the pulpit and sort of shoot the breeze. I can't do that."

As for the appeal to emotions, Duke said, "Some in my congregation would wish that I would be more forceful in pleading for a personal response" from worshipers. In revivalistic Baptist services, a minister encourages people to come forward to make a commitment to Jesus, usually against the background of a drawn-out "invitational" hymn. "Theologically I value the influence of the Holy Spirit to do whatever work is necessary inside the worshiper to invoke a response" without "a lot of pleading" from a worship leader, he said.

The format for worship at Kirkwood Baptist Church calls for Biblical texts, one from the Old Testament and one from the New, to be read aloud by male or female lay worship leaders. Although Duke will use the texts as the basis for his sermon, the goal, he said, is first to allow the text to communicate its own truth, "sacred word separate from sermon word." He lamented that Southern Baptists typically read little Scripture during worship services. Often, Duke said, a pastor will simply "weld the text onto a sermon" so that the text becomes the instrument of the preacher rather than the other way around.

Duke said ecumenical relationships had been helpful in recent years in overcoming "claustrophobia" produced by "being overwhelmed by the failure of your own denominational family. The less provincial my own relationships are, the freer I am to live inside my own tradition." He often chooses his texts for the day from the lectionary, the systematic series of readings used by liturgical churches—Catholic, Episcopalian and Lutheran—which have prescribed worship norms. But he also enjoys at times the "terrible freedom" that non-liturgical churches have to "just roll your own." Patting his heart, he said: "I'm Baptist enough to enjoy the freedom of choosing a text that speaks to me here. But I'm also constantly asking myself, 'Is my congregation dealing with the whole breadth of the canon? What theme or text has not been heard enough lately?'" He added, "Part of it is more haphazard. I'm constantly reading, and what I'm reading conveys an idea. You try to work off whatever is working on you and balance it with what you've forgotten to let work on you."

Duke also alternates heavy texts with lighter. He chose Psalm 16, a testament to personal satisfaction, as antidote to his sermons on Job. ("We ate our vegetables, now we get to eat dessert," he told his congregation.) After the 8 a.m. service, he remarked privately that his delivery had been flat. Perhaps he was tired, or perhaps because for a minister who says he still has a tendency to sadness, the image of Job is far more vivid than that of the faceless psalmist.

Pain and mystery are words that punctuate Duke's sermons as well as realities at the heart of a theology that takes with the utmost seriousness human struggles and the questions they inevitably arouse. Linda McKinnish Bridges, who teaches New Testament studies at Baptist Theological Seminary in Richmond, Va., an alternative seminary established in 1991 to escape fundamentalist control, describes Duke as one of few pastor-intellectuals among Southern Baptists. "That is his gift," she said, "he can package heavy stuff in a communicable fashion, and people don't realize they're getting heavy stuff."

A young woman in Duke's congregation who has talked with him about her interest in ministry said she had been impressed as well by Duke's capacity to tolerate questions she had raised, even of basic Christian beliefs, without becoming defensive. He is "a scholar-pastor," she said, who showed by giving her frequent gifts of books that he takes seriously her intellectual quest, and who shows in his sermons that he understands "theological complexities and how those relate to the complexities of people in the congregation."

Duke said he writes out his sermons word for word, drawing from his reading, often novels, for illustrations. He keeps references to books on cards, by topic, and files away sermons and material related to the Bible by texts. He considers the Gospel "too wonderful to communicate haphazardly." He equates good preaching with "good strategy," meaning that he chooses each word with care. One of his motives is pastoral. Language, especially in worship, is dangerous language," he said. "A careless preacher's words can go stomping around on people's hurts. I believe in shaping language so that it does not wound." But he also finds it helps him to convey images, to draw pictures with words so that the texts come to life and evoke a response. He finds the Baptist tradition of preaching, geared toward "making three points" to be too rational an approach to communicate complex truths.

"I live with the curse of a hyperactive imagination," he said. "I think in images. I feel that my sermons have clear movement, but it's not always linear movement." A narrative preaching style has been the strong preference among homiletic experts in recent years, a coincidence that has been fortuitous for Duke, who is often called upon to preach or write and teach about preaching.

After laboring over his sermons, Duke said he usually knows them so well by Sunday morning that he rarely has to glance at the text. But having it before him helps him to pace his words for effect. As in music, silences, "spaces between the words," are as important as sound and are unlikely to be effectively used by a preacher who talks off the cuff, he feels. "When a sermon is carelessly worded, the room fills up with a clutter of verbiage," he said.

Although Duke struggles to avoid words that "wound," he doesn't balk at challenging his congregation. Raising awareness of social problems and injustice is "terribly hard, but crucial," he said, a core element in communicating the Gospel, just as community involvement is a key to living it. Recently, Duke, who is a member of the NAACP, joined an interfaith committee seeking solutions to racial polarization in St. Louis. He tries to bring a social dimension to every sermon. "When he doesn't come at it directly, he does it indirectly," said John Tyler, who heads the congregation's leadership council.

But Duke was quite direct in expressing opposition to war in the Persian Gulf in January of 1991. Kirkwood Baptist Church opened its doors to an ecumenical "service of prayer for peace" on the eve of the U.S.-led attack against Iraq. Those leading worship ranged from Catholic and Episcopalian priests to a Unitarian minister, and in Sunday bulletins throughout the seven-week war, Duke warned members of his congregation to avoid triumphalism and "public simplifications" such as the term "just war," which he told them is a contradiction in terms.

"Given what we know of God's love, we acknowledge that every war is a civil war, kin killing kin," he wrote. "So we pray not only for the brothers and sisters and sons and daughters that we know, but for our 'enemies' whom God made also our brothers and sisters."

In an article, he described his personal struggle between two dimensions of ministry, both Biblical: the "priestly," which nurtures, and the "prophetic," which points toward justice. "A priest brings the people's grief, their anger, their need to God; a prophet brings God's grief, God's anger, God's need to the people," he wrote. He said he finds the image of the shepherd, often used as a symbol of a pastor, to be appropriate. "In the shepherd's bag is a flute for soothing and a sling for killing. In one hand a rod, in the other a staff."

It was 9 a.m. and Duke was already revising his plans for the day. He had just returned from two days in Chicago where he and Cathy had celebrated their 17th wedding anniversary. Now he was immersed again in church matters. A mother of two young children, Janet, had died just before her 28th birthday from a blood clot that developed after a bone marrow transplant, a risky medical procedure used to treat leukemia and systemic cancer. Janet's body had been cremated, but a memorial mass would be held in early afternoon at a Catholic church about 20 miles away, and her husband's family, which had ties to Kirkwood Baptist, had asked Duke to speak at the service. He was also distressed over news of a troubled marriage between two church members that was unraveling. He was rescheduling his afternoon to deal with the marriage, which had reached a crisis, he said. "If I don't see them today, I'm going to lose them," he said. Yet another matter pressing for his attention was the failure of an in vitro fertilization that a couple in the congregation had been hoping would lead to parenthood.

Duke said he is sometimes exhausted by the pain that comes his way. Yet he is loathe to diminish the image he wants to keep before his congregation: "that people are welcome" in the pastor's office. He worries that too much talk about ministerial stress will sound like "whining," as if there were something "uniquely draining" about pastoral work. At the same time, he knows that to refuse to talk about his discomfort is to foster an idealized image of himself or his ministry. "I want to be honest about it, because bearing other people's pain is part of the cost," he said. But "if people are hurting, the tendency of many of them is to become secretive, to hide the wound. I don't want to encourage that."

Duke wonders to what degree the cost is simply a function of his difficulty in balancing intimacy and distance. People in his congregation often cite compassion as one of the qualities they most value in him, but he often feels that he is too inclined to empathize and unable to achieve the clinical distance that professional counseling, at its best, requires. Sometimes he tends to overcompensate by becoming aloof, he said. "The growing edge for a pastor like me is learning what I can't do," he said. "I can listen, I can recommend reading or resources, I can point in certain directions, I can pray. But I can't make people stop hurting so much. I'm learning to be more appropriately distant so people can find their help within the community and more personally, with God. But I still go home aching for the needs that go unmet."

A day or so later, Duke offered another perspective on his battle, a theological insight rooted in the image of the crucified Christ. He found himself grieving after the couple revealed serious problems in their marriage. "As I was going to sleep last night, I began to realize that our particular faith"—the Christian faith—"means a certain bearing of pain. Whatever appropriate distance a pastor ought to find, it's held in tension with a calling that isn't clinical."

All told, pastoring evokes "a strange and wonderful mix of emotions," he said. "I don't know of any profession that invites access to so many different dimensions of life, that permits you to have a hand in shaping responses to life and death. You are with broken people who are getting better, sick people who are getting well." To balance grief, there are "incredible births," such as a child born to a woman who had asked Duke to pray with her during a process of in vitro fertilization. "We have a joke that I'm a full service pastor; I was present at the conception," he said, grinning.

As Duke deliberated about his part in the memorial service for Janet, he was uncertain of the message he would deliver. He wouldn't be able to prepare and refine it because his remarks would follow the priest's homily, and he had no way of knowing what the priest would say. He decided to trust his intuition and theological resources.

The message that Duke delivered that afternoon was driven by a theology rooted in this world. He spoke of mystery and pain, life and love, and he assured mourners that when one walks in darkness, all that can be relied on are memories and hope. "It is most appropriate that we weep, and for some of us that we weep for a long time," he said. "It is also appropriate that questions emerge from our tears, questions for which there are no answers." Yet Duke spoke of Janet as an enduring personality, a real person with quirks and a woman who, in giving birth, had transmitted life. "I understand the family had a saying, 'Janet will be Janet.' Whatever the mystery of life and death, it does not take from, but adds to the mystery that Janet will ever be Janet," he said.

Recalling that on the following Sunday, Janet would have been 28, Duke said, "This coming Sunday, in human terms, is Janet's birthday. And this year on her birthday, there is just one thing to remember: that death is no longer the last word. Life and love are the last words."

Afterwards, driving back to Kirkwood, Duke said he had been charmed in some ways by the service. If the focal point of worship for Protestants is the sermon, for Catholics it is communion. "I was struck by how right it was, the bread placed upon the tongue, to walk away from that kind of remembrance with more than words ringing in your ears; with a taste in your mouth." But Duke clearly cared deeply about the words as well. He said he had decided on his own message in reaction to being "scandalized—theologically scandalized" by a strong suggestion in the priest's homily that Janet would be better off in death and that her dying had been God's will. Duke was distressed that the priest, an elderly man with little personal knowledge of Janet, had idealized her so much that she seemed unreal.

Linda Bridges, noting that Duke's doctoral dissertation on the Gospel of John, published as *Irony in the Fourth Gospel,* has earned wide respect, believes he could have had a successful career as an academic. Indeed, the Kirkwood congregation, recognizing his need for in-depth study, provides him with a sabbatical of two months every three years. Duke admits that he used to fantasize about an academic life when clerical duties wore him out. "I live with an abiding ambivalence about this vocation, because of some personal limits," he said. He dislikes conflict, is "forgetful" and "not good with brass tacks"—the kind of pastor who could "kill a congregation" if others weren't in place to provide administrative strength, he said. Duke also finds it hard to live with constant demands on his time, the frequent feeling that he is shortchanging his family. He reflected:

"We bought a puppy once. We were the first to take a puppy from the mother. She was a big Labrador retriever, and she had more puppies than she had teats. I will never forget the weariness of her walk as those puppies pulled on her and tried to find more sources of nourishment than were there. There have been days when I have known that dog."

The ministry amid late 20th-century expectations of expertise is especially hard for a person "with the least bit of perfectionist instincts," Duke said. A pastor is expected to be not only a "shepherd of souls—the way we used to talk," but also manager, counselor, psychologist, social worker, liturgist and expert preacher. He used to wish that he could do only the part of the work he was best at, the part he liked the most.

"Then it occurred to me one day that in baseball I don't believe in a designated hitter," he said. "I think everybody should run and throw and catch. So I decided to be a little smarter about running and throwing and catching in my own profession. I told myself, 'This is how the church has decided a pastor is called to live, so suck it up and go.'"

Duke said he feels exceptionally well-matched to the Kirkwood congregation, with its strong, active laity and talented ministerial team, and says the relationship "feels long-term." Programs tend to be "mission-oriented," he said, in the sense of serving people, rather than designed simply to bring new people in.

If Duke fantasizes less of late about other options for his life, he said it is "an indication of love and respect for the congregation with whom I live, the real friendships they offer, the freedom they give me to be less than perfect, and the wonderful affirmation they give me for the gifts that are there." The congregation for him is an extension of his relationships in Louisville, a place where he tries to model "absolute commitment . . . obedience and faithfulness not only to Christ but to each other." He added, "What keeps this work from being as exhausting as it might be is members of the church who work hard at being the church."

Duke said thinking about his future in ministry reminds him of a story about stories—the story of Sheherazade:

"He was the sultan who was chopping off all his wives' heads. One wife starts telling him a story, and he thinks he might chop off her head one day. But in the meantime, he doesn't, because the story's good. And that's why I keep hanging on. The story's really good."

John Huston Ricard

Free At Last

by William R. MacKaye

*Now while he was at table in the house it
happened that a number of tax collectors and
sinners came to sit at the table with Jesus and
his disciples. When the Pharisees saw this, they
said to his disciples, "Why does your master eat
with tax collectors and sinners?" When he heard
this he replied, "It is not the healthy who need
the doctor, but the sick."*

—Matthew 9:10

Father Joseph Doyle remembers the night vividly. It was
1964. There, facing the Lincoln Memorial in silent vigil, he
stood with his classmate John Ricard, both of them students at
St. Joseph's Seminary in Washington. Hour by hour, around the
clock, seminarians from the Washington area's many theological
schools had appeared at the vigil site, bearing voluntary witness to what they held to be a moral imperative: the duty of
Congress to act without further delay to adopt national civil
rights legislation extending to all Americans the right to use all
public facilities in every state. Now it was the vigil time of the
two black-suited young candidates for the Roman Catholic
priesthood: Doyle, a white man from Philadelphia, and Ricard,
a black man from Baton Rouge, Louisiana.

On any night the Lincoln Memorial, viewed from where
the two seminarians stood, is an awesome sight. On that occasion, in that time of national crisis, the sight had even greater

power to anyone who placed hope in America's ability to summon up the will to choose the right action. Across the street, facing the two seminarians, rose a long, broad flight of marble stairs leading to the open side of the memorial's great hall. And there, in the midst of the hall, bathed in light, brooded Daniel Chester French's heroic statue of the seated martyr-president. Behind them stretched the Reflecting Pool, and further in the distance, shone two other grand icons of the Republic, the Washington Monument pointing to the heavens and the Capitol on its hill, pregnant with the promise of justice to be done.

And then a car came rolling by, slowed to a stop, and discharged its menacing passengers. "I think they were from the American Nazi party," Doyle recalled nearly 30 years later. "They were getting into an argument about the inferiority of blacks. John just handled himself with such coolness and poise and intelligence that they didn't know what to do . . . He handled it beautifully, without losing his composure or anything. I think John's always been that way. I think that scene represents for me the kind of priest and bishop John is."

"I was very fortunate to grow up in the church and in the seminary at a time of great turmoil," said the Most Reverend John H. Ricard, titular bishop of Rucuma, auxiliary bishop of Baltimore, and one of the dozen living African-American bishops of the largely white Roman Catholic Church in the United States. Sitting in his office in Baltimore's Catholic Center, he was musing on the events that shaped him on the way to the priesthood and since. Ricard and Doyle were ordained in 1968 as priests of the Society of St. Joseph of the Sacred Heart, a religious community founded in Baltimore in 1893 with a specific mission to minister among black Americans. Sixteen years later, in 1984, Ricard was ordained bishop, the second black Josephite to reach the episcopate. A third black Josephite, the Most Reverend Carl J. Fisher, would be ordained auxiliary bishop of Los Angeles in 1986. No white Josephite has ever been made a bishop, but then no black Josephite has ever been elected superior of the society.

"When I was in seminary, the five years that I was in theology, the five final years of my seminary formation, everything was completely turned upside down," Ricard said. "So there was

a constant imperative to keep on questioning, to keep on rede-
fining. . . . That stayed with me, and that's been there. I don't
know how successful I've been in terms of doing it, but I think
the seed was sown and the ground was set for that."

By some measures John Ricard and the eleven other black
bishops have been handed near-to-impossible assignments. Indeed, one, the Most Reverend Eugene Marino, the senior
Josephite bishop, has already left office and now lives outside
the public eye. In 1990 he resigned as archbishop of Atlanta,
the highest office in the Catholic Church ever held by an African-American, after it was charged that he had had an affair
with an Atlanta woman. Marino was succeeded in Atlanta by
another black prelate, the Most Reverend James P. Lyke. Another of the twelve, the Most Reverend Joseph Lawson Howze,
is bishop of Biloxi, Mississippi. The rest are all auxiliaries, as-
sistants to other bishops, and equipped only with such authority
as their bosses choose to delegate to them. Slotted in these cir-
cumscribed positions, they are expected to symbolize the growing leadership role of black Americans in the Catholic Church,
to enhance the increasing recognition and value the church
places on the black cultural tradition as a legitimate part of its
diversity and universality, and—as protectors of orthodoxy—to
hold the line against reforms that would undermine essential
aspects of the Catholic faith.

Ricard appears to thrive in the complex dynamics of his
job, juggling without ostensible effort the demands of a half-
dozen or more projects at a time. He cheers the opportunities
his work provides him to point to signs of hope and to promote
the good, and shrugs off the backbiting, small-mindedness, and
lack of vision he sometimes encounters. Preaching one Sunday
in the small chapel of a community of contemplative Carmelite
nuns in a Baltimore suburb, he seized on the evangelist
Matthew's homely agricultural parable to explain why he is so
ready to accept the bad along with good.

"The reign of God consists of wheat *and* weeds," he told
the little congregation, a dozen nuns or so, and perhaps 30 lay
people clustered in what seemed a grove of low arches. "Jesus
affirmed life in its inconsistencies and its discrepancies. . . .
Nietzsche once said life should not be, since we have to kill to

eat, but Jesus affirmed—he took on himself our woundedness, our brokenness."

In his visit to the Carmelite monastery to celebrate mass and to preach, the bishop was performing one of his duties as a staff assistant to the Most Reverend William Keeler, the archbishop of Baltimore: staying in touch with members of religious orders resident within the archdiocese. Under Catholic law, religious communities of men and women like the Carmelites, the Franciscans, the Jesuits, the Josephites, and so on, work largely outside the direct supervision of bishops, reporting instead to the superiors, or "ordinaries," of their own communities. Generally speaking, however, the local bishop still has the right to determine whether a given religious community may set up shop within his diocese and to exercise broad oversight over its activities. By visiting that summer Sunday, Bishop Ricard carried out the oversight role; he also solved a more immediate problem for the sisters. He filled in a slot on the rota of celebrants of the community's Sunday mass, a schedule many Catholic groups without a resident priest are finding increasingly difficult to fill as the church's supply of priests continues to dwindle.

Ricard's principal assignment in the Archdiocese of Baltimore is to be urban vicar of the Catholic churches in the city of Baltimore. Pastors of these churches report to the archbishop through Bishop Ricard, while pastors of the archdiocese's churches outside Baltimore—the Archdiocese of Baltimore embraces all of Maryland west of the Chesapeake Bay except the counties surrounding and south of Washington, D.C.—report to other episcopal vicars. Among his more ticklish tasks in this role is his supervision of small Corpus Christi Parish, which has not had a resident priest since 1986. Since then, its on-the-spot management has been in the hands of a nun, Sister Jane Coyle, who is called "pastoral director" of the 350-family congregation.

Sister Jane has husbanded the activities of her band of worshipers—60 or so attend the regular Saturday evening mass, while between 150 and 200 worship at the Sunday mass, depending on the time of year—working up to six months ahead to make sure a visiting priest will be on hand to preside. She's raised money and overseen a slow but steady renovation of the parish's handsome century-old building. "When I came on board, we put in the new furnace and air conditioning, changed the lighting, and started on the whole inside thing," she said. "That's what I've been doing. We just finished the painting in December and I'm working now on trying to start another campaign. Some of the stained glass windows at the top are pretty wobbly and not in good shape." She examined her interviewer with a slight twinkle in her eye. "Now all I have to do is scrape up something like—I'm looking for $60,000 if you know anybody. You look like a prosperous man."

Sister Jane's initial appointment as pastoral director was made by Archbishop Keeler's predecessor, the Most Reverend William Borders, who retired in 1989. It is not clear that Keeler, who is generally more conservative and cautious, is entirely comfortable with her assignment, though he has made no move to change it. What is clear is that some are keeping a close, and suspicious, eye on the congregation's activities. Sister Jane offered an example: "I guess every parish has what they call ex-priests. Some of ours have been very active. There is a policy that they are not to be lectors [readers of Bible lessons at mass] or communion ministers. And I didn't realize that. Someone came for one of our liturgies and recognized the person who was up there and apparently reported it downtown, so Bishop Ricard came and told me about it. And then left it to me to handle it as carefully and nicely as possible with as little hurt as possible."

Mainly, Sister Jane said, Bishop Ricard has been "utterly supportive in every way," trusting her to manage the congregation wisely but responding immediately when she had questions. Usually she sees him only at meetings they both are attending, such as sessions of BUILD—Baltimore United In Leadership Development—a coalition of city churches working together on urban problems. Civic affairs take up another segment of Ricard's schedule. Since 1988, in one such task, he has served as chairman of the Mayor's Homeless Relief Advisory Board in Baltimore.

In contrast to the experience of most auxiliary bishops, national activities consume a major portion of Ricard's time. Most of these have to do with developing the self-awareness of black Catholics and representing their concerns within the councils of the wider church. The African-American bishops formed themselves into a coalition in 1984, the year Ricard was ordained to the episcopate, and issued an unprecedented group pastoral letter titled "What We Have Seen and Heard." The 36-page document, addressed "to our black Catholic brothers and sisters in the United States," was largely drafted by the Reverend Cyprian Davis, a black Benedictine monk who is professor of church history at St. Meinrad Seminary in Indiana. In it the bishops announced that the black Catholic community had reached adulthood. "This maturity," they went on, "brings with it the duty, the privilege and the joy to share with others the rich experience of the 'Word of Life' " to be found within the black community. The bishops described what they said was a distinctive black approach to Catholic spirituality, rooted in the black community's gift for spontaneous and pervasive prayer, its instinctive rejection of dualism (and "any notion that the body is evil"), its sense of joy and celebration, and its understanding that a Christian's identity is not to be found alone but in community with others, especially with one's extended, and sometimes informally adopted, family. They encouraged their hearers to develop distinctively African-American rites of worship within the Catholic liturgical framework. And they called on them to commit themselves wholeheartedly to the cause of justice for all.

"Our own history has taught us that preaching to the poor and to those who suffer injustice without concern for their plight and the systemic cause of their plight is to trivialize the Gospel and mock the cross . . .," they wrote. "As Black people in a powerful nation we must have concern for those who hunger and thirst for justice everywhere in the present world. . . . As a people we must have the courage to speak out and even contribute our efforts and money on behalf of any people or any segment of the human family that the powerful may seek to neglect or forget as a matter of policy."

The stance assumed by the black bishops contrasted dramatically with the growing inclination of many white bishops to focus their social justice activities almost exclusively on making abortion illegal, to continue to root their moral theology in suspicion of the temptations of the flesh, and to discourage freewheeling liturgical experimentation in favor of close adherence to the norms, mostly European in origin, laid down by authorities in Rome. Ricard decided early on in his episcopate that he would devote a major portion of his energy to issues of concern to black Catholics.

"I think black bishops, in particular, today play a much more expanded role," he said, looking back over his seven years as a bishop. "First of all, we're identified collectively as one, as *the* black bishops. There is a consciousness—there was and there is now—a consciousness within the church that something else needed to be done for black Catholics, so we assumed that responsibility. Part of my early experience of being a bishop, and it continues today, is this outside involvement, a kind of national focus on activities that would affect all black Catholics. Specifically, that means coordinating training workshops for clergy who are working in black parishes. That means this black Catholic assembly that we're going to have next year. That would mean advocating for black Catholics at the U.S. Bishops Conference. That means anywhere from that to umpteen invitations to speak, brother bishops who ask you to come to their dioceses. You become the symbolic person for them."

Father John Harfmann, the director of the Josephite Pastoral Center in Washington and a fellow member of Ricard's religious community, is one of the bishop's closest associates in his national activities. They were major planners of the National Black Catholic Congress in New Orleans in July 1992, a three-day forum for lay people, clergy, and members of religious orders to discuss the role of the family in the African-American community. It was the second such gathering; the first, which Bishop Ricard also chaired, attracted 1,500 participants to a gathering in Washington in 1987.

To some it might seem odd that Harfmann, who is white, was so involved in the design of an event for black Catholics. But he said he felt no discomfort, as he chatted one afternoon in his office at the Josephite Pastoral Center in the huge building near Catholic University in Washington that once housed the classes of St. Joseph's Seminary, where both Ricard and Harfmann were educated for the priesthood. "People always knew I was not there dictating anything, I was there giving options," Harfmann said. "I think that's what safeguarded both the integrity of what I do and also made sure that whatever was being done was being done by African-Americans."

Harfmann believes Ricard is able to manage the complexity and diversity of his interests and responsibilities because of his ability to tap a wide variety of colleagues and associates for ideas, information, and energy. "I think his secret is that he never really, from what I can see, really allows things to rest," he said. "He's always going from one to the next and keeping the pot boiling by questions: 'Where are we on this?' 'Have you thought this out?' 'Did you read this? What is it saying?' If I were to call him right now and say, 'Bishop, I just heard something—' 'Find out what it's about, call me tonight.' When you're in that kind of relationship with him, you can call him day or night—eight o'clock in the morning and eleven o'clock at night or twelve o'clock at night, and he'll jump in if he feels the concept is one he can work with. . . . By working like that you involve lots of people, and you get lots of people to do lots of thinking. He knows, for example, if he says something to me, I'm going to ask two or three other people what they think. He's got the advantage now of three people rather than himself alone. I think his ability to do that has been his success."

The Josephites recognized Ricard early on as a member with promise. After his ordination to the priesthood in 1968—he and his two black classmates, Joseph Rodney and Samuel Daisy, who were also Louisianans, were separated from their eight white classmates and ordained in a special ceremony at the cathedral in Baton Rouge—he was assigned to an assistant's post at St. Peter Claver Church in New Orleans. Then he was sent to Tulane University, where he earned a master's degree in psychology and became an associate professor. In 1972, at the age of 32, he was appointed to his first pastorate, Holy Redeemer Church in Washington. Three years later he was transferred to the pastorate of Holy Comforter-St. Cyprian's Church, also in Washington, a larger congregation.

In those first years of Ricard's priesthood, the black members of the Josephites were struggling, along with the whole black community, Catholic and non-Catholic, to identify and legitimate a black culture that was distinct from the white culture that hitherto had dominated American life. "There was a sense that the African-American community was changing, radically changing and radically coming into its own," is how Ricard described the process in later years.

Even while the 1968 ordinands were still students, said his classmate Joseph Rodney, "you had chaos in the seminary. A lot of that had to do with the fact that the blacks began to contend that we weren't being trained to be black people. We were really being trained to be a middle-class kind of white people. . . . You see, the faculty always considered everybody the same, whereas the blacks began to say, 'Well, there are two different people. . . . Our history is different, and we don't have any of our history being taught.'

"And we didn't," Rodney added firmly, speaking in his office at Prince of Peace Church in Mobile, Alabama, where he is pastor. "We didn't have any of our own history being taught in the seminary. The things we learned about being black . . . were things that you learned on your own, and read on your own, and I think Ricard and all of us did a lot of that on our own. We learned it on our own because I don't think it's really fully accepted in the Society right now, even up to today. They might kill me for saying that, but that's the truth.

"Tensions were high and there were times you didn't even know what to say to certain guys because you didn't know how he was going to react to it. Even some of my own classmates, even though we remain great friends and whatnot, but some of them—because of the tension—everybody seemed to have been on the defensive for some reason or another. At that particular time just being a black in the seminary was kind of hard, and a lot of guys quit right at that time. You could see why they quit—because nobody was listening to them."

In Ricard's recollections, the turmoil of that era gave rise to a spiritual turning point of sorts for him. "The year I was ordained a deacon, we had gone home the previous summer and vacationed, and I came back and half the seminary had left," he said. "That was a real trauma, just to deal with that, because you had to deal with the question, 'Well, why am I still here?' . . . I can remember reading an article in *America* magazine—I'll never forget reading that—where there was an older priest talking to a younger seminarian, and telling him, 'Be decisive, take the step!' You know, take the risk, be ordained, and I thought he was talking to me. And I made the step. I said that this was going to be a decision that *I* will make, not my parents, and not the community, not even the church. This is one that *I* am going to make. That was, I think, a real moment."

That diaconal ordination marked the end of an era. Ricard and his surviving classmates were ordained with students from other Washington area seminaries in a mass ceremony at the city's vast National Shrine of the Immaculate Conception, 85 of them altogether made deacons at the hands of the Most Reverend John S. Spence, an auxiliary bishop of Washington who, as Ricard recalled it, was seeking to preside over a record ordination. "That was the last year deacon ordinations were like that," Ricard added. "Then everything kind of fell apart after that."

In 1978 Ricard was named consultor general of the Josephite Society, the first black to hold the office. The job was ill-defined—he was to be a sort of deputy without portfolio to the superior general—but the assignment was seen as an honor and a strong vote of confidence in Ricard's ability and value to the Josephite community. Ricard, approaching the age of 40, had staked out a cautiously independent posture by then. He had a side job as an adjunct associate professor at Catholic University. He had experimented with a modified Afro haircut, the bushy hair style then popular among many black men and women which emphasized the coarse stiffness of the curl of Negro hair. He had grown a mustache (which still survives), a facial adornment generally frowned on for Catholic clergy. He was a man who liked to be handed an assignment, given the authority to accomplish it, and then left alone to carry it out. Sitting in an office in Baltimore, working at the beck and call of the Josephite superior general, was a bad fit.

To Harfmann, it's no surprise the consultor's job didn't work out for Ricard. "He's a hands-on guy, and it wasn't that kind of job." It's no surprise to Rodney, either. Noting that all the consultors general but the first two have been black, he said: "I guess a lot of the guys have got the feeling that since it doesn't have a definition, and it doesn't have any authority really connected to it, that's why one of us gets elected to it."

Ricard points to the vagueness of his duties. "The expectations were entirely different from what I had been experiencing as a pastor, and also as a community leader, or activist, or psychotherapist. I had lived a fairly self-defined life,

I kind of set my own schedule, and I felt myself to be somewhat of a fairly astute manager and administrator. This position was clearly subordinate. It was going to be one of intense subordination and ill-defined. That was the biggest difficulty."

In addition, Ricard sensed resistance among his fellow Josephites to coming to terms with the new black self-awareness. That made the discomfort he felt as consultor general even worse. "Being a black priest, a black person, that was an extremely painful position: to be part of the administration and find the incapacity to respond to, or inability to deal with, some of what I thought was important," he said. He struggled on for a time, but finally in 1981, in an extremely unusual move, he resigned as consultor. In later years he wondered if he shouldn't have tried harder to make the job work. At the time he felt that he had probably wrecked his promising career with the Josephites, that he would never again be anything more in the Society or the wider church than a rather obscure pastor.

During the closing months of his time as consultor general, Ricard had been made pastor of Our Lady of Perpetual Help Church, also in Washington, a larger, almost entirely black congregation in the city's impoverished Anacostia section east of the Anacostia River. He plunged into his pastoral duties and concurrently enrolled for doctoral studies in psychotherapy at Catholic University. He began an internship in the practice of psychotherapy at the D.C. Institute for Mental Hygiene, an unusual private organization that offered low-cost, psychoanalytically oriented therapy for poor people. Ricard found the training a powerful experience, particularly because—as he said—"it came at a time in my life when I was having a lot of questions about my own skills to deal with problems that were presented to me, especially with problems of individuals and people relating to other people, and problems of living." Under those circumstances, looking deeply into the problems of others seemed to lead him fruitfully into examining his own situation. "When you're dealing with people with psychological difficulties," he said, "it forces you to some self-reflection. . . . As you build your capacity to observe people in the depths of their soul, it also builds the capacity to understand one's own self and to distance one from one's self."

Ricard, characteristically, swiftly acquired broad respect from colleagues and wide responsibility in the Institute's clinic in Anacostia. He soon specialized in working with severely depressed women, a group he had already met in large numbers in his earlier work at Holy Redeemer and Holy Comforter, which were also inner city congregations, and was encountering again at Our Lady of Perpetual Help. "They were women in their 30s," Ricard recalled, "typically, mid-30s or early 30s, with two or three children and feeling stuck with these kids, with an image of a husband or boyfriend footloose and fancy free, doing his own thing or doing what he wanted to do. 'I'm stuck with these kids, I could have been a nurse' or 'I could have been a school teacher,' they were saying, 'I could have been something else but my parents didn't motivate me to do this sufficiently' or 'He came into my life'—the boyfriend—'and now all of this is coming down on me.' That was a constant theme I kept hearing, and not really knowing how to respond to that adequately."

Dr. John Love, a psychiatrist who was director of the Institute's Anacostia clinic and Ricard's supervisor, draws a vivid word-picture of the situation that the priest encountered when he arrived, and how he handled it. "We were in an area of huge, massive migration, where the people were rootless," Love said. "They had come from the South, and had virtually no chance for jobs. They were thrown into a large, anonymous group, primarily determined by the housing projects most of them lived in. To say that these people were lonely and vulnerable is to put it as an understatement.

"I had gone there with the feeling that the application of a model of intensive psychotherapy which included an intense relationship [with the therapist] could be applied there as well as in the other clinics in the town. That's the philosophy of the clinic. It was that not only do we treat them organically and biologically, but that a relationship would develop that included an understanding of their experience. . . .

"In that setting, there was Bishop Ricard, then a priest, who was given a list of people who were in no way different from the ordinary list of patients. These were the kind of patients that in the past I had seen, in other settings, to be a tremendous challenge to men of the cloth, something they had a great deal of trouble tolerating. I think that John Ricard was a more experienced person. He seemed to be able to shift into our language, and to be able to try to understand things in the way that we would try to understand things without being apparently challenged. He was a very handsome, striking man, so that he was considered fair game, particularly since he wasn't in the cloth in our office. He would come dressed immaculately in street clothes. I think it was part of his character: he wasn't wearing protective garb, and the women came after him hammer and tong.

"I'm fortunate to have few problems in this area"—indeed, Love is a rumpled, somewhat overweight man unlikely to attract admirers on the basis of his physical appeal—"so I certainly wasn't bothered by this. He had numbers of people who came after him. I never saw him be unpleasant to the other people. I never saw him do anything but give a loving rejection to them. . . .

"He certainly stood that test very well, and, I think, came to understand a great deal about what we would call an erotic transference, understand it in an intellectual way that would serve him in the future. . . . If I were going to be a priest and be celibate, it wouldn't be a thing I would choose, to be tested that way. I wouldn't choose that myself, but he did, and he seemed to learn from it and to gain from it, rather than to be brought down by or in any way depressed by it that I could see."

Despite Ricard's junior status on the therapy staff—Love recalls him as being one of a dozen or perhaps fourteen clinicians, each seeing eight to ten patients—he was soon exercising considerable leadership in the operation. Partly it was a consequence of his being a black male, a category of professional in short supply and sorely needed at the clinic, almost all of whose patients were black. Partly it was a result of his efficiency and his ability to tolerate stress and responsibility. Many therapists confronted by the seemingly intractable problems suffered by the Institute's clients—unending tales of grinding poverty, depression, violence, neglect, and abuse—sank into depression of their own. Ricard protected himself by throwing himself harder into his work both at the clinic and at his church, as Love recalls it. "I felt he was someone I could draw on," said Love. "Perhaps it was as much for my own purposes as his that I became his supervisor in psychotherapy, as well as running that particular clinic, which I did for about ten years."

Charges began to circulate that the clinic, where whites made up most of the administrative and professional staff, was a racist institution. Black employees—the clerical and support staff was largely black—and some of the radical white professionals questioned particularly the policy of requiring therapists in training to serve their first six months without pay, a policy the critics said biased professional staff recruiting toward more affluent, white candidates. "It could be seen as exploitative," Love conceded, looking back. "We felt the education made up for some of it, but there was nothing we could really put up to justify it altogether except our need, our incredibly pressing need."

The showdown came at a tense staff meeting conducted in the only space at the clinic large enough to hold everyone, a carpeted room slated to become a therapy room that at the time was entirely bare of furniture. Some participants sat on the floor, others stood, and the protestors voiced their complaints. "They were angry," Love recalled. "They were getting a chance to say how angry they were, and to put forth their view that we too were a racist organization. It was very difficult to listen to the angry charges: the points that those people in charge should be models to the children, and should be black."

For a long time Ricard listened silently, Love recalled. But then, finally, he spoke up. He said he did not believe the clinic was a racist organization. He said he "felt that we tried our best to get as many black people on the staff as we could," the psychiatrist continued. "I think that by saying that in his calm way, he turned the tide and was able to reassure people that pretty much what we were doing was all we could in that area. . . . I saw that as a piece of very necessary support for me, very needed. He didn't come in any too early, he waited awhile, and people had a long time to discuss it, and they had at me, but then he did come in to stop what could have been a pretty messy business."

John Ricard lived a tightly scheduled life in those years, as Love recalled it, and usually was able to work with only a minimum number of patients because of the demand for his time at Our Lady of Perpetual Help. There, in addition to the usual round of pastoral chores and crises characteristic of life in a good-sized congregation, he embarked on renovations. His colleague John Harfmann recalled discovering on one occasion that Ricard had recruited some men of the congregation to paint the outside of one of the church's school buildings, a three- or four-story structure. Ricard was up on the scaffolding with the others, painting away. "People were amazed that here was the pastor doing this, the same pastor who was just about finishing his doctorate. He's counseling at the D.C. Institute, running this very large parish, doing all these things, and he's out *painting*! There's never a case where it will be said with him, 'That's below me. I don't do that. I won't lift this. I won't move the chairs. I won't set up the podium, the bishop doesn't do that.' He's more at ease pitching in."

What with all the competition for his time, Ricard, like many another Ph.D. candidate, found it difficult to keep moving ahead with his dissertation, a study of the treatment of depression among black women. More than once Eugene Marino, his fellow Josephite, who was then an auxiliary bishop of Washington, admonished him to finish the degree. But there was so much to do. The parish planned a huge dance as a fund-raiser, hoping to attract 2,000 participants, and the pastor threw himself into that as well. Calamitously, the fund-raiser was a flop— only about 200 people turned up.

Not long after that, around ten o'clock one morning in late May 1984, the rectory phone rang. It was Cardinal John Hickey, Washington's archbishop, asking Ricard if he could come downtown for lunch. "Can you tell me what this is about?" Ricard asked a little nervously, wondering if he was about to get clobbered for the failed fund-raiser. The cardinal just urged him to hurry on downtown. And there, in Hickey's office, Ricard heard the news: He was about to be appointed an auxiliary bishop of Baltimore.

" 'Baltimore!' I said," said Ricard, recalling, "just spontaneously, because you know how people in D.C. look at Baltimore. I argued with him about the wrong choice—'Don't you think you ought to consider Father—' I mentioned a few other priests. I was in total shock, complete shock. . . . That was the last thing I was aspiring to. But anyway, that happened, and I came to Baltimore." The reason for Bishop Marino's puzzling anxiety about the dissertation's getting finished had become clear.

The bells of Baltimore's Cathedral of Mary Our Queen rang out on July 2, 1984, and a congregation of more than 3,000 worshipers thronged in to assist at the ordination of the nation's tenth black Catholic bishop in the 20th century. John Ricard's mother, Albanie St. Amant Ricard, and his six living brothers and sisters had gathered from across the country for the occasion (their father, Maceo, had died in 1977), and as he prepared to leave for the cathedral for his ordination, the bishop-elect was reflecting on the rigor with which his parents had practiced their religion.

"Why do you suppose Mom prays three hours a day?" he asked one of his sisters, Dolores Chustz. Chustz chuckled as she recalled her answer, another question: "Why do you suppose you were named a bishop?"

Indeed, the Catholic faith, intense and traditional, did lie at the heart of the Ricard family life throughout the future bishop's childhood. He was born on leap year day, February 29, 1940, about 30 miles north of Baton Rouge in New Roads, Louisiana, a town of about 2,500 in those days. New Roads, the seat of Pointe Coupee Parish, crouches on the shores of a lake formed by a loop of the Mississippi that the main channel of the great river later abandoned in one of its recurring changes of course. A few days after the baby's birth, he was baptized Sam Huston Ricard at Immaculate Conception Church in nearby Lakeland, Louisiana, where the Ricard family worshiped in the mulatto section of the segregated nave. Blacks, mulattos (as persons of mixed Creole ancestry were known), and whites all attended the church, carefully sorted into separate seating areas depending on their skin tone. Albanie and Maceo Ricard named their new child after Louisiana's new reform governor, Sam Houston Jones, who had been inaugurated a few weeks earlier. In later years, by now a priest, the namesake regretted his parents' choice and dropped his given name in favor of John, though members of his family still call him Sammy.

The elder Ricards customarily spoke French with each other and with many of their neighbors, but the children were English speakers from their schooling. Life was rough in New Roads, especially for persons of color who had no land—a little share-cropping, a little fishing—but then World War II began and brought with it new opportunities. In 1942, eager for a better life and better schooling for their children, the Ricard family moved down the road to Baton Rouge. Maceo Ricard got a job with Standard Oil (now Exxon), and the family became pillars of St. Francis Xavier Church, a church staffed by Josephites. All the children attended the parish's elementary and high schools, and for many years Albanie Ricard was a daily communicant at the parish mass, walking twelve blocks each way from the first house the family lived in. After he retired from Exxon, Maceo Ricard was a daily communicant as well.

One of John Ricard's vivid memories of childhood, a memory shared by his brothers and sisters, is gathering as a family in his parents' bedroom each evening for the recitation of the rosary. "We were Catholic to the bone," Ricard said recently. "I knew I was Catholic and I knew I was part of this church"—the image of the church imparted by his parents—"and I know it now. Somebody else might have come along and said, 'This is what it ought to be,' but I knew better. That says to me that the formation that occurs in the home—a definition occurs there that is much more lasting than what you're going to read about later."

A second aspect of Ricard's upbringing also had a powerful impact on the bishop-to-be. "I grew up in a very rigid society, comparable to South Africa. As a child I can remember my parents finding it necessary to protect me from stepping over the boundaries, the racial boundaries, of saying 'Yes, sir' and 'No, sir.' I saw through all of that. I used to hate and resent my parents' telling me to do that, but I know, in retrospect, they were doing it for my own protection. So I grew up with a self that questioned throughout. We weren't allowed to feel that we were part of the system that we were in. You weren't part of being an American, you weren't fully a part of the society or the culture. That stayed, and it was bound to affect my feeling for the church."

In time, after Ricard was ordained to the priesthood, he sensed that his conception of the priesthood was richer than that held by some others. "I didn't belong to how 'they' defined priesthood. Because of my background, I had a capacity to look beyond that and see the church was much more than the way 'they' defined it." Asked who "they" were, he paused, and then replied, "White clergy."

Some of that background, some of that shaping arises from his membership in the Josephites, Ricard said, and that helped especially in his ability to adjust to being a bishop. Members of religious orders generally do not become bishops except in missionary areas, and hence order priests do not aspire to the episcopate as perhaps diocesan priests do. "Nobody put a gun to my head and told me I had to say yes," he said. "The decision was really mine, and I assumed ownership of it, and I think I thus got a bit more of a grasp on things." But some of the confidence with which he moved into the job came from his years with his fellow Josephites. "I found, as a priest, enormous personal support from the Josephites," he said. "I think I found people that were inherently sympathetic to African-American Catholics, intuitively sympathetic and intuitively identified with them. I felt a lot of affirmation by the Josephite community. . . . They identified with the struggle, and I think that is what made a quality difference and made my own struggle as a black person easier. I could always feel we could discuss anything with impunity, even when we disagreed, even when they didn't want to do it. They were one with us, and I was one with them."

Although, as bishop, John Ricard has been detached from formal Josephite membership, he lives in the rectory of St. Francis Xavier Church in downtown Baltimore, a historic Josephite parish. He acquired his PhD in clinical social work in 1985, his credential to practice psychotherapy though he does not practice. He's a familiar figure on the city's streets. As John Harfmann says, "The drunks and dope fellows don't have to see him in cope and miter and red hat to know him, to say 'There's the bishop, hey man, don't do that, that's the bishop.'" In a suit, or in running sweats, they know him just as well. Indeed, after he'd been bishop a while, Ricard noticed people doing double-takes on the sidewalk as he came jogging by, saying, "Haven't I seen you—" in questioning tones with voices that then trailed off. "The last straw came when this guy, a priest who was visiting from New York, told me he had seen me. I said that's the end of that, so I went and found one secluded track at one of the high schools." The bishop is still a jogger, but in private.

Ricard gives every sign of ease when he functions as a public person. Watching him in action with a Catholic youth group, for example, makes it easy to understand why the organizers invite him back year after year. When he spoke to 50 teenagers at the High School Leadership Institute held at the Monsignor O'Dwyer Youth Retreat House in Sparks, Maryland, on a hot Saturday morning, Ricard began not by telling but by listening. "It's vitally important that the church listen to people like yourselves," he told them, "You are the church." The conversation began, and the bishop listened.

But before the hour and a half was over, the bishop had served his enthusiastic, mostly white, audience some significant food for thought. He noted that black Catholics in the United States cut a relatively small swath, that he is one of only 300 black Catholic priests in the entire country. "But there are 75 million Catholics in sub-Saharan Africa," he added. "That's going to influence how the church develops." That thought led, after further exchanges with the participants, to his recalling the wonderment of an African priest he had met at how quick Americans are to throw things away. "As Americans we need to do a lot of soul-searching. What is really important to us?" Ricard said. And he added after a time, "I really think we have to return to the concept that life is very important. Jesus pursued everyone whom he met. You can see that, if you read Matthew slowly and carefully."

Behind the Most Reverend John Ricard the public person is John Ricard the private person, and that private person is very important to Ricard. Those who know him well comment that behind the friendliness, the quick incisiveness, the compassion and concern, there is a distance, someone they never quite get at. "Because of my background, both in psychology and in my early formation, I have always felt a capacity to step back," he acknowledged. It helps him to avoid being shaped by his job. "I still do feel freedom, and I think it's a very liberating experience."

It is perhaps that free person who looks clear-eyed at flaws in the churchly institution, at flaws in the organization of its priesthood, and remains wholeheartedly in its service. "I stay," said Ricard, "because I feel affirmed by what I'm doing. I feel I have made a commitment and I think the commitment is meaningful to others and, certainly, to me."

It is perhaps that free person who looks back at his ordained ministry and says: "I hope that I've been able to make a difference in the lives of many people and that that would prompt them to make an affirmative choice in service to the church. I see my role as bishop as one of service. I felt that in becoming a bishop you have to go all the way, you have to go native. If you don't go native, if you don't throw in your all, you aren't very effective. It may be a weakness on my part that I haven't encouraged others [to enter ordained ministry] as much as I perhaps could or should. I think I would like to convey to people, by what I do, a basic optimism towards life, a basic sense that despite all of the difficulties and painful experiences they may go through that there is a kind of purpose and meaning underneath all of it. And that there is redemption in suffering, that—especially for African-Americans—this does in a way make us stronger from the struggles and difficulties."

It is perhaps that free person who talks to seminarians like this: "My overall message is that it's worth the struggle. Nothing comes to you without a struggle and it really is worth the struggle. My basic message too is that the alternative that our faith offers, and a religious life offers, is far greater than anything else out there."

It is surely that free person who chose to end his homily for the Carmelite nuns by telling a story first told by England's Cardinal Basil Hume. Hume said he had been unnerved since childhood by the image of God's eye, an image familiar to Americans from the Great Seal on the back of the dollar bill. Such an image had hung in Hume's boyhood dining room, where the young Basil saw the eye watching him as he helped himself to an apple his mother had forbidden. And then one day an old woman turned his view around. She told him she loved having God's eye on her wall. Why? "Because he loves me so much he can't take his eye off me."

Carol Anderson

Female and Charismatic in Beverly Hills

by John Dart

"All of them were filled with the Holy Spirit and began to speak in other languages, as the Spirit gave them ability."

—Acts 2:4

The adult class inside the Episcopal church in Beverly Hills was completing its Bible study of the "gifts of the Holy Spirit." The list of divine gifts included talents as prosaic as wisdom and mercy and as sensational as the phenomena usually associated with Pentecostal churches—speaking in tongues, healing and exorcism. Mentioning gifts that some parishioners had cultivated, the rector teaching the class then came to: "Giving money liberally for use in the Lord's work." She let hardly a second elapse before adding, "I don't know of anybody who has that gift." The three dozen people in the chapel classroom burst into laughter.

She then responded to an earlier query that she had sought to put off. "Okay, I'll talk about raising the dead," she said, "which we're going to practice after class."

After the laughs subsided, the rector, Carol Anderson, admitted that her "skeptical buttons" were pushed by accounts of raising the dead emanating mostly out of Africa and Latin America. Anderson declared herself an agnostic on the subject unless she saw it herself. But she also noted that the Gospels have Jesus telling his disciples they will do what he did (and,

165

by implication, so will all Christian believers). Western culture was generally not attuned to the spirit world, she said. To the rapt class of parishioners, she told of a memorable brush she had had with spirits six years earlier, when she was guided through an apparent exercise in casting demons out of a black-jacketed motorcyclist.

This was the way that the Rev. Carol Anderson, rector of All Saints' Episcopal Church in Beverly Hills, tiptoed intellectually through the ordinary and the extraordinary, occasionally speeding up the trip with bursts of humor. One could imagine theological tremors reverberating through the tall walls of the church, a handsome white-stucco building with Spanish-tile roof, as Anderson used theology long associated with the lower-economic strata of Pentecostalism. This, after all, was not what parishioners were accustomed to hearing in an Episcopal church nestled near the homes of the rich, only two blocks from the expensive shops of Rodeo Drive.

Yet, this religiously and politically conservative parish had first surprised itself in 1989 simply by hiring a female priest—a confessed Democrat at that, who had lobbied prominently for women's ordination years before the 1976 Episcopal convention lifted the ban. Now, the congregation, excited over a new-found vitality with Anderson at the pulpit, was being drawn gradually but willingly into an Anglican-style charismatic renewal. Not that no wariness remains. During the evening class on "gifts" of the Holy Spirit, a new parishioner asked, tactfully but suspiciously, "Is what you're teaching mainstream? Is it Pentecostal or charismatic?"

"In other words, should you get scared?" said the rector, as if to acknowledge the offbeat images she conjured up.

Charismatic movements tend to be restrained, mainstream versions of Pentecostalism, a global phenomenon that erupted in 1906 at the Azusa Street Mission, 20 miles away in downtown Los Angeles. The most distinctive feature has been the evident recovery of glossolalia, or utterances in an unknown or foreign tongue. The New Testament says the earliest apostles practiced speaking in tongues, courtesy of the invigorating Holy Spirit. In mainline churches, its importance is somewhat downplayed.

Half of All Saints' governing vestry was speaking in tongues, "quietly and not making a big deal of it," according to Anderson. Sunday Communion services at All Saints' were typically Episcopal. But one night a month, Anderson led a low-key Prayer and Praise service. Arms were raised in characteristic Pentecostal prayer poses and hands were laid on those kneeling at the altar.

To the class member worried about the orthodoxy of this quest, Anderson put it this way: "The oldline churches in the orthodox tradition are opening themselves up to the work of the Holy Spirit that are talked about in Scripture" while maintaining their worship style and traditional sense of church order. "We're trying to be open in ways that enliven and empower the church," she said.

Yet another newcomer, his voice catching with nervousness, asked if the parish's newly formed prayer healing team would act responsibly and not make unwarranted claims.

"That's why we spent nine weeks helping them to know what they are doing and what they are not doing," Anderson replied. "Experience will show that seldom is someone healed just like that," she said, snapping her fingers. "Sometimes it happens, but if that person does not seem in any way healed, hopefully we will pay attention to know God is working in other ways."

Anderson, in her mid-40s, has an ample, 5-foot-11-inch frame that is often blurred under dark-color jackets and nondescript skirts. Her light brown hair falls in a simple pageboy cut. It is her amiable face, quick to smile and raise eyebrows in seeking assent, that engages the listener as words pour out, rapid-fire and without loss of clarity. She was the first Episcopal woman to preach at the National Cathedral in Washington and in Westminster Abbey, and her sermons and classes have won admirers wherever she has given them across the country.

Her preaching is no less a drawing card for the Beverly Hills parish, whose average Sunday attendance has climbed by 100 people to 600 since she's been there. "She's inspiring," exuded Susan Hartzler, 32, a publicist who grew up in a Methodist church. "She doesn't preach above people. She might preach about the Bible, then say personally how something affected her life."

Tom Foster, the music director for 15 years, called the parish a "sleeping giant" transformed by Anderson's vision to the way church "ought to be." Anderson said Foster at first objected to some of the charismatic-style music she wanted in the Prayer and Praise service, and she backed off. "I valued his opinion," she said. "But over a year's time, he's opened up to it. He's not afraid of it anymore."

Many of All Saints' 1,850 members were comfortable about the parish's new directions because of the legitimacy lent by the rector's connection to the charismatic movement inside the Church of England. Several Anglican priests befriended Anderson during her pivotal, three-month sabbatical in England in 1978. They were involved in an evangelical-charismatic movement in which speaking in tongues was merely one possible "gift"—not the dramatic signal of classic Pentecostalism that one had been baptized by the Holy Spirit. For this Anglican version of the charismatic renewal she cited the books of Michael Green, who was then a parish priest near Oxford and now teaches at Regent College in Vancouver. Anderson felt this movement has "significantly touched" one-third of the nation's 12,000 or so active Episcopal priests. Not all are card-carrying charismatics, she added, but 3,000 priests have identified with the movement's U.S. organization, the Episcopal Renewal Ministries.

While in England, Anderson encountered another proponent of the renewal, "a guy with a Ph.D. in theology who could really kind of kick back and forth with me all the struggles I was going through theologically." That parish priest, George Carey, with whom she corresponded over the years, was later elected a bishop, then the Archbishop of Canterbury, the spiritual leader of the worldwide Anglican Communion.

In early 1991, Anderson was one of six Americans, including the Episcopal Church's presiding bishop, invited to Westminster Abbey for Carey's enthronement ceremony. At a private reception following the rites, Carey donned an All Saints' Choir baseball cap presented by Anderson for a photo of the two that made the front page of the All Saints' newsletter. "We spark with each other," she said. "George has got the same kind of creative mind-set as I do. We're rooted the same way theologically. We both sort of push out at the edges—ask questions, fuss and carry on."

Anderson said she made friends easily. That was demonstrated no more clearly than when All Saints' called her to the pulpit in 1989. Bishop Frederick Borsch of the Los Angeles Diocese said he had submitted to the parish a list of possible candidates that included several women, although not Carol Anderson. "The [parish's] response in so many words was that they were not interested in a woman priest," Borsch said.

However, Rob Kass, a surgeon at Cedars-Sinai Medical Center, who chaired the search committee, said the panel had not ruled out a woman rector during its process of whittling down a long list of possible candidates. "She was one of about 20 people on our list to interview," Dr. Kass said. "We were impressed with her."

Businessman Don Allison, a member of the search committee, said the vestry was loaded with oldline Episcopalians and Republicans in their 60s. He remembered with relish the winning over of one vestryman, an ex-Marine captain whose wife had worked in the Reagan White House: "Carol, I want to talk politics with you," said the retired officer during one dinner-interview.

"No, you don't," Anderson replied. "I not only voted for Gov. Dukakis willingly but I also voted for George McGovern happily," she said, referring to past Democratic Party presidential candidates. "But you will never know my politics from the pulpit." Rather, she said, social-political issues would come up only in settings where parishioners could exchange views with the rector. When it was clear that Anderson would be offered the position, the ex-officer, Edward Borcherdt, said he confided to others on the vestry, "I'm going to have to go home and tell my wife that I'm voting for a woman who is a liberal, went to Harvard, is a Democrat and is opposed to everything I stand for, but I am so impressed by the spirituality of this person that there is no question in my mind about what I should do."

Sitting in her office with the windows open to the church's inner courtyard and to the noise of church school youngsters, Anderson said the military man also surprised some parishioners in a lecture he gave at the church during the crisis before the Persian Gulf War. "This man stood up and opposed going to war—from theological directions!" she said. "People looked around and wondered, 'What's going on here?'" Borcherdt himself remembers his position coming more from mixed, personal feelings—he had business friends in Iraq and a Marine son stationed in Saudi Arabia. He said he doesn't know if his stance, or the way he expressed it, was affected by his exposure to Anderson's ministry.

But Borcherdt is unequivocal about her effect on him otherwise: "I am 59 years an Episcopalian and have been a member here 25 years and I never really understood what Christianity was about until Carol came."

By everyone from Borcherdt to Bishop Borsch, Anderson is also praised as an excellent administrator. She indicates part of that task is performed by "spreading out the ministry" among lay members. Church law, for instance, requires the rector to chair the vestry meetings. "I will not do them," she said. "The senior warden does them. I say almost nothing at the meetings." The parish has expanded its community outreach to include volunteering at a Los Angeles center for homeless women and taking lunches to AIDS patients waiting in long lines for treatment at the huge USC-County General Hospital. "We may extend that to include grief counseling, and maybe housing; we'll let it develop in a natural way," she said.

Anderson's mix of a liberal-to-moderate social perspective and theological conservatism places her a bit awkwardly between two camps in the Christian world. She has resisted invitations from a southern California association of Lutheran, Presbyterian, Episcopal and Methodist charismatics to join in their meetings. "I've always had a love-hate relationship with the charismatic renewal movement in this country," she said. She disagrees with some of its beliefs and practices, especially those related to classic Pentecostalism. "And I cannot stand their political conservatism."

All Saints' Church has racks near the front entrance filled with small, evangelical booklets on faith questions available for the taking. Charles Colson and best-selling evangelical author Charles Swindoll are among the authors; topics include "How to Be Born Again." Missing, at Anderson's direction, are booklets on two topics that the evangelical camp sees as sinful scourges—abortion and homosexuality. "I happen to be personally against abortion, but I like to talk it through with people . . . about abortion being the last option," she said.

Also, her left-of-center position on gays and lesbians puts her at odds with mainline charismatics. An Episcopal parish in nearby Burbank that is fully involved in the charismatic renewal, for instance, prays for the healing transformation of homosexuals. "I've come to the conclusion that some people are born that way," she said. Her study of Scriptures suggested that the seemingly anti-homosexual passages in Paul's letters actually were much narrower—against promiscuity and lasciviousness in the sexually liberal Greco-Roman society. She said she welcomed gays to a parish she had in New York and that gays are on the staff at the Beverly Hills church. "I try to introduce people to Christ and let them sort it out," she said. "That position is different than that of my two clergy associates, and perhaps of a lot of people in the parish. What I'm trying to say is, 'Drop the prejudice. Get to see them as human beings.'"

Anderson knew several lesbians who were fighting for women's ordination in the New York Episcopal Diocese during the 1970s. "Not being one myself, I backed away from some of the feminist movement when it seemed to be synonymous with being a lesbian," she said. "I may care about women's rights but I don't think you have to be a lesbian to do that."

Through anecdotes, Anderson readily reveals her past fears and failures as a woman trying to gain a place in the priesthood. But her basic self-confidence also comes through— whether talking matter-of-factly about an upcoming service which President and Barbara Bush were to attend or about what it takes to be a successful clergywoman.

Anderson believes that more women priests will be called to posts such as the Beverly Hills church if they demonstrate the desired gifts and skills. "I think there is sexism in the institution, but women should become at ease with the skills they have, and develop them."

She said that she worked hard on improving her sermon delivery early in her ministry. Anderson quickly gained repute as a good preacher although she was never gifted as a writer. "I could write okay, but it was sheer agony for me," she said. One of her few published articles, not surprisingly, was a book review critiquing 15 supposedly exemplary sermons. Anderson termed them "flat" and devoid of storytelling touches. Her review continued: "They did not inspire me, breathe life into me, help me to breathe. They are controlled and reasonable, like the writings of a good country editor. But, it seems to me, a sermon needs to draw the listener into dialogue."

Her own journey to the priesthood, tough enough in a denomination that had an all-male priesthood when she entered seminary, was made more difficult by her tendency to seek trouble—in the form of potentially discouraging challenges. Yet, she declared that she grew up as a shy, introverted person. Her first 17 years were spent in rural northwest New Jersey. She was born June 18, 1945, across the Delaware River in Easton, Pa., and was raised in Asbury, N.J., a town named after Francis Asbury, the first Methodist bishop in the United States. "The town had 300 people and you were either a part of the Methodist church or the volunteer fire department. One small grocery store, that was it." In the town's four-room school, a Methodist hymnal provided the only material for music lessons. She could hardly read when she got to high school. "Neither of my parents were churchgoers," she said, and even her brief exposure to Sunday school was uninspiring. "I was bored to tears; I always thought there was more out there somewhere."

After high school graduation, a new world opened up in 1963 when she was accepted at Lycoming College, a small Methodist liberal arts college in Pennsylvania. The civil rights movement was in full swing. Within months she took part in demonstrations in Philadelphia aimed at opening a private boys school to blacks. She also took a required religion course and liked it, prompting her to study more with a faculty that linked liberal theology and social action.

Anderson had a scare once while working summers with inmates at the New Jersey State Prison for Women. A riot broke out one day. "Everyone who worked in the prison was subject to attack, but these women, all black and very tough, stood around me and wouldn't let anyone get near me," she said. "I think they probably saved my life."

During her senior year as an exchange student at all-black Claflin College in South Carolina, student riots erupted in that state. Walking one day with her black roommate, Anderson was beaten across her knees with a baseball bat by a white man. As she retold the story years later, she remarked that one knee was "acting up" from the injury. "For the first time, I ran into raw evil—that I couldn't explain," she said. "So much of what I had been studying did not address this evil. It began to form questions in my mind."

She decided to do university graduate work in theology, but advisers who were aware of her penchant for working with people suggested instead that she go to a seminary. Impressed by the number of Episcopal priests she saw in the civil rights movement, she went to the Episcopal Theological Seminary in Cambridge, Mass., knowing that she would then be able to take courses at Harvard as well. In three years there, she was arrested for involvement in civil rights and anti-war demonstrations.

For her mandatory practical experience as a church intern, Anderson demanded to be assigned "to the toughest parish you got to offer," namely one that might discourage an aspiring priest from entering the pastoral ministry. "If I'm going to do this with my life, I've got to know what it's like," she recalled thinking. So, they sent her to an "old, Yankee curmudgeon rector" putting in his time until he could retire. The rector at the troubled parish in Needham, Mass., told her he didn't want a woman on his staff.

"Look," Anderson said she replied, "if I can put up with you, then you can put up with me." She spent three years there, and the parish was supportive in her lobbying for ordination despite the denomination's ban on women priests. "I could have been ordained in the United Methodist Church—that was one of the things I had to struggle through," she said. But, after graduation in 1970, she was still "pushing at the edges to find out what life was about." Anderson became a chaplain at Massachusetts General Hospital in Boston, working for a year with heart surgery patients and terminally-ill children in intensive care units.

Though enjoying the work, she felt unprepared when a patient facing heart surgery requested prayer. "I had put this very formal prayer together and I'm not sure I even believed to Whom I was saying it," she said. God was to her at that time a vague creative force without any personal quality or power.

During her prayer, however, something unusual happened. "I felt this enormous jolt of energy going through me and into him. It left me baffled and scared." The man refused surgery the next day. After tests showed that the blockage had disappeared from his heart, he was sent home.

However, it was the fight for women's ordination, not an unexplained healing, that concerned her then. "I discovered five minutes after I began my job that I would need ordination to do the job properly," she told a reporter a few years later. "I was called to the bedside of a dying woman who needed the sacraments. I could not bring them to her, and I could not find a priest in time." Deciding that she could not get backing in the fight for women's ordination from the Diocese of Massachusetts, she approached the New York bishop at the 1970 national convention and told him that he "needed me." "It was the boldest thing I ever did," she admitted. She also had a contact in New York City—the Rev. John Coburn, the former dean of her seminary and then rector of St. James' Church, a parish on Manhattan's affluent Upper East Side. She was assigned temporarily to the Episcopal Mission Society in New York.

The 1970 triennial General Convention of the Episcopal Church okayed women as deacons, but delegates resisted change in the all-male priesthood. In 1971, Anderson became one of the first women deacons in the country and the next year she joined the staff of St. James as an associate rector. "It was a big jump for me," she said. Ex-mayor John Lindsay was a member. "A lot of the Fortune 500 people were floating around," she said.

At the first service she did on her own, she fainted. "I was trying to say, 'The Lord Be With You,' and the word 'the' came out, and the rest got stuck somewhere in my chest cavity," she said. Feeling increasingly lightheaded, she collapsed over the altar rail. "I was petrified about public speaking—not a good thing to be afraid of when you're in the ministry," she said. Nevertheless, she learned by necessity to talk publicly after she met at a bar on Second Avenue with three other female priest-aspirants and formed the advocacy group called the Episcopal Women's Caucus.

She stepped back from the radical edge of the campaign, however, when 11 Episcopal women decided to defy the denomination and be ordained in 1974 by a willing bishop. "I was the only one who already had a job in a parish, and I knew I would lose it if I got involved in the conflict," she told the *New York Post.* At the 1976 convention, the Episcopal Church altered its laws to allow for the ordination of women priests. On Jan. 4, 1977, Carol Linda Anderson was the first woman priest to be ordained in the Episcopal Diocese of New York and the third in the country, apart from the unauthorized ordinations of 1974. A profile of Anderson in the *New York Times* on that occasion said she was "regarded by her parishioners as congenial, unassuming and highly intelligent."

Despite her triumphs, Anderson remembered that latter period at St. James as a time when her "liberal theology went belly up." She found it intellectually unsatisfying and inapplicable. Simultaneously, she was intrigued by an evangelically-oriented Anglican bishop who spoke at St. James. "Here was an intelligent, socially involved man who was not a fundamentalist," she said. This led her toward the Anglican-style evangelical movement. She attended a conference of evangelical Anglicans in England, then plunged into reading classical Christian writers. Her "life-changing" sabbatical in England in 1978 was the time when she met the future Archbishop of Canterbury. "I realized the orthodox tradition of the Church was alive—it was not thoughtless or anti-intellectual," she said. "There was really a God who transformed peoples' lives."

Returning to New York, she wanted to apply these ideas in a parish "where nothing else was working." In 1979, she got her chance at All Angels' Church on Manhattan's West Side. Once a fashionable church, its membership had fallen drastically from its peak of 2,000 parishioners. Thirty people met in a social hall, its church building having been sold. "Rats were all over the place," Anderson recalled. "You could only have one set of lights on at the same time. It was a drug-infested neighborhood. People were dysfunctional, angry, crazy. . . ." After fixing up the building and introducing her own style of ministry, Anderson attracted disenchanted churchgoers, Jewish residents, self-styled revolutionaries, gays, one vocal Republican, Columbia University graduate students and professors, and a whole group from Julliard. "We had a wonderful music program!" she said, laughing.

The place was a revelation for Bob Craft, who was to become a location manager for motion picture productions. He first went to the church in 1979 when he was a film student at New York University. "My parents raised me as an atheist, and I had all these preconceived notions about Protestant fundamentalism," he said. "But here was a mainstream Protestant church that made Jesus Christ come alive. I was there four or five nights a week. The average age was about 35. They had a soup kitchen and other outreach activities. One of the things that I thought was wonderful was Carol's interest in theology and spiritual issues—it wasn't just a social club."

Indeed, Anderson was trying to elicit "gifts" from the Holy Spirit for the parish and herself. A prayer team prayed daily for nearly a year for a woman diagnosed as having brain cancer. The team claimed success when Memorial Sloan-Kettering Cancer Hospital gave her a clean bill of health.

Anderson hadn't spoken in tongues while she was with her charismatic Anglican friends. But one day while strap-hanging on the subway in New York, she started praying silently in English. "The first thing I knew this language was coming in my mind. Since then it has been part of my prayer life."

She also sensed contact with evil spirits not long after discovering the charismatic renewal. Before leaving St. James' Church in 1979, a parishioner innocently invited her to a dinner with a dozen of his astrologer friends. But Anderson said that it turned out to be "a real battle of spirits, not just of personalities." Taught in seminary to regard evil spirits as pre-scientific notions, Anderson changed her mind through such chance encounters and reading M. Scott Peck's *People of the Lie.*

In 1985, while still rector at All Angels', Anderson became convinced of the reality of the spirit world. She took a study month to observe independent charismatic Pastor John Wimber, a southern California advocate of healing and miraculous signs who had started churches called Vineyard Christian Fellowships. "I came away with good things and bad things," she said.

She swears, though, that a couple of weeks later she encountered the demonic during a healing seminar led by a Wimber associate at Westmont College in Santa Barbara. When a motorcyclist, wearing leather jacket and chains, burst into the meeting, the instructor commanded the man to stop. Anderson said the intruder tried to move but couldn't. The instructor then directed Anderson to "minister" to the man. "I got up to about 15 feet from where he was and I walked into what felt like a spiritual force field," she recalled.

"It was not an emotional or psychological thing going on; the term 'spiritual warfare' suddenly became real to me."

The seminar leader told her, "You can finish this."

"What did you start?" asked Anderson, confused. "I don't know what's going on."

The instructor told her to ask the man to name himself.

"Name yourself," Anderson mumbled.

"Murder," he said.

"In the name of Jesus I cast you out," said Anderson, following her instructions.

"Name yourself," Anderson said again.

"Pederasty," the man replied.

Anderson said about 15 things "came out" before the subject said, "No more."

At the bidding of the instructor, she said, "Come, Holy Spirit, and fill up his life." When Anderson touched him, he fell to the floor. When he got back up, he professed ignorance of what had been taking place.

Told what had happened, he said to her, "I feel like a new person." He then urged her to minister to his blind sister, who was seated in the balcony. Anderson went up and prayed for the woman, who started reporting seeing vague figures. But Anderson said she walked away without doing any more. "There was so much of God's power going on, I was scared. I couldn't deal with it anymore and I had to go out and walk around," she later recalled. Pressed years later on whether she could have been duped, Anderson said firmly: "No, I can smell a setup a mile away."

In her seven years at All Angels' Church, she brought the membership up to 500 people—winning admiration from church leaders in a mainline denomination that was in the throes of a long membership decline. New Yorker Ann Dewey, a friend of Anderson since her St. James days, said that Anderson was known among Episcopalians as an evangelical and charismatic minister—but no one put her into an oddball category with TV evangelists or Pentecostal revivalists.

"I never heard anyone at the local, regional or national level say a derogatory word about her, and a lot of people didn't know we were friends," Dewey said. Anderson had more spiritual leeway, of course, at struggling All Angels' than she would have had at the well-established St. James, Dewey said. "She was known as someone whose theology was solid," she added. In terms of deeds, Anderson's strongest suit was in "getting it done right or not at all," according to Dewey. "She also learned a lot about church politics and how to handle things with grace."

She was elected a clergy delegate from the New York Diocese to consecutive national conventions in 1979, 1982 and 1985. She either chaired or served on several national committees on evangelism. "But I burned out at the same time. All Angels' Church was a horrendously difficult parish to work with," Anderson said. "I spent 16 hours a day on the job, eating fast foods on the run—and I gained 80 pounds, which I have never been able to get rid of."

Anderson's lively parish attracted a stream of wandering clerics looking for answers to personal and parish problems, and that gave her an idea. She proposed creation of the Institute for Clergy Renewal. "I called in a few chips. I went to Trinity Church on Wall Street and got $45,000, and All Angels' gave me $30,000," she said.

A parish in Fairfax, Va., agreed to provide office space and some living support. "It was not a lucrative thing," she said. "We lived from hand to mouth for three years." At the same time, her trips to conferences and diocesan seminars piled up her airline frequent flier mileage, providing a few free trips to her spiritual feeding grounds in England. From relatively liberal surroundings in the New York diocese, Anderson was now based in a very conservative, anti-abortion, tongues-speaking charismatic parish called Truro Church. That church would receive the spotlight in the summer of 1991 when it was learned that Supreme Court justice nominee Clarence Thomas—Baptist-born and Catholic-raised—attended that parish with his wife.

Anderson's message then to fellow clergy on what the Episcopal Church needed was an echo of her own religious discoveries. It went along these lines: "The church must be radically rooted in Jesus Christ, but during the last three decades the Episcopal Church has been rooted in good works. We thought that with social action we had a complete theology when in fact we had only traded half for the other. We were still operating with an incomplete theology. . . .

"What the liberals need to hear is that to do social action without the Holy Spirit is to rob it of its power. What the conservatives need to hear is that the empowerment of the Holy Spirit is never for private use and [that] not to employ it for justice is to commit theological abortion. It's a crime either way."

Anderson's national exposure and self-confident manner led to 19 dioceses asking if they could nominate her as a bishop—which was the ecclesiastical frontier for Episcopal women in the late 1980s. "I tried to honor the process and the colleagues who were pushing me in that direction; I stayed in two processes before dropping out," she said. She chafed at the idea of being "the woman candidate." Mostly, she couldn't envision herself welcoming "the administrative nightmares" of the bishop's office.

On the other hand, she was ready to return to the parish ministry after the three-year hiatus. She happened to be preaching at an ordination service in Lompoc, Calif., when search committee members from All Saints' Beverly Hills went to hear her and were struck favorably. Anderson told them she would not accept a call to the Beverly Hills parish unless it was a unanimous bid. She got her way.

Relatively few All Saints' parishioners live in Beverly Hills. The city's small population (32,000) is mostly Jewish and may include as many Muslims as Christians. Nevertheless, most parishioners were from the affluent west side of Los Angeles and they had been paying the senior rector a salary of $75,000 in addition to providing a home. In view of the parish's growing expenses and some large salary inequities, Anderson took a 30 percent pay cut. She raised the pay of associate rectors and the church staff. "The lay staff, which was making hardly anything, also got pensions for the first time," she said.

One associate she hired was to fill an admitted gap in her ministerial abilities—pastoral counseling. "I'm okay in an hour-long session with somebody who has some resources," she said. "Your garden variety neurotics drive me crazy."

Not long after she started in Beverly Hills, she received a nasty letter from a man who detected too much humor and laughter in church services. Anderson wrote back, citing every conceivable Bible verse relating to humor. Dissatisfied, the parishioner complained to the bishop. Anderson met with the man in an effort to resolve the problem, but to no avail. "He and his family left the parish because they decided they couldn't stand all the laughter here." Then, smiling, she added: "His wife left him the next month, which pleased me no end!"

Anderson is serious about humor, and the cordiality and cooperation that it usually engenders. At the Tuesday staff meetings in the parish hall, the reports were often accompanied by bantering and joking. At one such meeting, the church administrator was one person who never seemed to crack a smile. He lost his job two days later. He was fired, Anderson said, partially for his humorless manner, but mainly for what she called an arbitrary decision-making style that irked co-workers.

Despite the fact that Anderson enjoys her highly placed Anglican friendships, her national reputation and her popularity in Beverly Hills, she occasionally insists that she does not want to draw attention to herself. At that same Tuesday staff meeting, Bonnie McClure, the senior vestrywoman, asked why All Saints' did not have Anderson's name included in the *Los Angeles Times* "religious directory." Many churches advertised their location, telephone, service times and pastor, but the space for the All Saints' rector was blank, even after 20 months with Anderson in the pulpit.

"Why is that?" McClure asked. "Other churches list their pastors."

"Well, I . . . bluh, bluh," Anderson said, exaggerating her stumbling attempt to answer.

"It looks like we don't have a rector," said McClure.

"It was on purpose," Anderson said. "I can't remember why."

"I think it looks silly," said McClure.

Finally, facing up to McClure's persistence, the rector said it was because of "my obsession with not having a clergy-centered church."

Later, in private, she elaborated: "Southern California has got more superstars in pulpits than any place I've ever been in the country. I know people scream at me when I'm not preaching on Sunday, and I've got two first-rate associates, but there is this whole fixation on the rector. I want the lay ministry developed to such an extent that the place is not known for me but known for the parish itself. My desire is for people to have a real living encounter with God, be formed in that—spiritually, emotionally and intellectually—and then move out, make an impact in social kinds of things."

Anderson answered quickly when asked how many people she has guided into the ordained ministry: "Fifteen." Then, just as swiftly, she added how she is against encouraging many people into the priesthood. "I think priests are necessary, but I just go to town on people who think ordination is required for ministry. I think very few people ought to be ordained," she said. Too many seminarians "are on spiritual quests; they're wounded and responding to Christianity as pastoral care and 'God loves you.' They are not people who are engaged intellectually with issues of faith. They are not very well grounded in Scripture or able to get excited about the dramatic stuff in Scripture."

Too many seminaries, in her view, tend to one extreme or the other. She said they are either chiefly academic or heavily immersed in pastoral care. From the latter seminaries, she said, "you've got all these pastors going out for whom the one-on-one relationship is so significant that they can only take care of 150 people. That's why you have all these small churches all over the place." A parish ministry is more effective, she believes, when the duties are spread through the congregation and the staff is large enough not to be consumed by counseling needs.

Her desire to reach and teach large numbers effectively undoubtedly comes from the evangelical component in Anderson's post-1978 ministry. It should be no surprise that Anderson said she liked the approach at Fuller Theological Seminary in Pasadena. "They have a marvelous ability to know what people in parishes are concerned about," she said. Fuller is a large, conservative Protestant school noted, among other things, for facilitating the cross-fertilization of the evangelical and Pentecostal/charismatic movements. That blend was labeled "the third wave" by C. Peter Wagner and other Fuller professors. Anderson pointed to a "fourth wave"—those like herself who emerged from a liberal tradition, were influenced by Anglo-Catholic and charismatic ideas, and are trying to combine them all. "There are more of us around than most people think," she said.

Without being asked, she said she tried not to be manipulative or to foist a charismatic agenda onto the Beverly Hills parish. The church vestry adopted a new mission statement under her leadership that began with a description of All Saints' as "a community of disciples seeking to glorify God, to grow in Christ and to be empowered by the Holy Spirit." The expressions of "glorifying" God and seeking the "power" of the Holy Spirit would signal to knowledgeable Christians that this is probably a charismatic congregation, but the rest of the 170-word statement speaks in customary church language about worship, discipleship, pastoral care, service and evangelism. In Anderson's words, she wanted to teach "the fullness of biblical faith and life . . . I try to be naturally supernatural here without seeming to be abnormal."

Carol Anderson, the small-town product who suffered through a "boring" youth, said she loved the kind of challenges she deliberately chose in Boston, New York, the Washington area and Beverly Hills, as well as the excitement of big-city life. "I think I have to live near all this," she said.

In her younger adult years, Anderson dated and was engaged once to be married. "If I found somebody who cared about the things I care about, I'd be happy to be married," she said. She indicated, however, that a man would have to share her single-mindedness on the priesthood. "When I get up in the morning, what I'm thinking about is the Kingdom of God. I really do," she said, expecting skepticism. "That's what I'm about."

Jeb Stuart Magruder

Death and Life After Watergate

by John C. Long

Amazing grace! how sweet the sound
That saved a wretch like me!
I once was lost, but now am found,
Was blind, but now I see.
——John Newton, 1725-1807

Over salads at lunch, a criminal lawyer in Lexington, Ky., told his new pastor why he had opposed him—opposed calling to the pulpit of one of the state's oldest churches the man who had supervised the Watergate cover-up and gone to prison for it. The Rev. Jeb Stuart Magruder remembers the lawyer's explanation: "You were supposed to be dead."

The lawyer doubted that G. Gordon Liddy's old boss, a convicted perjurer, was the ideal choice to become the moral model for parishioners of Lexington's First Presbyterian Church. He thought Magruder should have had the good grace to remain out of sight and out of mind—for all intents and purposes, "dead." But lawyer Steve Milner's view was not shared by the seven members of First Church's pastor-nominating committee, who unanimously chose Magruder from among 228 applicants after an 11-month search. The congregation overwhelmingly endorsed Magruder's selection, by secret ballot, 254-5.

So on Nov. 1, 1990, Magruder became senior minister of the downtown church that in 1784 was among the first three Presbyterian congregations formed in what eight years later would become the state of Kentucky. Because Milner made no secret of his feelings, Magruder, two months into his pastorate, approached the lawyer at church and invited him to lunch to clear the air. "Jeb had mentioned that I had been identified as a project," said Milner, who told him that with Watergate, "You forever cured me of being a Republican."

Magruder had encountered doubters before, himself first of all, and the doubts raised questions central to the Christian faith: Does God really love everyone, no matter what? Does God really forgive sin? Do Christians, including the sinner, really believe that God forgives? Can Christians really accept a redeemed sinner as authentically whole, as unreservedly morally credible—even as a moral model? Or, as Steve Milner confessed to Magruder over lunch, is the sinner supposed to go away—to prison would be good—to die and to stay dead to the consciousness of the morally offended? Magruder's moral and spiritual journey—before and, especially, after the June 17, 1972, break-in at the offices of the Democratic National Committee at the Watergate office-apartment complex in Washington—provides one set of answers to those questions.

The journey continues. Magruder's call to the Lexington church was his first to be a senior pastor; he said he wants to serve there until his retirement, and he will be 65 in 1999. So his arrival at what he perceives to be a destination furnishes a possible conclusion to this story of Magruder, but—with its Lexington chapter just under way—his story does not neatly end here. Nor did it neatly begin.

Magruder's situation was never so heavily ironic as those of television evangelists Jim Bakker and Jimmy Swaggart, who purported to be moral leaders, and highly visible ones, at the very times of their falls. Yet the uneven path of Magruder's journey brought forth doubters, whether a disgruntled parishioner, a former ethics professor disappointed in his old student, or, in city after city, a succession of skeptical news reporters. After all, Magruder is the guy who once proposed that the Federal Communications Commission "license" individual broadcast journalists to protect the public from "misuse of the airwaves." And in any case, when a person has admitted to lying under oath, skepticism might be expected.

After the cover-up began to unravel, Magruder came clean with the prosecutors, accepted the prospect of his punishment and asked for, and said he felt he had received, God's forgiveness, in an experience that would be his life's turning point. Once Magruder regained his moral bearings and became committed to tell the truth, he rapidly regained his credibility with the court and earned high marks for his testimony in the Senate Watergate hearings. And he wrote two remarkably forthright books, *An American Life: One Man's Road to Watergate*, in the months before he went to prison, and *From Power to Peace*, three years after his release.

As Magruder acknowledged in the second book, religious conversions of celebrity sinners *invite* skepticism. And his fall and rise were harder to explain because he had experienced Christianity and its teachings before he strayed and stumbled into Watergate. In his early teens he was a faithful churchgoer. And later, as a student at Williams College, he had many long talks about issues of right and wrong with the college's young chaplain and teacher of ethics, the Rev. William Sloane Coffin, Jr. Still later, before Watergate, Magruder became a Presbyterian elder, and he and his family attended church regularly. But back then, he said, he kept his religious life and the rest of his life in separate compartments.

Magruder described his religious reawakening, while he awaited sentencing, as much deeper than his earlier experiences of church. His understanding of, and commitment to, Christianity grew in prison and after, and he became an executive of an international Christian youth organization, received a seminary degree, was ordained, and became an associate minister in California. Then he encountered another quagmire in his journey: His wife left him, and—shortly after he moved on to join the staff of a church in Columbus, Ohio—he suffered a bout of severe, disabling depression. That painful time was Magruder's second death. But it led to his second resurrection, with his recovery in Columbus, aided by a supportive senior minister and congregation, one member of which became his new wife. And now, with his own senior pastorate in Lexington, Magruder at last can employ his full range of talents to lead a congregation—one that chose him to do so despite his past errors.

Jeb Stuart Magruder was born on Staten Island, N.Y., on Nov. 5, 1934, to a family once well-off. His father, a quiet, well-liked man, owned and operated a job-printing shop. His mother was a homemaker. His brother, Don, four years older and to whom Jeb was never close, has lived out of the public eye. Jeb's parents were Presbyterians, but—perhaps discouraged by wartime gasoline rationing—seldom traveled to their church, a distance of several miles, when he was a child. Young Jeb, however, joined an Episcopal church just two blocks from home. He became an altar boy. But the church had no youth group, and he dropped out. Magruder did well at his public high school, but left Williams after his sophomore year to serve a two-year hitch in the Army, mostly in postwar Korea. He returned to Williams to earn a degree in political science. To resolve a dilemma in his love life, Magruder sought out Coffin, who later became chaplain at Yale and then pastor of Riverside Church in New York City. Their discussions of ethics, in and out of class, ranged to other subjects, notably the racially discriminatory fraternity system, of which Magruder was a part and Coffin a strong critic.

Soon after his college graduation in 1958, Magruder joined Crown Zellerbach Corp. in San Francisco as a sales representative. He began dating Gail Nicholas, a graduate student at the University of California at Berkeley, whom he had met back East when she was at Vassar College. They were married in Los Angeles in 1959, just as the firm was transferring him from there to Kansas City, Mo.

In Kansas City, Magruder began his political involvement, as a ward chairman for Richard M. Nixon's 1960 presidential campaign. Motivated to consider his future by the birth in 1960 of the couple's first child—and tired of crisscrossing Iowa, Kansas, Missouri and Nebraska to sell paper bags, gummed-label tape and the like—Magruder enrolled at the University of Chicago to get a master's degree in business administration. He took classes by night and worked as a management consultant by day. He got another taste of politics in Chicago in Donald Rumsfeld's successful 1962 congressional primary campaign. And that fall he joined Jewel Tea Co., a food-store and drugstore chain, as the first trainee in its new program for MBA recipients. His sponsor and mentor was Donald Perkins, soon to become company president. Perkins taught him, Magruder said, that the best management style is "team-oriented," that "the chief executive officer . . . sets the tone," and that "if the tone is set correctly, . . . the corporation will run that way."

In the 1964 presidential campaign, Magruder headed the Goldwater for President organization in Rumsfeld's congressional district, but in 1966 Jewel refused Magruder a leave of absence to work full time in a local political race, so he made "the worst mistake of my business career" by quitting Jewel. Ironically, he missed that campaign anyway, because the new job he had to find turned out to be with a California department-store chain, and he left for Los Angeles.

In 1968, with two partners, he started two companies—one to sell cosmetics, the other to manufacture a cosmetic product and a hosiery product. He left the retail chain early the next year to run the new companies. In the meantime, Magruder was southern California coordinator of the 1968 Nixon for President campaign. Word of Magruder's organizational ability reached H. R. "Bob" Haldeman, President Nixon's chief of staff, who recruited Magruder to help improve the president's public image by reorganizing the White House communications operations. On October 1, 1969, Magruder went to work at the White House, with the title of special assistant to the president.

Magruder soon found that Nixon regarded the news media as enemies to be conquered and manipulated. Magruder's most successful public-relations project was to promote the president's image as anti-drug and, ironically, anti-crime. After a year, he wearied of being under "the direct, day-to-day thumb of Bob Haldeman." So when Magruder was asked to direct the operations of the president's re-election campaign, under the chairmanship of Attorney General John Mitchell, he eagerly accepted, and on May 1, 1971, moved across Pennsylvania Avenue to the Committee to Re-elect the President. With his marketing experience, Magruder initiated techniques for advance planning, for advertising and for gathering and analyzing voter information that made Nixon's 1972 campaign a model of effectiveness. But as the world has long-since known, the campaign went far beyond such above-board strategies to include covert operations that centered on infiltrating and spying on the campaign operations of opponents.

To direct some such operations, a lawyer and former CIA agent was brought in, ostensibly as the campaign committee's counsel. His name was G. Gordon Liddy. Liddy proposed tapping telephones of the Democratic National Committee at the

Watergate complex, and Magruder and Mitchell approved. The wiretapping was botched on the first try, and during a second break-in, the re-election campaign committee's security chief, James W. McCord, Jr., and four fellow burglars were arrested. Mitchell assigned Magruder to plan how to keep the prosecutors, Judge John J. Sirica, the Democrats, the press and the public from connecting the break-in to high re-election officials or the White House. At Mitchell's suggestion, Magruder burned the file containing the burglary plans in his living room fireplace. He concocted a cover story, which he and others—including an assistant whom he persuaded to do so—fed to the prosecutors and a federal grand jury.

Liddy, McCord and E. Howard Hunt—another ex-CIA agent who helped plan the break-ins—and the four other burglars agreed to go along with the cover-up and take the blame. Those seven were indicted; Magruder and the aide were not. Magruder went on to direct the activities of Nixon's second inauguration in January 1973 and won wide praise; even the parade ran on time. Three days later, Magruder lied at the trial of the seven, who were convicted that month.

Magruder then took a job at the Commerce Department, as director of policy planning. But just before the convicted seven were to be sentenced, McCord, hoping to receive a shorter prison term, began to talk. With the cover-up cracking, Magruder retained lawyers, but told even them the fake story. One of his lawyers, Jim Sharp, sensed he was lying and told him, "Jeb, pretty soon you're going to have to tell me the truth." Magruder did so the next day, and three days after that, on Friday, April 13, 1973, he agreed to plead guilty to a felony charge of conspiracy to obstruct justice. His maximum penalty would be five years in prison. He began to tell the prosecutors all he knew.

"I felt a tremendous sense of relief, I felt almost happy, to be finished with the cover-up and all its lies," Magruder wrote soon afterward. "I felt as if I'd been seized by madness for a long time and suddenly I had become sane again." Ten months before, when he had sat in front of his fireplace watching the "Gemstone" file burn to ashes, he had wondered if his life would go up in smoke as well. Now, by telling the truth, he was beginning to rise from those ashes.

He accepted the prospect of his punishment in some measure as a way of helping to restore the integrity of the justice system he had abused. He had to resign from his Commerce job only six weeks after it had begun. Less than a month after his guilty plea, his mother died unexpectedly, and he still regrets that he did not get to say goodbye or to clear the air with her about Watergate. A month after that, Magruder had his day in the spotlight before the Senate Watergate committee. He came across as cooperative, sincere and remorseful, and, as he finished his testimony, received the praise and good wishes of one of his interrogators, Democratic Sen. Joseph M. Montoya of New Mexico.

> SEN. MONTOYA: Well, Mr. Magruder, I believe that you have told a very complete story. I believe you have been most frank. I believe you have comported yourself in an admirable fashion before this committee. . . . Now, I ask you this final question: Does it not amaze you that after all this allegiance [to the president] and blind devotion to duty, now you have been relegated . . . to stew in your own juice?
> MAGRUDER: Well, Senator, let me just say I have had to take the attitude, and I have taken the attitude, that this is certainly a very unfortunate period of my life. I am not going to let it destroy me. I have a wonderful wife and four children.
> SEN. MONTOYA: I understand that you do, Mr. Magruder.
> MAGRUDER: And I am not going to lay down and die because of it. I think I will rehabilitate myself, I guess is the best word. I think I am in that process and I hope to be able to live a useful life. I would not recommend this as a method of re-emergence, but in this case, I think I can and I will.

His lawyers believed him, the prosecutors believed him, the judge believed him, and now the senators—and probably most of his national television audience—believed him, but Magruder himself found something impossible to believe: that God still loved him and would forgive him. Magruder's moral deck may have been clear, but his spiritual deck still needed work. Workers were on the way. Chief among them was the Rev. Louis Evans, pastor of National Presbyterian Church. When he and his wife saw Magruder testify on TV, they believed they could help, and invited him to their home. Evans brought Magruder into a men's Bible-study group that became his support while he was awaiting sentencing and in prison. Evans became Magruder's spiritual mentor, leading him for months toward God's forgiveness in the weekly study group and in talks during their rides home together. In his *From Power to Peace*, Magruder described the moment when forgiveness finally arrived, while the two men sat and talked in Evans' small car after Bible study one night:

"You know, Jeb, your problem is that you still think you have to do twenty years' penance before you can even ask his forgiveness. Well, that just isn't true. He already has forgiven you—and Jesus Christ can tell you that, if you'll allow him to. . . .

". . . All you have to do is ask Christ, right now, to forgive you. Tell him that you accept him and ask him if he accepts you." He bowed his head. "I think we ought to pray about it."

While Evans did so, Magruder later wrote, "I found myself speaking to Christ as if he were in the car with us." Magruder said he had never before felt Christ so close or "spoken to him so directly." He said he asked for forgiveness and offered to "give my life to Christ . . . if he would accept me." Neither man spoke for a while.

. . . Then Louie asked, "Jeb, what did he say?"

"He said yes! Just like that—as clearly as anything I ever heard. He said it was okay!"

"See! What did I tell you!" Louie said.

I leaned back as far as the Toyota would allow. A feeling of relaxation was beginning to replace my excitement. I couldn't remember ever feeling so good. . . .

This is the moment that skeptics will examine for evidence of a pre-jailhouse conversion. Did Magruder seek salvation with a quick fix of cheap grace? Let's see: He was sought out by Evans, who pursued him, dragged him to forgiveness, then smote him over the head with it before he would accept it.

Having offered his life, Magruder wondered what God wanted him to do with it. God did not immediately smite him with the answer.

On May 21, 1974, Sirica sentenced Magruder to a term of 10 months to four years, and ordered him to report two weeks later to Allenwood federal prison camp in north-central Pennsylvania; he would also serve part of his term at Fort Holabird, Md. Magruder was concerned about the effect of his imprisonment on the children—daughter Tracy, 10; and sons Whitney, 13; Justin, 12; and Stuart, 7—and he worried about how long he would be away from them. Sirica would release him after seven months and eight days. Prison was the strongest direct exposure to human suffering that Magruder had experienced, he said. Affected by his awareness of the other prisoners' needs and grateful for those who visited Allenwood to offer comfort, Magruder said he came to believe that God wanted him to serve people, as individuals. His journey would take more twists and turns before he would learn how.

After his release, he explored several options for Christian service, then accepted a position as director of communications for Young Life, a non-profit Christian organization for high school youth, based in Colorado Springs. His favorite part of the new job was the seminary coursework that Young Life officials were offered for eight weeks each summer, and that whetted his appetite for still more knowledge of the Bible, the church and theology. After three years in Colorado, he enrolled at Princeton Theological Seminary, back East in New Jersey.

Magruder was awarded a master of divinity degree in 1981, but his feelings about Princeton were mixed. "I enjoyed the intellectual experience," he said, but the training "was somewhat unrealistic; . . . much of the preparation, though interesting theologically, was not very helpful practically." So "I had to start over again when I got out in a parish." Also, he said, "there were issues with the marriage" that made the experience less positive than it might have been otherwise.

While he was at Princeton, Magruder, as a candidate for the Presbyterian ministry, encountered a skeptic in the very person assigned by what is now the Presbyterian Church (U.S.A.) to be his guide, his official liaison, during his studies. Appointed to that task was the Rev. Vin Harwell, a pastor in

Alexandria, Va., who held special credentials for his skepticism: He had been an anti-Vietnam War activist, and on the night Nixon announced his resignation, Harwell had stood on the sidewalk in front of the White House to savor the moment.

He recalled the essence of what he told Magruder when they first met: "You need to know that I have a lot of questions about whether you should be a Presbyterian minister, . . . and frankly I don't very much like the idea. I feel . . . as if you and a lot of people like you taint the profession. . . . And I have real questions about people who do wrong and then seek to win credibility by citing some particular religious conversion or experience." But Harwell, now a pastor in Wilmington, Del., said he became a believer that Magruder was repentant and felt called to the ministry. "One of the clear bases for our Christian faith is an understanding that a person can change" and have one's life "affected by an encounter with God," Harwell said. "The validity of that is always difficult to determine," but with Magruder, "we've had to . . . face up to whether we really believe what we say." Harwell said he realized that if Magruder had wanted to capitalize on his conversion, he could have formed his own high-profile evangelistic organization instead of seeking to serve in a mainline denomination. Magruder seriously considered confining his ministry to counseling, saying "he never wanted anyone to become part of a church . . . because Jeb Magruder of Watergate was his pastor," Harwell said. Now as then, he said, "I think Jeb wants to be a Presbyterian pastor, not a former Watergate conspirator."

In 1982 Magruder became an associate pastor of the 1,300-member First Presbyterian Church in Burlingame, Calif., which accepted his past and supported his ministry. But no amount of support could have protected him and his family from the lingering effects of Watergate, about which, Magruder said, his wife still harbored anger. As his ministerial career was beginning, his marriage was ending. Gail filed for divorce. (Later, she, too, would be ordained a Presbyterian minister.) The three older children had long since gone off to college, and Stuart, their youngest, a senior in high school, was about to.

Shaken and alone, Magruder arrived in Columbus in September 1984 to become executive minister of the second-largest congregation in the United Church of Christ—the

3,800-member First Community Church in the comfortable suburb of Marble Cliff. Magruder said he found First Community's call especially compelling because he felt he needed to move onward and upward without delay in the career to which he had come so late in life. Under Presbyterian rules, he could remain a minister of that denomination while serving outside it.

Magruder's new boss, the Rev. Barry Johnson, First Community's senior minister, said he felt the attention that Magruder's past would bring to the parish would, on balance, be beneficial. But after just a few weeks in Columbus, Magruder found he was so depressed he could barely function. He offered to resign, but Johnson insisted that he stay, and take as much time as he needed to mend. Magruder sought psychiatric help, but the psychiatrists could find nothing wrong, other than what one might expect in a man who—besides all he had endured before—now had lost his wife, was separated from his family, was alone in a strange city, and was facing a demanding new job. Drawing strength from an outpouring of support from the church's members, Magruder decided to persevere, opening the way for the transformation that was to be his second resurrection.

What happened to Magruder in Columbus and how he affected First Community and its members were vividly described by four of those supportive members of the congregation—including the one he married—in a series of far-ranging interviews.

Richard Wood, Sr., a member for 30 years, said First Community's hiring a person of Magruder's notoriety fit its tradition of being "on the cutting edge." For example, the church was one of the first in the nation to offer a complete counseling center for members, said Wood, a now-retired businessman. Robert Wandel, a member for 37 years, said that for him and his wife, Sally, Watergate "was not an issue . . . at all." More important was Magruder's anxiety level, said Wandel, an architect. The Wandels had volunteered to welcome Magruder, and they went on to make their home a haven for him. During Magruder's first nine months or so in Columbus, Wandel said, "we always made sure we were available. . . . Generally, he'd say, 'Can I come over and watch football?' " Wood said he, too, reached out to Magruder, because he was in pain and needed a friend. He appeared nervous and stressed, and showed a vulnerability and an appealing quality of openness and honesty, Wood said. "It's an irony, a paradox," he said of the man best-known for a cover-up.

Of all the members of the Columbus congregation to whom Magruder was sent to minister, but by whom he was also ministered *to*, the most significant was Patricia Ann Newton. Magruder was starting once again to socialize with women, but, being depressed, he was not a fun date. He recalled with a chuckle his first—and last—date with a woman who told him she did not want to hear about any problems. Magruder, of course, *needed* to talk about his problems. Enter Patti Newton, a tall, dark-haired schoolteacher, divorced, with two young children—and a very good listener. Magruder was a tough assignment. "In fact," she recalled, "our first date was on what would have been his 25th wedding anniversary, and he was . . . a very sad man. Probably the first thing I said to him after we met—to go out to dinner—was, 'You're not doing very well, are you?'" She laughed as she recounted the moment. "He said, 'No, I'm really not.' So we talked about it. And we talked about it and we talked about it. And I think he needed someone to say to him: 'You're fine. You're all right. . . . It feels terrible, but you're going to be fine.' . . . He's a different man today than he was then," she said. "He was just a very, very sad man," understandably: "He was alone." With his divorce, "Watergate finally, really hit," especially because "Jeb is very much a family man. . . . He likes his family around him."

Patti succeeded where Valium had failed. "I am a pretty down-to-earth, direct, cut-to-the-bottom-line person," she said. "Jeb tends to be a very circular person. You don't always know where he's going. *He* doesn't always know where he's going. I think . . . he appreciated my directness," she said with a laugh—"*most* of the time! . . . I also tend to be a very positive person, . . . and I think that helped Jeb, because . . . Jeb can too easily see the clouds. . . . But I would always show him the sun."

Soon after she and Magruder began dating, her assignment with a suburban public-school system changed from the teaching of developmentally handicapped children to guidance counseling. Richard Witter, another First Community member, believes her professional training as a counselor, along with her openness and strength, helped her to help Magruder. And "Patti has a mind of her own," Witter said. "She is a strong personality, and she is a great balancer. . . . They are both very, very lucky to have found each other," he said. "Each one has strengths . . . that the other one needs." Johnson, the senior minister, said she "has made a big difference" in Magruder's "ongoing project" of forgiving *himself* for Watergate. Wandel said she was able to help Magruder heal because her friendship and, eventually, her love were "totally unconditional." She and Magruder were married on February 28, 1987, two and a half years after they met.

After four years of marriage, with quick brush strokes, Patti Magruder added detail to her husband's personality portrait: He is determined. "I've never met anybody who pushes himself so hard," she said. "He truly, truly believes you should never give up. . . . And I think there are times you should!" He has come to terms with his crime and imprisonment. "He enters a room with his head up, feeling good about who he is and what he's doing with his life. And even when he meets people who are still angry [about Watergate], it hurts him, but he doesn't lower his head a bit. It's nice to see that he put that in perspective." But "the pain always shows." He is exceptionally realistic. "I think the experience of Watergate has made him much more cautious. He has a much . . . clearer view of human nature and of life than many people, because he looks at every person and knows there's both good and bad . . . that life is gray," with "no extremes . . . no black and white."

Magruder was called to First Community primarily as a manager, but he became a leader in education, missions and counseling as well. His first accomplishment at the church, Wandel said, was "to organize it so . . . decisions were made in an orderly fashion." He made sense of the church's complex budget, balancing an operating deficit, and later, with Johnson, he would lead a drive that raised a $6 million building fund. He got the church's operations computerized. "But then the surprise for the congregation, who anticipated somebody who would just do administrative duties, was that he . . . began a very, very strong adult-education program," Wandel said. The heart of the program was a "Spiritual Searchers" series, featuring big-name speakers such as authors M. Scott Peck, and Rabbi Harold S. Kushner. The adult-education program became a model, Witter said. "Other churches would come to find out how we were doing what we did." Wood said that a Roman Catholic sister he knows once told him, with an angelic smile, "I'd kill for a program like Jeb Magruder's got at First Community."

The adult-education program attracted new members and activated old ones, including Witter, a 40-year member inactive for a decade because of his wife's illness. He became involved again after his wife's death, when Magruder invited him to join him in teaching Eastern religions, Witter's specialty. "We would get up and debate and argue," he said, and "the congregation loved it, because here's a minister not threatened by this layman . . . spouting off Eastern points of view. . . . It was such a surprise to run into a Christian minister who was not just open, but . . . a spiritual searcher." After the adult-education program was under way, Magruder led the congregation into mission work, including a Habitat for Humanity homebuilding project and support, with both time and money, of an inner-city shelter for the homeless. Magruder's "surprise gift," Wandel said, "was his desire to take the congregation farther" than anyone expected.

In both his preaching and counseling, Magruder found assets in his experiences—in Watergate, divorce, depression, even in business. He found that his sins and suffering were gifts, and he said he came to know what it meant to be, as Henri J. M. Nouwen had put it, a "wounded healer."

As a preacher, Magruder has a low-key, conversational style, and delivering sermons in Columbus only once every six weeks limited his opportunity to become polished there. "His preaching wasn't great," Wood said. But his style had a genuine, engaging quality; he seemed to be talking directly to each worshiper. The people in the pews were engaged also by his vulnerability, Patti Magruder said. "It just does something to you. It opens you up. It enables you to hear. You feel in tune with the person that's hurting, and the message they have to give you."

For counseling, parishioners felt comfortable in bringing their worst problems to Magruder because, he said, they knew their mess couldn't have been any worse than the ones *he* had been in. Their sins could be no worse than his. If God had forgiven *him,* God could forgive *them.* If you have had problems of your own, Magruder said, "people are more willing to come and talk to you. They know you won't think poorly of them." Those seeking Magruder's aid could believe that God redeems not only the sinner, but also the sin, putting it to use for good. A thank-you letter from Dave, Nancy, Charles and Jim Evans, one of dozens Magruder received from First Community parishioners when he left Columbus, said that "through your sharing and teaching, you clearly show us how to change . . . things that we see as dooming us to failure into launching pads for greater experiences, through an application of faith and a reorientation of perspective."

Those suffering the agony of family breakup knew they could find comfort in a man who had been through it. And "he had a wonderful ministry to men," Patti Magruder said. Sometimes people wonder what a minister "knows about real life—life beyond the church." But "with Jeb's experiences in business and politics—and divorce—men knew this was a man who could talk to them about their problems." Many people depressed about business failures sought Magruder's counsel. "Nobody will ever know the depth of that pain" that Magruder still feels because of his felony conviction, Wandel said, "but you will also never know the joy he has come to receive from being able to help people . . . with issues similar to what he has had to deal with."

Magruder can help people understand ethics and morality "because he has dealt with those issues with such fierceness and depth," Witter said. Magruder does so not only as a confidential counselor, but also as a public speaker, which Patti Magruder said he regards "as part of his ministry." During the Columbus years, she said, he would accept almost every speaking invitation. "He is at his best with business groups," according to Witter, "because he can speak their language . . . and they listen." He still accepts two or three speaking invitations per month locally and perhaps a half-dozen per year out of town, typically on the need for religious and ethical values in American public life. Magruder tells his audiences that the separation of those values from public life led to Watergate—

that most of the conspirators possessed *private* morality, but that working together, in an atmosphere in which the presidency reigned supreme, they were devoid of *public* morality. They believed their cause was good, then became convinced that therefore all they did in the name of the cause was good.

When Nixon came to First Community in 1987 for the funeral of former Ohio State University football coach Woody Hayes, Magruder was assigned to escort and sit with the ex-president, whom Magruder had neither seen nor heard from since the cover-up collapsed. Nixon told Magruder he was pleased to see that he was doing well. Neither man mentioned Watergate. But Watergate and Magruder's involvement in it were thrust back into the headlines that same year by a freak accident that brought the ethics issue to the fore in Columbus. When more than $1 million in currency dropped out the back door of an armored car, and Columbus motorists grabbed and kept most of the money, Mayor Dana Rinehart appointed a Columbus Commission on Ethics and Values—and made Magruder its chairman. The commission was a diverse group—of university, business, religious and political leaders—and Magruder got them "talking to each other at a different level than they had been before," Witter said. At the same time, he said, Magruder "was able to deal with the press in a responsible way." Journalists "seemed to respect Jeb, because he was honest with them."

Magruder's record in Columbus may have been impressive, but Wood believes all his accomplishments there combined are equaled by one that Magruder did not even intend: the effect on the congregation of his transformation from brokenness and depression to wholeness and health, right before their eyes. "People could perceive this person as coming in one way and going out another," Wood said. "You could watch him change. . . . It was more powerful than his other skills, . . . to see the power of the Spirit working on a human being." Wood sums it up in a single word: "salvation."

In his sixth year at First Community, Magruder felt the time had come to move on to a senior ministerial position. First Church in Lexington was near its deadline for pastoral applications when Magruder's arrived, and it quickly rose to the top of the "yes" pile. The priorities Magruder listed for the church

almost exactly matched those of the pastor-nominating committee: First Church needed a strong administrator who would re-
vitalize its education programs and ministry to the community.
And being a downtown church with an emphasis on Sunday
worship, the top priority was preaching. Despite Magruder's
lack of polish, the committee liked his style, and felt he would
get even better once he was preaching every week.

Still to be faced were questions about Watergate. Would
the church's members vote for Magruder, and if so, would they
then give him a chance to succeed? Would the inevitable publicity be good for the church? In the end, the nominating committee decided that if Magruder "actually was our choice and
we didn't . . . recommend him . . . then we had not done our
job," said Cecil Dunn, the lawyer who was the committee's
chairman. And "of the 228 people we were able to evaluate and
consider," Dunn said, "he clearly was the top choice." The committee overcame its Watergate doubts, he said, when it realized
that "if you can't forgive people, you ought not to be in the
church to start with." Looking "at any situation in a forgiving,
redemptive manner . . . that's what churches are all about. . . .
We were content in our own mind that, through God's help, we
had done the right thing."

The night before the committee announced its nomination
of Magruder in a letter to the congregation, its 24 deacons and
24 elders gathered at the church to meet him. "He was probably
in the room three or four hours," Dunn said, and there were
some tough questions, but when the meeting was over, "I don't
believe there was a person" there who "did not feel that we'd
made the right choice."

In his first few months in Lexington, Magruder reorgan-
ized the church office and instituted long-range planning. Hospital and emergency visiting were revitalized. New emphasis
was placed on adult education. At Magruder's urging, members
volunteered for Habitat for Humanity, and he joined the board
of Lexington's homeless-aid agency. "And there are other outreach programs that he's working on to get our church to quit
worrying about what goes on completely inside [its own] walls
and get out and worry about what goes on in the community,"
Dunn said. Giving increased; after one year under Magruder's
leadership, First Church's annual pledges had risen by 37 per-

cent, from $293,000 to more than $400,000, and a $1.5 million capital fund drive was under way. If Magruder had failed, Dunn said, "everyone would have used the excuse of Watergate and prison" and said "you never should have chosen him," despite his good points. "So we felt some pressure" on the pastor-nominating committee. "But as it turned out . . . anytime you see any of the committee members in church, they just kind of look at each other and grin." Even skeptic Steve Milner, though he remains "philosophically uncomfortable," said he feels "very positive" about Magruder's accomplishments. "I think he's done an excellent job and motivated the church."

Patti Magruder also found a challenging new job in Lexington: helping to plan the implementation of Kentucky's sweeping school-reform act in the Fayette County school system. She also continued as a candidate for a doctorate in family studies at Ohio State. The Magruders rented a three-bedroom Cape Cod in an established neighborhood near downtown, from which they frequently ride away on bicycles, to stay fit and to work off tensions. Although Magruder is much more at peace than he once was, he takes a muscle relaxant for back pain, and his friends speak tongue-in-cheek when they call him "calm and collected." Magruder's four children from his first marriage are grown, with college degrees—two have MBAs—and careers. And "he has become a wonderful father" to his two stepchildren, Patti Magruder said. She said that when one of them, Jennifer, was assigned in school to write about whom she admired most, her stepfather was one of her choices, because of "his ability to overcome what must have been a very, very difficult time in his life and to be doing so well."

First Church, its red-brick Gothic edifice next door to Henry Clay's old law office, had been without a permanent senior minister for nearly two years. The church claimed 900-plus members when Magruder arrived, perhaps one-third of them inactive. The sanctuary often had been only half-filled for Sunday services. For Magruder's first, the sanctuary was packed. That was no surprise; his arrival had been heralded by the news media in Lexington and across the state. Magruder thanked his new flock for entrusting him with leading them, and warned them that they could expect to be asked to work harder at serving the needs of the Lexington community. Afterward, he wondered how much of his opening-day crowd, without the media and the curious, would return. The crowds kept coming. More people came to hear Magruder the established pastor in December 1991 than had come to see Magruder the new celebrity curiosity in December 1990. In Magruder's first 16 months, 165 new members joined, swelling the congregation to more than 1,000 for the first time in its history. Attendance at Sunday worship more than doubled, to an average of more than 400. And that took place in an old, downtown, mainline congregation in a denomination that in 25 years has lost one-third of its membership.

Over lunch at the same table at which a few months earlier he had been told he was supposed to be "dead," Magruder, the resurrected Christian, talked excitedly about his resurrecting congregation. "This church was you," his luncheon companion ventured. Magruder pondered the thought and smiled.

A few weeks later, on a sunny Sunday morning in June, Magruder, ruddy-cheeked and ready for business, hung the coat of his gray plaid suit on a wrought-iron candelabrum in the church's ground-floor fellowship hall and wished that his adult-education class, like the inaugural parade, could begin on time. "What's *with* church people, anyway?" he quipped, as more members straggled in. At 6 feet 2 inches and 210 pounds, he towered over the small lectern. He was wrapping up his six-week series on "Who Do Men Say That I Am?" Magruder fired Dietrich Bonhoeffer, Rudolf Bultmann, Hans Küng, Edward Schillebeeckx and the Holy Scripture at the 60 parishioners, and several fired back, pushing and pulling to get at the nature of Jesus. "We are a Resurrection faith," Magruder told the group.

Afterward, Jean Monaghan, a member of First Church for about 20 years, said that she had attended Bible studies in the past, but that Magruder's classes are more demanding: "If it won't stand to be looked at in the light, then it's not valid. That's Jeb—just straightforward and honest." And "very much in the process of becoming who he's going to be. I think his journey is just beginning, in some ways."

At the worship service that morning, in the old sanctuary, with its soaring, vaulted ceiling and dark woodwork, nearly every space in every pew was filled. Magruder preached about the Good Samaritan, about Mother Teresa's recognizing "Jesus in the guise of the poor," about friends who would not desert him after Watergate. And he installed 22 more new members.

As the worshipers filed out, their conversations buzzed with talk of the renewal in their midst. Carla VanHoose, a non-Presbyterian visiting for the third time, said she would be among the next group of new members, because Magruder is "human enough to relate what he says about Scripture to everyday lives. . . . He makes it a living thing." As Anna Ray Faulconer made her way out of the church, she spoke to a companion: "We're going to need to have two services!" she said. (Three months later a second service indeed would be added.) Outside, she lingered a moment in a knot of parishioners. "Do you know," she said to the others, "I've been a member here 25 years, and I told Jeb, I said, 'What a blessing to see things happening in this church once again!'"

"Because," she said, "we've been dead."

James Reed

This May Be the Day

by Kenneth A. Briggs

"When the Son of man comes in all his glory,
and all the angels with him, then he will sit on
his glorious throne."

—Matthew 25:31

A half hour before the start of the Sunday morning worship service, the Rev. James Reed unlocked the front door of Community United Methodist Church, flicked on the vestibule lights and felt a wave of hot air. The heat told him instantly that the group which used the building on Saturday nights had again neglected to turn down the thermostat. Somehow the carefully posted instructions weren't getting through, he concluded benignly, as he adjusted the device to shut down the oil-guzzling furnace.

Continuing his quick inspection tour, he stopped in the cramped room which served as the church office. There he found a hand-scrawled note reporting that someone had smashed the red light with a rock ("What red light?" he wondered). He tried the telephone. It had not worked the day before. It still did not work. Those nuisances could wait. Moving on to the spacious sanctuary, he seemed only mildly surprised that half the ceiling lights were out. Without a moment's pause, he dashed to the circuit breaker, resetting it to restore full power. Meanwhile, a church member had arrived and promptly went about ironing a banner to hang behind the altar table. Its message read, "Give Thanks to the Lord." Ten minutes later, shortly after 9:30, Mr. Reed, in his white robe and red, white and blue stole, led a handful of worshipers in the opening hymn, "Beneath the Cross of Jesus."

Community Church, a functional one-story brick building with no religious symbols on the outside, lies within the "back-of-the-yards" neighborhood of southwest Chicago once dominated by the city's teeming stockyards. Nearby are the bustling streets featured in Upton Sinclair's muckraking novel about the meatpacking industry, *The Jungle*. Earlier this century, the rows of sturdy houses in the district were occupied by thousands of Eastern European immigrants and their descendants. Gradually those groups were replaced by Hispanic people from Catholic backgrounds and the church's rolls steadily declined. Most members today are widows who vividly recall the church's glory days.

Reed has taken upon himself not only the task of trying to breath new life into that expiring congregation but of reviving another struggling parish as well. His day began earlier that morning in the parsonage attached to Union Avenue United Methodist Church, where he also serves as pastor and functions as his own support staff: secretary, treasurer, janitor, whatever. Before setting out for the early service at Community, he had already done housekeeping chores for the 11 o'clock worship at Union Avenue: vacuuming the rug around the altar, removing bows left over from a wedding the day before, muscling the long, unanchored pews into a cozier configuration, folding the bulletins, brewing coffee and picking up litter from the sidewalk in front of the church. "Caring for a church brings out all the neuroses in you," he joked. "All the Boy Scout."

The picturesque steepled Union Avenue church with its ornately wooden interior is situated in Canaryville, a working-class enclave, largely Irish, about two miles east of Community, near Lake Michigan. Established in 1877, five years before Community, Union Avenue's principal founder and benefactor was Gustavus Swift, the meatpacking pioneer, a burnished photo of whom hangs in the church vestibule. For decades, the church was a stronghold of Swift company managers of English, Scottish and German descent. As this Protestant stock gradually vanished, the church's fortunes had, accordingly, fallen. It, too, is fighting for survival.

To this dual assignment, Reed brings stores of faith, talent and skill cultivated over nearly four decades in the ministry. He was just shy of his 63rd birthday when he took up this challenge in the summer of 1988. Describing it as "the toughest thing I've ever been involved with," he foresees shuttling back and forth between the two parishes until he reaches the denomination's mandatory retirement age of 70.

The problems he encounters in the two churches are ones he has faced in varying degrees since his ordination in 1952. They are inherent to the pastor's central task of fostering a congregation whose members worship together, care for one another and serve the wider world. At Union and Community, Reed has undertaken that mission with less to build upon than he had available at his previous three pastorates. According to 1990 United Methodist statistics, Union carries 101 members on the rolls; Community, 95. Active membership, however, was scarcely a quarter of those totals. The rest had either long since dropped out or moved away. Neither church could support itself financially; both were subsidized by the Northern Illinois Conference, the Methodist territorial equivalent of a Catholic diocese.

For all the difficulties, Jim Reed was doing what his heart desired, ministering to working-class people in the city he loved. He was born in 1925 at the western fringe of Chicago, in Oak Park, and as a young man had been entranced by the sights, sounds and smells of the city. He knew its history, its jazz, its movie houses, its honeycombed neighborhoods, its fabled political intrigues and especially its miseries. Early in his ministry, he had cast his lot as an urban pastor. His passion for that calling still burned intensely.

As the concluding chapter to a remarkable clerical career, however, his shepherding of two pint-sized congregations constitutes an unusual coda. Ministers with his impressive pastoral record usually complete their professional lives in reasonably stable and comfortable surroundings as a reward for a job well done. Reed had that option but wrote a different script for himself. He had reached a pinnacle in 1982, when the bishop of the Northern Illinois Conference, Jesse R. DeWitt, tapped him to be a District Superintendent.

As the principal liaison between the bishop and the local churches, the "DS" oversees parishes within an area of the conference and, together with the other superintendents, sits in the bishop's powerful cabinet which determines all ministerial appointments. It is a mark of distinction and a highly visible position within United Methodism. Reed's selection was especially significant. Not only was it a recognition of his proven ability; it also represented a sort of vindication for the leftist, social activist wing of the conference which had long proposed him as its candidate to the cabinet.

He became a leading figure in that movement for human rights and social justice. While ministering to his first church, Washington Heights on the far south side, in the 1950s, he began to explore ways of overcoming racial barriers and easing a rising wave of black/white tensions. That led to his involvement in the South West Community Organization. This grassroots coalition for social change was initiated by followers of Saul Alinsky, Chicago's self-professed radical who sought greater political and economic clout for aggrieved groups and neighborhoods. From there, Reed had plunged into the burgeoning civil rights campaign, marching in Mississippi and recruiting clergy to the cause. The issues had changed over the years, but his commitment remained vibrant. One of his most recent efforts was to help organize a day-long conference to examine the implications for economic justice when factories close.

His zeal for human rights, he believes, can be traced to the only fistfight he ever got into. In the 5th or 6th grade, he recalls, he tore into a bigger boy who had taunted him. The bigger boy won. "I was both afraid of my own anger and aware that in normal fighting I wasn't going to be skillful," he says. "I had to find another way to deal with it. That's how I came to do it by standing for lost causes." Participation in city-wide, regional and national causes had paralleled his local pastoral duties from Washington Heights to the district superintendency. The question was, as his DS term ended, what should come next?

Customarily, the retiring superintendent returns to the pastorate in one of the stronger churches. But Reed asked specifically for Union Avenue and Community where his combined income of $21,848 is close to the conference's $18,000 salary minimum. Because both congregations were within the area in which he was superintendent, he had more than passing knowledge of their precarious condition. Reed made the unusual request, he says, in part because his wife, Pat Devine Reed, directs the Boulevard Arts Center located near the Union Avenue church. The move also demonstrated a penchant for prudent daring that has marked the length of his ministry. "I think most of us my age should consider taking churches that are in difficult situations and investing whatever wisdom and skills we have in them," he says.

In actual practice, he noted, most of the appointments to dying, impoverished churches were handed to pastors with the least experience. "If a young person gets appointed to a church with few resources, they're likely to think of themselves as failures," he says. "I can't imagine being assigned to these two churches just out of seminary. It would be very discouraging." Before Reed arrived, Community had had a student pastor and Union Avenue made do with the part-time services of a retired minister.

The title of his sermon this particular Sunday, "Risky Business," was borrowed from the recent, popular movie. It reflected both his personal theology and the fragile status of the two tiny congregations. At Community church, as was his habit, he stepped down from the chancel to preach on the level of the congregants. Even with that disparity eliminated, he was a commanding figure in a white robe cinctured at the waist with white vestment rope. His lean, big-boned frame made him look somewhat taller than his 6-foot 1-inch measure.

For his sermon text, Reed took Jesus' parable of the talents, in which two men receive blessings for making good use of their God-given gifts while a third is scorned for burying the one he receives. "This doesn't mean we should all be capitalists or play the lottery or practice hang gliding," he said, drawing smiles and chuckles. "It does mean that the Kingdom of God is a life, a plan of risk in faith, living a life that steps beyond what is absolutely clear and secure.

"In everyday life, we don't look for risk, we look for security and safety," he continued. "Jesus said that was the way of the world. But he taught us that the way of the Kingdom is constant, everyday risk." From the Bible he lifted out examples of risk-takers: Abraham, Moses, Ruth, Mary and Peter. He cited

Dietrich Bonhoeffer, the German theologian who had put his life on the line to plot against Hitler, and the madcap movie, *Risky Business*, which had, in a more lighthearted fashion, he said, also illustrated the point. Then he made the connection to Community church, which, in its perilous state was threatened with extinction. "Look at this congregation," he said. "We're a risky venture. I think God has big plans for us. But if we don't risk, we won't find out."

Reed's preaching voice was clear and sonorous. He used it to convey an array of feelings, punctuating comments and stories with bursts of spirited laughter. Strands of thinning light brown hair fell over a broad, high forehead and tufts of grey bordered prominent ears. His long, rectangular face with its straight, full nose and a solid, round chin suggested boldness. But there were hints, too, of shyness in his green eyes. Here was a man, these features seemed to say, who had learned leadership by overcoming a deep strain of reserve. His face retained hope and compassion, despite the dark furrows that spoke of life's trials. It was, on the whole, a remarkably youthful look, one that overflowed with good will.

In preaching, as in the rest of his ministry, he prefers to exercise leadership through suggestion rather than outright direction. "He never lectures you," says the Rev. Robert Harman, an official with the United Methodist Board of Global Ministries who once served as co-pastor of a Chicago church with Reed. "He has a way of informing you without telling you." The Rev. Bonnie Beckonchrist, one of the several female pastors Reed brought into the district while he was superintendent, says he was, in that capacity, "a friend, not a hierarchical kind of boss. That's his style. He's a person I still seek counsel from. I don't see him as someone offering advice. When you are struggling, you can call Jim and he'll give you some piece of wisdom that at first might seem ridiculous—but it's just what you need."

His handling of controversy has won him admirers as well as critics. Both supporters and opponents of his activism agree that throughout conflict he retains a calm graciousness, looks for value in the views of others, and displays a remarkable capacity to place people before partisanship. "He does what he believes," says Doris Rudy, the lay leader of the Northern Illinois Conference. "He's also very affirming. In the face of a lot of criticism, you can always depend on Jim to be supportive. Now he and I happen to believe about the same on issues and he acts that way to me. But he does the same for people with whom he would disagree."

Those who have seen him in action for a long time extol his talent for building alliances and coaxing consensus. The Rev. Frederick West, minister of University United Church of Christ, went into the ministry largely as the result of his involvement in a church pastored by Reed in the 1960s. Lauding him as "the only minister I know with impeccable integrity," West says he is especially impressed with Reed's skill at being either a mediator or provocateur, depending what the situation might call for. "He is known," says West, "as someone who can read a group intuitively."

Reed's wife, Pat, who met him when she was a community organizer, attributes his social and political finesse to his "amazingly wide range of respect for people. I see him being a mentor to all kinds of people. They trust him because they always know where he stands. He never lords it over people. He challenges and confronts people but the manner in which he does it wins them over. I'm amazed how he can do it."

Reed's gifts of political savvy and personal grace have cast him as the diplomat, the maker of compromise rather than a disturber of the peace. "My role," he says, "has been to be the person put forward to negotiate. I've been perceived by most of my opponents as reasonable, one who could be talked to. That's the way I hope I come across—someone with strong convictions but who people enjoy being with and would listen to them."

When Methodist inner-city ministers organized to press their concerns with the bishop, Reed was their spokesman. When the now-defunct national group, "Methodists for Church Renewal," attacked segregation within the denomination, Reed was a key go-between. Within his own conference, he says, "it was always clear that, if there was a breakthrough, and one of us got appointed district superintendent, I would be the most likely candidate." He adds, with a wide smile, "I don't know if that was a compliment or not."

In his current setting, Reed spends considerable time away from Union Avenue and Community pursuing broader causes through a variety of church agencies, committees and interest

groups such as the Hispanic Ministry Taskforce and Methodists
for Social Action. The balance of his week is devoted largely to
the kind of routines that sustain churches and, under favorable
conditions, enable them to grow. In his current circumstances,
where prospects are dim, he needs all the patience and faith he
can muster to practice those ingrained pastoral habits with a
measure of hope.

He goes about those rounds with customary attention to
detail. It is the kind of care that sees to it that Union Avenue
worshipers have freshly-made coffee with which to socialize
after the service and makes sure that Blanche Girard, a Community stalwart and inspiration for many decades, is given a
fitting tribute for her years of unstinting service to the church.
Plans for the tribute, which would be folded into the regular
Sunday morning worship, were set at a meeting one weekday
afternoon in the home of Judy McGinnis, one of Mrs. Girard's
daughters. Reed, dressed in a mauve open-necked shirt, brown
slacks and soft brown shoes, had brought two other women to
the meeting. His manner was as relaxed and informal as his
attire.

Presiding with a light, almost invisible hand, he moved
steadily through his checklist. Which hymns did she especially
like? Who would read Scripture? A room would be dedicated to
Mrs. Girard, for whom the event was intended as a surprise, so
someone was needed to read the inscription on the commemora-
tory plaque. "You should do that because you represent the
church," Janet Walker told him. "I do?" he replied jauntily.
"That's the nicest thing anyone ever said to me. How about if
Bessie and I do it together?" Agreed. Bessie Carey, a longtime
friend of the honoree and, like her, a widow, would also read
the letters of praise from those unable to attend.

The conversation was laced with banter. "What's your
mother's favorite flower?" Bessie asked Judy. "I don't know,"
she answered. "You don't know much about your mother do
you?" Bessie teased. "Come to think of it," she chirped, poking
fun at herself. "I don't think my kids know much about me." To
which Janet chimed in, "Judging from what my kids give me,
they've never even met me." The minister enjoyed the kidding
and joking. Such easiness resulted in no small part from his
uncanny knack for erasing distinctions that sometimes inhib-

ited lay people around clergy. Such barriers are contrived, he believes, and he strives to avoid even the appearance of supporting the notion that clergy somehow belong to a higher order.

Differences between the preacher and the preached-to are, as he sees it, based on practical needs rather than importance or degrees of holiness. "Baptism is the primary ordination for everyone's ministry," he says. "The purpose of ordaining clergy to lead churches is to make them accountable. [Theologian William] Stringfellow really gave me clarity about that. In one of his books, he says that priesthood and laity are both essential for the church. The ministry of the church belongs to the laity. The laity create the priesthood in order to enable lay people to perform lay ministries. I tell people that being a lay minister in the world is about as tough as anything can be. I say that some of us aren't up to that so they let us be clergy."

Reed was raised on strong, egalitarian convictions and rock-of-ages reverence. He was baptized with the middle name Merrill to honor a Methodist bishop. The household was devoutly Christian, infused with piety from both sides of the family, in which the church was a natural extension of the home. His father, a Bible school graduate from Iowa, managed a shoe store and later became a podiatrist. His mother was a Chicago native who attended the city's normal school before marrying, and caring for Jim and his younger sister.

From his mother, with whom he enjoyed an especially close bond until her death in 1982, he absorbed the rare ability to be both open-minded and resolute. "That's the way she was," he says. "For example, she had very strong feelings against alcohol, but when I came home from the Army after drinking 3.2 beer in Texas, I could tell her about that. She didn't make any judgment about it, though clearly it was something she would never do."

During his boyhood, his paternal grandmother, who became a lay preacher in the Church of the Nazarene, planted seeds that would help nourish in him a yearning for a life in the ministry. He vividly remembers one particular camp-meeting refrain of hers. "When I went to stay with her in Iowa as a young child of seven or eight, I'd wake up at what seemed like the crack of dawn," he says. "I'd smell things baking in the kitchen. Then she'd come in, wearing a dress with sleeves fully up to her wrists, her hair done up on top of her head, having finished many chores already, and she'd say, 'Wake up, Jimmy, this may be the day the Lord comes.'"

His decision to enter the ministry occurred with muted drama during the summer of 1942, between his junior and senior years of high school at a church camp on Lake Geneva in Wisconsin. "I was on Vesper Hill and had a strong conviction that I'd been called to the ministry," he recalls. "I went to the camp dean, who was pastor of my church and asked him if I could be sure about it. 'What are you waiting for, lightning to strike?' he said. 'Get on with it.'"

In following that inner prompting, Reed has been uncommonly hospitable to people, experiences and ideas from both inside and outside the church. Books, magazines (he is a longtime subscriber to the *New Yorker*) and movies point him to ways of understanding the surrounding culture. Travels to Latin America (he has studied Spanish on and off for many years) have sharpened his view of the developing world. All along, the interests and concerns of parishioners have appealed to his receptive, curious nature and drawn him in yet other directions.

Noting recently, for example, that many congregants in his two small churches were devotees of television preachers, he had set out one evening to find out for himself what the attraction was. A young couple that had been attending Union Avenue invited him to go with them to hear an up-and-coming media evangelist at an auditorium in downtown Chicago. What impressed him first of all was the size and make-up of the audience. The crowd numbered in the thousands, and, for the most part, it was composed of young, well-dressed couples, the kind that were in short supply in most established white-steepled churches. Moreover, Reed noticed with pleasant surprise, the attendees were more racially mixed than one would expect to find in the average American congregation on a Sunday morning.

Beyond the music, which he rated "pretty good," and the message on prosperity by the Pentecostal preacher, which he described as "simple, very basic stuff . . . giving the A-B-C's over and over again," it was the effectiveness of the whole production that struck him most deeply. "I think the thing that turns them on is the *professionalism* of it, the *success* of it." He came away "fascinated but turned off," thankful for the chance to better know the world inhabited by the young couple he hopes will join Union Avenue.

Getting inside the experience of people is a major theme of his ministry. Congregants sometimes are baffled by his interest in what they considered their humdrum work lives. He had been trying for weeks, for example, to arrange to spend a working day with a layman who was a truckdriver. The man seemed amenable but was having trouble believing that the minister could really want to spend a day in a truck cab.

Reed's reservoir of hope, fed first by his grandmother on those summer mornings—the possibility that the Second Coming could happen today—sustains him in the uphill struggle to find new sources of life for his two tiny churches. It is that hope that spurred him to spend a month of Saturdays going door-to-door in the Hispanic neighborhoods around Community with a lay associate, Gilberto Rosado, looking for potential congregants. Though this evangelistic effort yielded no gains, and Rosado has since moved on to other work, Reed believes Community can be a thriving Hispanic congregation if, somehow, the people can be drawn in. He is thinking of making the church a center for community issues such as schools and housing as one means of reaching them.

His belief in the ultimate, perhaps even imminent, triumph of goodness, inoculates him against the day-to-day difficulties and defeats. "I have never felt despairing," he says. "I came into the ministry with the sense from my upbringing that the world could be changed if enough people commit themselves to a decent and honorable life. It's never left me." West, reflecting on the core of Reed's faith, identifies its key element here. "If I were to choose a category of theology where he fits it would have to do with the Kingdom—he is convinced that the Kingdom is just about to come."

Reed's quiet confidence, energy, persistence and loyalty to the church's mission had a profound influence on the religious development of many younger clergy. The Rev. John Auer is one of them, as are West and Harman. In 1968, after the assassination of Martin Luther King, Jr., Auer had enrolled in a Unitarian seminary in an effort to do his part to carry on the work of the slain civil rights leader. By happenstance, he became a student assistant to Reed at his church in the Lincoln Park section of the city. He was awed by the older man's vision, humility and dedication to justice.

"It was the most pivotal experience of my life," Auer says, and it impelled him to become a Methodist as a result. Now pastor of Rogers Park United Methodist Church in Chicago, he considers Reed "the most singular influence on me," the person he would still consult if he had a "painful, personal need." In tribute, he gave a son the middle name of "Reed." Within the conference where they both serve, Auer proffers Reed the ultimate professional accolade, as "the one looked to as pastor by other pastors, even by those who are diametrically opposed to him politically."

Bishop DeWitt knew Reed as a compatriot in human rights campaigns before being assigned to head the Northern Illinois Conference (an area that includes 141,600 Methodists) from 1980 until his retirement in 1988. Bishop DeWitt attributes much of Reed's influence to his clarity of purpose. "He is the way he is because he knows who he is," the bishop says. "There is no question about his commitment to Christ and the church and no hesitancy on his part to declare it. He knows what it means."

Echoing that thought, Auer regards Reed as "the person I know who is most comfortable with his identity and his calling. Though his way of doing ministry can be costly, I've never seen Jim shrink from it." That identity coheres around a core of beliefs shaped profoundly by several theologians sometimes called "secular" because of their close attention to the religious nature of this world.

Reed was several years out of seminary already when the writings of these theologians appeared and began to remold his thinking into the form that would guide his mature ministry. *The Secular City* by Harvey Cox, the Harvard theologian, turned his attention to the presence of the sacred in the world. From the books of William Stringfellow, the Episcopal layman, he drew insights for witnessing to the Gospel in everyday life. In Bonhoeffer, the German theologian and Nazi resister, he encountered the enigmatic sounding term, "religionless Christianity," which probed the meaning of faith and courage in circumstances where Christians live out their convictions outside the artificially insulating trappings of the church.

A Methodist thinker, Colin Williams, contributed two important books to his rethinking, *What in the World* and *Who in the World*. In the "liberation" theologians of Latin America, who stressed the struggle on behalf of the poor and oppressed as a central imperative of the Gospel, Reed saw the cause of social justice through new eyes. Filtering those works and others through the sieve of his own experience, Reed has derived a personal credo which he sums up as "seeing the Word of God present everywhere." Whereas he had previously conceived of God institutionally and ecclesiastically he recalls that he began to see the church as only one among a multitude of locales where divine intentions were unfolding. More specifically, liberation theology radicalized and politicized his personal theology. He remembers an apt line from a speech Stringfellow gave at the inauguration of an activist clergy alliance in Chicago. "If you want to find God," he had said, "go to the hells of the earth."

Reed's response was to search for theological meaning in such places as politics, social causes and the arts. "It was like the scales falling from my eyes to see it all fit together," he says. "To see, first of all, that the church is imperfect—just another secular institution—and that my deeply felt faith was being brought together with my life. In reality, the Word is in the church, to be sure, but everywhere else too."

This awakening translated into his preaching. In his first church following ordination, he remembers delivering "brave sermons on abstract issues." The congregation gave him the freedom to say what he felt about such issues as racial justice, but also gave themselves permission not to pay attention. His shift in theological direction changed all that. "I began to relate preaching to the immediate situation, to put it in a social as well as religious context," he says. "I consider sermons as disposable art, so I don't ever use them again."

Their disposableness has not made them perishable. Listeners can recall images and emphases Reed invoked from the pulpit years ago. One cited an epigrammatic theme: "Some people plan trips; others go on them." Another was struck by an analogy Reed drew between Easter and D-Day, the World War

II Normandy landing. Each was an event, he had said, "after which things would never be the same again." His reputation for elegant, effective preaching studded with Biblical and contemporary illustrations had been long since established.

Reed became not only a spinner of inspiring sermons but a master of everyday churchcraft as well. He was, above all, a pragmatic artisan using the ordinary materials of parish life. Often young pastors overlooked these practical skills, he reckoned, in pursuit of what they saw as higher aims. "As I used to say when I was a DS," he says, "I don't care so much about a person's theology or personality but, rather, can he or she handle a church day-to-day? It seems obvious that in this area seminaries don't do a great job." Competence includes "some basic business skills," he says, such as the ability to keep church finances straight and work well within committee structures. It was at his first church, Washington Heights, that he learned the ropes. At the end of his seven-year stay in 1959, he says, "I knew how to run a church."

Another factor in his ministerial formation was the Ecumenical Institute, a high-energy center in Chicago which, through various innovative teaching techniques, sought to break down common assumptions that kept the church at arm's length from the world. Reed found the Institute at a time when he was ready to rethink his guiding theological presuppositions. It provided him just the climate of creativity and support that he needed.

Though he finds signs of God's activity in the ordinary, time-bound world, Reed retains a deep trust that the outcome is transcendent, beyond human efforts, resting finally with God. While human efforts are useful, he believes, God's Kingdom will arrive in its own way and its own form. Accordingly, everything can be taken seriously, including, of course, the church, but nothing should be taken with ultimate seriousness.

"I learned from Jim that acceptance of the . . . brokenness of life is fundamental," says Stan Hallet, a research associate at the Center for Urban Affairs and Public Research and adjunct professor at Northwestern who has known Reed since they were fellow students in theological school. "It keeps you from latching on to the false gods." The one God to which Reed attests is securely, mysteriously in charge.

The most crushing assault on that bedrock of faith was the death in 1982 of his first wife, Jane, when he and she were driving to Oak Park to inspect the home into which they were to move when Reed took over as a district superintendent. Jane was seated on the passenger side placing stamps on thank-you notes to supporters who had just helped elect her to a second two-year term on the Will County Board of Commissioners. From the opposite direction, a car suddenly crossed in front of theirs, bounced off the guard rail and smashed into them, killing Jane instantly.

Reed not only lost his wife, companion and mother of their son, Stephen, born in 1956, but a powerful voice of conscience as well, a soul-mate who had prodded him beyond his cautious instincts into action on behalf of various causes. She had been a social worker, teacher and perpetual gadfly. She could be far more confrontational and outspoken than he.

"Jane pushed him on feminist issues and other things," says Hallet, who accompanied her to many protest demonstrations. "She was lively enough and so bright that you couldn't ignore what she had to say. She pushed Jim to follow up on things." They complemented one another and gave each other a hard time. He was even tempered, she was intense. Everyone who knew them, it seems, saw them as an extraordinary, if sometimes dissonant, team. Their names were often spoken together, signifying how deeply their identities were linked. "For all of Jim's distinct features," says Harman, "Jane had the capacity to make them richer and stronger. They were always out in front. The marriage had tensions, but the marriage bond kept getting stronger."

During the early years of their marriage, the civil rights movement was in its beginning stages and the young minister jumped aboard by heading a human relations council and joining the Alinsky team, becoming a vice president of the South West Community Organization. Reed's bishop, Charles W. Brashares, shared a widespread suspicion that Alinsky's motives and tactics were dangerous, even un-American. In an effort to sever Reed's tie to SWCO, the bishop ordered him out of the area where the group was active. Reed refused to budge, explaining his stand to the congregation. He relented, he says, only when the bishop dispatched a special delivery letter demanding that he take up duties as pastor of a small church on Chicago's north side. "It was supposed to be punishment," he says wanly. But like B'rer Rabbit, for whom the briar patch was a godsend, the new parish brought rich blessings, affording ideal circumstances for the unfurling of his energy, idealism and creativity.

Throughout the tumult of that transition, Jane stood by him as his main support, reassuring him of the rightness of his stand. Years later, it was Jane who had overcome Jim's initial reluctance to accept appointment as a district superintendent. "Jane thought it a crowning tribute to him," says Harman. "In a way it was something she thought couldn't happen. For her it was recognition of what they stood for. Then for him to have to live with the burden of the district superintendency without having her to enjoy it with was tough."

By his own account, he lost his bearings in the months following Jane's death, trapped by "the tendency of clergy to think we can handle anything." Waking to that illusion, he sought counseling to cope more adequately with his grief. The crisis eased. Soon he began dating Pat, a friend and "movement" comrade of his and Jane's for nearly 20 years. They were married in 1984.

She was an organizer, teacher, political activist and artist. To make possible her goal of establishing an arts center for minority youth, she had gone back to school to earn a master's degree in art. The idea materialized in the establishment in 1983 of the Boulevard Arts Center. Pat's religious identity had taken a sharp turn. Born Roman Catholic, she had abandoned adolescent thoughts of becoming a nun and attended Alverno College, a Catholic school, where she received her baptism in radical student politics of the 1960's from fellow undergraduates. After college, she went to Chicago with a group of young Catholic activists where she met the Reeds. Her cooperative efforts with Reed sparked an attraction to Methodism and she became a member.

By comparison, Reed had trod a steady path. He graduated from high school during the Second World War and shortly after was drafted into the Army, ending his hitch in a military government company that helped preside over vanquished Japan. Following his discharge, he entered DePauw

University, a Methodist school in Indiana, at the urging of his
father. There he met Jane and they married in the summer of
1947, before his senior year. After he graduated, he went off to
Boston University School of Theology for three years. By late
spring of 1952, he was fully ordained and assigned to his first
church.

The heyday of Reed's ministry was inaugurated by his
forced exile to the north side after the row over his involvement
with Alinsky. His church, Wesley Methodist, warmly welcomed
him, the audacious young minister who had stirred the conference waters by defying the bishop. Soon, the church began ex-
ploring merger talks with a nearby congregation of the
Evangelical United Brethren (the E.U.B. and Methodist denominations had joined together in 1960 to form the United Methodist church).

By 1963, the merger was complete. The new church was
more than a sum of both parts. Called Holy Covenant, it was a
distinct new creation which, under Reed's inspired leadership,
became a vibrant, experimental model of church renewal and
community outreach. Exacting membership standards were put
in place, requiring, among other things, completion of two
courses at the Ecumenical Institute and participation in a "mission" group with specific objectives for neighborhood improvement.

The situation called on Reed's every resource, both realized and latent. The congregation caught fire, it initiated all
kinds of ministries from innovative worship to community action. Jazz became part of the Easter celebration and theatre
groups performed in the sanctuary. It became a staging area in
the fight against urban renewal, which congregants saw,
rightly, as an effort to displace low and moderate income people
with upscale real estate (the opponents lost). With the civil
rights campaign at full throttle in the South, Reed and many of
his cohorts went to Mississippi to support integration. When
they did, some prominent, affluent members, including a state
legislator, left Holy Covenant in protest. The leaders of the
church did not desist, joining marches for desegregation in Chicago. Reed, meanwhile, was helping to spearhead a drive to
eliminate the clustering of black Methodist churches into a sep-

arate Central Jurisdiction. (The effort to abolish it succeeded in 1964.)

After 13 highly stimulating years at Holy Covenant, during which the church became a showcase for urban ministry, Reed felt he was getting stale and that it was time to move on. Jane took a job with the Methodist Board of Global Ministries in Washington and they moved to D.C. with their son, by then a high school senior. He returned to the conference the following year for a different kind of challenge, the pastorate of Richards Street, an all-white church in a black section of Joliet. While Jane avidly pursued politics, he strived to integrate the congregation and to draw people from all areas of the city. By his estimate, progress was modest at best in the seven years of his ministry there, but his affection for the people was strong. From Richards Street Church he went on to the district superintendency.

His earlier pastoral positions matched him with the constituents he wanted: upwardly mobile working class people. Now the congregants in his two tiny parishes are mostly either elderly or content to stay where they are. They are delighted and still amazed that this decorated ministerial veteran wanted to be their pastor. "God knew what He was doing sending him to us, says Bessie Carey, echoing a common sentiment. "We're very lucky to have him." Reed admits sometimes getting dismayed by the slow pace of change and the reverses. There are no obvious sources of new members. But the moments of dismay give way to a more powerful, enduring sense of hope.

It is late on a Saturday afternoon and he has just finished doing a wedding. The situation is typical: The bride was baptized in the church but grew up outside of it; the bridegroom is a former Catholic. The couple wanted to be married in the handsome old sanctuary of Union Avenue, the house of worship Swift built, but had no intention of becoming part of the congregation. Regardless, Reed was his usual accommodating and gracious self, helping the wedding party to feel at ease, warmly greeting the families and friends, joyously conducting the ceremony, exulting that, despite the difficulties, this was the best of times.

"I'm an unstylish optimist," he says, folding his stole after the ceremony and gazing across his cozy office. "It's finally in God's hands. We might not be able to see the evidence of good things. The problems may seem insurmountable. But you go on doing what you need to do as co-creators with God. I have to struggle more with optimism now. Part of it is getting started in these new parishes. It takes time for things to fit together. Sometimes I wonder if I'm the person who should be here. But more and more I'm feeling it's okay. Remember Anthony Quinn as Zorba? He built this slide to pass logs down the mountain. When the first log went down, the whole structure shook—and fell down. What did he do? He danced. It's a strong image, full of faith in God. In the face of death, you dance."

E. Eugene Meador

Pentecostal Pastor Blends Past And Present

by Margaret M. Poloma

*"This is what was spoken by the prophet Joel:
'In the last days, God says, I will pour my Spirit
on all people. Your sons and daughters will
prophesy, your young men will see visions, your
old men will dream dreams.'"*

—Acts 2:16

Pain has a paradoxical quality. It can destroy the human spirit or it can bring life. In the case of E. Eugene Meador, a childhood filled with poverty and hardship gave birth to an adulthood of compassion and caring. A youngster who could claim no heroes grew into a man whose life has inspired others to commit themselves to pastoral vocations. A youth whose life was clouded by loneliness has become a pastor who sees his greatest achievement as sowing the seeds of love in his church family.

Meador is senior pastor of First Assembly of God, the oldest and one of the largest of some 50 pentecostal churches in the greater Akron, Ohio area. First Assembly was founded more than 70 years ago by C. A. McKinney, a Christian and Missionary Alliance pastor who left his denomination to become a charter member of the newly formed Assemblies of God. First Assembly is a blend of the old and the new, with members who are second and third generation Pentecostals worshiping alongside new converts. Meador has been able to retain aspects of the old-time pentecostal tradition while accepting more modern practices that attract charismatics and evangelicals who were never exposed to the earlier ways.

Meador's public countenance bespeaks a successful Pentecostal preacher. When he approaches the "platform" (as he terms the pulpit area of the church) on a Sunday morning or evening, his demeanor would be familiar to any who frequent pentecostal services. Whether leading the congregation in loud and fervent prayer, preaching a heartfelt sermon, or praying quietly with those who come to the altar, Meador exudes a fervor that is little understood by those outside Pentecostalism. An animated Meador puts body as well as soul and spirit into the prayers he leads and the messages he preaches. He eschews intellectualism, never straying far from a straightforward interpretation of Biblical passages. In content as well as style, Meador's public pastoral profile is one that reflects his second-generation pentecostal heritage. Among members of his congregation Meador is warm and outgoing, seeming to enjoy the responsibility of pastoring his flock.

His mien changes once he leaves the ministerial platform. The public persona of exuberance and effervescence gives way in private to a cautious reserve. He is much more likely to ask a question and to listen carefully for a response than to promote his own views. An astute observer might wonder how well his people really know him. Meador—away from the platform—is a somewhat shy man, quick to listen but slow to speak—especially about himself.

During the past three decades, Pentecostalism has shifted from society's fringes and moved closer to the mainstream. Meador has accepted some of these changes, but seems to be resisting others. His impeccably decorated office and well-tailored suits reflect the increasing affluence of a denomination that can no longer be described as comprising the disinherited. Yet Meador clings to some of the old ways, cherishing much from the pentecostal tradition, particularly the role of pastor. Meador, who is uncomfortable with the term "reverend," refers to himself in public as "Pastor Meador," much like the leaders of earlier congregations. "The word 'pastor' is my favorite word," he said. "It speaks of a shepherd, of someone who will leave the

99 and go and look for the one sheep that is hurting, to try to reach him, to touch him."

Meador was born in 1934 in St. Louis and was raised in rural Missouri, far from any of the safety nets that might have attenuated the poverty experienced by his family. His father was a pentecostal preacher, a shepherd to the poorest of the poor. The tiny congregations pastored by the elder Meador rarely comprised more than a few dozen followers, most of whom were barely able to support themselves, much less provide ample financial remuneration to keep the Meador family of ten above subsistence levels. "My dad always pastored very small churches," Meador said. "I think the largest church he ever pastored in his life was 75 people. The income from that was very small. Dad never felt that God wanted him to work a job and pastor on the side. He felt God had called him into full-time ministry and that He would provide for us. Whatever it took, Dad felt he needed to be faithful to the call. So we lived off the ministry, and that was hard."

The poverty that blanketed rural Missouri during the Great Depression impacted the small church congregations served by the elder Meador and caused great pain to his family. Meador's most vivid memories center on having grown up as the son of a pentecostal preacher amid "great hardship, poverty, and loneliness." These feelings were fed not only by financial struggles but by the bickering and squabbling that often besets the pastor of such churches. Meador described the people who attended the small rural pentecostal congregations of his childhood as "very dogmatic, very judgmental, and very legalistic" and the atmosphere they produced "was always focused on the negative."

What Meador remembers most from these churches is seeing his parents disappointed by the very people they sought to serve. He, his four brothers and three sisters saw their parents toil without complaint, while receiving few rewards for their tireless effort. Meador noted, "All too often someone would get upset with Mom and Dad about something trivial, and in a small group like that it wasn't long until Dad would have to move on."

Eugene Meador attended 11 schools in 12 years, an unsettled and unsettling childhood in which the family was constantly moving, pulling up roots and going elsewhere. He recalls the names of no childhood friends, no teachers, and no adults who impacted his young life. The loneliness stemming from these frequent moves was compounded by the isolation of the rural Pentecostalism of his childhood. Pre-1950 Pentecostalism was far removed from contemporary urban versions that have acclimated to the dominant culture. There was no radio and no "worldly" amusements intruded from the outside. "We were so isolated," Meador recalled. "We weren't allowed to go to any kind of sporting events or any other kind of school activities. Since school activities were not planned by our church, we weren't allowed to attend. I was completely sheltered and isolated."

It was in this atmosphere that the seeds of Meador's faith were firmly planted. Although he says the negative memories are a blur for which he is able to provide few details, memories of times when he felt touched by the power of God are vivid. He remembers the day as an 8-year-old when he "got saved," accepting Jesus as his personal savior. He also remembers the Sunday morning when as a 10-year-old he was "baptized with the Holy Ghost" (as old-time Pentecostals would say). "I had made up my mind that I was going to receive the Holy Spirit that day, regardless of how long I would have to stay," he said. "I really got earnest around the altar, so earnest that I didn't even realize that everyone had gone home and left me there. (The Meador house was next door to the church so the family wasn't worried.) I was so caught up in praying and seeking the Lord! Suddenly I began to speak in other tongues. It went on for a number of minutes. It was such a beautiful experience that I ran over to tell Mom and Dad."

Meador was perhaps most deeply impressed by the faith of his parents, especially his father. Time and again he saw his father rely on what the poverty-stricken pastor believed to be the "supernatural power of God" to provide for basic family needs. Meador recalls sitting down to dinner when the only food available for the large family was some corn bread that his mother had just baked. He remembers feeling somewhat cynical when his father told the family to pray over the meal. Just as the prayer was finished, someone knocked at the door, bringing the family the best meal they had in weeks. Meador says that his father's unwavering faith taught him to trust in God and showed him that prayer was important.

The young Meador, while he had no desire to separate himself from God or from the church, said he knew that he never wanted to become a pastor. The emotional pain and physical poverty of growing up in those pentecostal churches in rural Missouri took its toll. Over the objections of his parents, Meador eagerly left for the big city of St. Louis shortly after graduating as valedictorian of his high school class at the age of 16. "I had no goals, no vision for my life," he said. "All I knew is what I didn't want. After seeing what my parents had gone through, I did not want to ever be a pastor."

Meador took a job in a shoe factory, and joined Berea Temple, a rather large (for the time) and successful Assemblies of God church of some 400 members. For the next two years, work and especially the church were his life. The pastor provided him with the most emotionally affirming relationship the young teenager had ever experienced. Meador described this first hero: "For the first time in my life, I met a man who truly cared about me. I was just a 16-year-old boy from the country who knew nothing! And he took time with me. He would let me come into his office, and he would pray with me. I became the leader of the youth group within nine months after coming there. There was just a camaraderie that I had with him. He must have seen something in me that was sincere because he gave me an opportunity—he gave me a chance. He was a man of prayer and a good preacher."

Meador's life was changed by his experience at Berea Temple. The congregation not only provided a very different model from the 11 rural churches he experienced as a child, but it offered him opportunities for personal growth. He had come to St. Louis with "no thoughts, no direction to my life—I just knew what I didn't want" and with little of the self-confidence that would permit him to dream about his future.

The insecurity waned, Meador said, as he took on volunteer roles and felt needed in the church. One job for which he volunteered was the bus ministry, helping children cross the street and assisting older persons on and off the buses. Part of the ministry also involved going out on the bus route, knocking on doors to tell people about the bus service, and asking if they would like to be picked up for church. Meador felt this sort of job was adequate for him.

A turning point came one night when his knock on a door led to the conversion of an entire family. "It so touched my heart that I could do that," he explained. "As I saw them pray and turn their hearts to God and then watched them grow in the Lord over the next year, it did something for me spiritually." Meador wanted to be more involved in church activities, feeling he had something to offer that went beyond working the bus route.

While serving as a church volunteer, Meador heard the unmistakable call to the ministry. It became impossible, he said, for him "to deny the call of God." He gradually gained a certainty about his vocation that remains with him to this day. It began to happen one night after completing the church bus rounds, when the teen-age Meador returned home and tried unsuccessfully to fall asleep. He finally dozed off and had a dream in which he was a student on a college campus. He had no idea where the campus of his dream was and eventually he just put the dream aside.

Two months later, the pastor sent word that he wanted to talk with Meador. He entered the pastor's office, went over to his desk, and looked down at an open book. "I couldn't believe what I was seeing!" Meador recalled. "On the double-spread pages of a book that lay open on his desk was a glossy picture of the campus of my dream. I had no doubt that it was exactly the one I had dreamed about." Meador found that the campus was a Bible institute in Springfield, Missouri. The call intensified.

Meador's job in the shoe factory provided only a subsistence living. He could in no way afford to give up the job and attend the bible institute. Then, the appearance of a benefactor who had no knowledge of Meador's dream seemed to reaffirm the call. The benefactor was a handicapped woman whom Meador had helped on and off the church bus for two years. Meador was surprised when the woman asked him to meet her in the pastor's study. "God has laid it on my heart to help finance your education," she told him. "I want to give you a loan for you to go to school to prepare for the ministry. If you don't make it through school, if you drop out for some reason, or if you feel the ministry is not for you, just consider it a gift. If on the other hand you go into the ministry, at whatever time you are able, you can pay me back as you see fit, without any interest." Meador is still somewhat awed by the timing of the woman's offer: "I couldn't believe it! It was one of those miracles!"

Miracles continued to be part of his experience during his years at Central Bible Institute as he was forced to trust God for his daily bread just as he had earlier witnessed his father's reliance on providence. Although his benefactor paid his tuition, he still needed money for other expenses. Some miracles came disguised, as the one that arrived in the form of an offer to work part-time in a cafeteria. Some incidents he considered miracles a more skeptical person might term "coincidences." Once, when he needed money to purchase textbooks, he asked God specifically for the $20 it would take to cover the cost. The response came within three days in an unexpected envelope containing $20 from someone in St. Louis. With the help of his benefactor, part-time jobs, and his faith in God's providence, Meador said he was able to finance his ministerial training.

Meador loved the three years he spent at the Central Bible Institute (now Central Bible College), and it was there he met his future wife, Mary Louise. Meador took an elective in sign language, and started attending a church where services for the deaf were held. Mary Louise, the child of two deaf parents, also was attending the church. They also were both active in the sign-language club on campus in which he served as president and she as treasurer. They became a team in their ministry to the hearing impaired as Meador's empathy for handicapped people focused on the deaf.

He readily credits Mary Louise with improving his self acceptance and self-esteem. "Mary Louise has been a very, very supportive person," he said. "She has been the positive affirmation that I never received as a child growing up. There is nothing I can do that is bad in her eyes! I can flub up—and she will always say it is great. When opportunities would come my way, I would want to turn them down. I would always feel that I wasn't qualified. She would encourage me, and it was her encouragement that helped me to see myself in a different light. Without her, I don't know where I would be."

Following graduation and marriage, the young couple took a part-time assignment ministering to the deaf in an Assemblies of God congregation in Oklahoma City. Unlike his father, who refused to take a secular job while ministering, Meador worked for the Chamber of Commerce and pastored part time. Within two years he shifted to a full-time pastoral position and Mary Louise took over the part-time position working with the hearing impaired. They established a ministry for the deaf that continues to this day.

A "burden for the deaf," as Pentecostals often express their ministerial concerns, is something the Meador couple carried with them to Akron's First Assembly of God in 1970. First Assembly, a congregation of approximately 600 persons, is the city's oldest Pentecostal church. Situated in one of Akron's more affluent areas, it bears more resemblance to Berea Temple of Meador's adolescence than to the tiny rural pentecostal churches of his childhood. Within six months after arriving in Akron, Meador was able to invite a young graduate of Central Bible College, John Sederwall, to pastor a deaf community that began meeting at First Assembly.

Sederwall is now the pastor of Calvary Church for the Deaf, one of only a dozen or so Assemblies of God deaf congregations in the country. He credits Meador for making possible his dream of pastoring a self-supporting deaf church. Sederwall was a senior at Central Bible College when he learned of Meador's concern for this special ministry. Sederwall sought to work with Meador in fashioning a ministry for the deaf and accepted an invitation even though First Assembly was not in a position to pay him a salary. He came to Akron "by faith," grateful for the indirect support that Meador and First Assembly was able to provide for his work.

Sederwall describes Meador as "very supportive—very encouraging" and as putting "no limits on us—no reins on us or anything." This kind of independence, according to Sederwall, is not typically offered to those who would minister to the hearing impaired. He said that most frequently the pastor will not permit deaf members of a congregation to hold separate services, forcing them to settle for an interpreter at regular church services. In contrast, Meador not only permitted the fledgling deaf congregation to conduct its own worship, but allowed them to be a "separate church within a church," preparing for the day when they could totally separate.

As the deaf congregation slowly grew in size, the members pursued their dream of autonomy. After reaching the point of being able to support Sederwall as their full-time pastor, they began to seek their own church property. In 1982, with the blessings of Meador and his congregation, Calvary Church of the Deaf purchased a building and "cut the apron strings" to First Assembly.

The founding of Calvary Church for the Deaf illustrates Meador's pastoral influence beyond the walls of his congregation. He has often played the role of being a "pastor's pastor." For 12 years he was a district presbyter for the Akron area, giving up the post when he felt the demands of the position began to detract from pastoring his congregation. He also has been supportive of those in his congregation who have experienced a call to the ministry.

Meador had a role in promoting the ministerial vocations of at least 18 men. One of them, Roger Larrison, the pastor of a growing Assemblies of God congregation just outside of Akron in nearby Wadsworth, was an unlikely candidate for the ministry when he felt the call in 1978. He was 30 years old, married with two small children, and ostensibly happy in a new career as an engineer. "The Lord was really dealing with me—and I was arguing with him," Larrison recalls. "The timing was off, from my vantage point. Finally, after these years of married life, we were seeing some light at the end of the financial tunnel. We were feeling a bit more comfortable, and God seemed to be asking me to do something that was very uncomfortable!"

Larrison spoke of his struggle with his pastor, Meador. Not only did Meador encourage him to pursue his vision, but he invited him to sit with the church staff on the ministerial platform for Sunday worship. He also urged Larrison to begin taking courses through Berean School of the Bible, a correspondence school that allows men and women to prepare for ministry with the Assemblies of God without having to leave their communities. Within a few months and reportedly after much prayer by both men, Meador then asked Larrison to join the pastoral staff, an offer that Larrison accepted. Larrison moved on in 1985 to pastor Wadsworth Assembly of God.

Jim Arnold, Meador's current assistant, tells a story similar to Larrison's. He, too, felt drawn to the ministry at the age of 30, was married and had two small children. It was while serving as a manager for a grocery chain, where he had been employed since he was 16, that he began to feel "that the Lord wanted me to do more than I was doing." This feeling developed into a desire to become an ordained minister. Once again Meador confirmed the "call" and eventually asked Arnold to join the staff.

"This opportunity would be a prospective minister's dream—to be able to serve under an accomplished veteran pastor who has been here 21 years and who knows the ins and the outs, who is a good teacher, who is willing to take time with his staff," Arnold said. "I find myself in an enviable situation where I have a pastor who helps me, who guides and trains me so that somewhere down the road I will be ready to be a senior pastor one day. This is a tremendous opportunity."

Historically the Assemblies of God has emphasized the "call" over formal ministerial education. The credentials of most of the denomination's ministers are from Bible colleges and are sometimes earned through correspondence courses. Rarely do Assemblies of God ministers pursue advanced training in a seminary. There is an uneasiness in this rapidly growing denomination over how to reconcile formal theological education with what is considered the purity of the pastoral call. Meador seems to personify the ambivalence on this question. Although he has facilitated the non-traditional paths of those who he perceived to have received a calling, he wishes he himself had more education. He concedes that if he could do it again, he would extend his three-year Bible training, sensing that he "missed a lot." He feels particularly weak in history and writing skills, both being areas in which he would like to have had more formal training.

At the same time he notes the importance of on-site instruction, pastoral skills that come not from the classroom but from life. "When I try to apply what I learned," he said, "I don't know that the classroom prepared me for the ministry as much as life experience. I know the Assemblies of God places more emphasis on education than it once did, but education of and by itself does not make one successful. You go to our theological seminary and Springfield, and 75 percent of those attending our seminary will never be pastors. They will be administrators and teachers, but they will never be pastors. I guess it's the ego. I don't know that education would have helped me to be a better pastor. But when I hear people talk about their degrees, I feel somewhat at a loss at not having one."

Meador's acceptance of different modes of education is reflected in the educational paths of his own children. In an age when many evangelicals, including pentecostals, promote Christian education, Meador remains committed to the public school system. All three of his children went to public schools before pursuing advanced education in different colleges. Alan, the eldest, who is now 32 and living at home, attended the state-supported University of Akron. Eugenia, the older daughter, followed in her parent's footsteps, graduating from the Assemblies of God's Central Bible College. The younger daughter, Janine, pursued a business degree at the Assemblies of God's liberal arts college and is now a CPA.

Of the three children, it is Eugenia who is clearly most like her father. Married to an Assemblies of God pastor and the mother of a toddler, she is a licensed minister who holds a full-time position as a children's pastor. Eugenia and her husband are one of a small but growing number of dual-career couples within the Assemblies.

Eugenia said she was called to the ministry as a young teen-ager. "I didn't know exactly what God wanted of me," she said, "whether he wanted me to be a pastor or a pastor's wife. I just sensed that God was calling me." Her mother and her father prayed with her and for her, and she credits them for affirming her and teaching her to recognize God's call in her life—a call she says was reinforced by the way her parents lived out their service to God and to the church. "My mother especially sensed that God had placed his hand on me in a different way than he did on my brother and my sister," Eugenia said.

Meador seems to delight even more in Eugenia's success as a wife and mother than in her ministerial role. He concurs with her decision not to pursue (at least at this time) full ordination in the Assemblies of God. Meador commented: "She doesn't know why she would need ordination to be a children's pastor. At this point at least, being licensed is as far as she wants to advance." He paused and then with a slight chuckle he added, "giving the high honor to her husband, as I taught her."

Meador's attitude on the role of women fits into a larger worldview in which he has attempted to reconcile secular values with a simpler religious perspective. He is partial to the supernatural emphasis given to the faith by Pentecostalism's founders that led them to grant ordination to women even at a time when mainstream denominations denied women access to the pulpit. The Assemblies of God leaders maintained that the spirit of God flowed through women and that the manifestation of such spiritual gifts was more important in ministry than gender, degrees or ordination itself. It was an age when pentecostal men "dreamed dreams" and their "daughters prophesied," as promised in the book of Joel.

Meador compared the past and the present. "My dad came into the Assemblies just five or six years after the movement began," he said. "The miracles he saw, I don't see in Pentecostalism today. I see them in other countries—in Brazil and Argentina, just to name two. In third-world countries there is a move of the Holy Spirit very similar to what I knew as a child. I don't see that kind of thing happening in our churches today."

Although Meador does not feel that the old pentecostal legalisms are identical to the signs and wonders to which he is referring, he does lean more toward the old-time pentecostal past than do many of his colleagues. The denomination no longer officially forbids movie-going, but Meador never goes to the movies. He still mirrors the taboos of his early childhood and young adulthood that forbad even such innocent pastimes as enjoying a swim at a public beach ("mixed bathing," was the pentecostal term), playing cards and social dancing. And despite the increase in divorce and changes within the denomination that permit ministers to officiate at second marriages, Meador still cannot find it within his conscience to preside at the wedding of a divorced person.

Although he employed a woman on his pastoral staff for many years and accepts women as ministers, Meador has not encouraged women to enter the ministry the way he has mentored young men. His non-pastoral contact with women is limited by older pentecostal taboos that lead him not to be seen in public with any woman other than his wife—even over a business lunch. He believes that to behave otherwise is to court scandal.

Some might call Meador old fashioned in his concerns about the compromises the Assemblies of God has made since the 1950s. There is another side that needs to be told. Meador's respect for tradition is coupled with a tenacious loyalty to his congregation. He regards this unwavering commitment as the greatest single achievement of his pastoral ministry, feeling that once God has called a pastor to a congregation, that pastor should remain there "refusing to yield to frustrations and pressures" until God calls the person elsewhere. His personal reward, according to Meador, is that he has been able to see a second generation of people in the church and pastors and evangelists called from within the congregation. Unlike his father, who was forced to move from small congregation to small congregation without seeing the fruits of his labor, Meador has stayed in one place to enjoy some of the rewards of his efforts.

Meador said he went to First Assembly only after repeated invitations. The church was without a pastor and a board member encouraged Meador to apply for the position. Initially, he rejected the request but eventually agreed to preach at the church one weekend. Meador wondered whether the board member's persistence might be God's way of speaking to him. "So I came," he said, "more out of a feeling that I didn't want to miss God than anything else."

Even before he had a chance to fully appraise the situation, Meador felt he heard the inaudible voice of God. "You know," Meador said, "I have never had such an experience before! Mary Louise and I got off the plane, and we were met by a member of the church board at the airport. When I walked off the plane and we were going toward the car, I said to Mary Louise, 'We are going to wind up here.' I said this out of the blue—and she looked at me as if I were crazy. We had talked a good deal about this on the way up to Akron, and she knew how I did not want to leave Oklahoma. I didn't want to make a change."

Meador regarded the call to Akron and First Assembly as God's will. It was not as dramatic as the call into the ministry, but Meador is just as certain that God led him to this congregation. This certainty fortifies his devotion to the ministry at First Assembly. He likens his commitment to the congregation to his fidelity to his wife. "A commitment to a congregation is like a commitment to marriage," he said. "It is for better or for worse. Any pastor who stays in a church for 21 years ministering to the same group of people is going to experience times when he is hurt and circumstances that are not what he wants them to be. There are many times when I sense a feeling of frustration and a lack of accomplishment (at least in my own eyes), and yet I am able to rest secure in the bonding that God has given me and this congregation. That bonding is very strong today; it hasn't weakened."

The time of greatest frustration at First Assembly for Meador was during the first eight years. He describes the congregation as being very "divided" then, with "lots of hurts and animosities." His predecessor had been forced to resign by part of the congregation and the residual effects caused Meador great concern. He says he spent eight difficult years trying to unite a divided congregation. Throughout this time he felt as if no one was listening. "I was preaching my heart out, and I didn't seem to see any change," he said.

A turning point came when Meador attended a Minister's Institute in 1978, a time during which he says he experienced a change within himself. This change took the form of a deep conviction that God was about to move in the congregation. He felt that God was speaking to him about plowing, planting, watering and waiting for the harvest. "He showed me that I had been faithful in sowing the seed through the Word I was preaching," Meador explained. "It had been in a time of waiting, but the harvest was near." This sense of God speaking to him about his situation moved Meador deeply. He was convinced that something was about to happen. This feeling of expectation increased as he was preaching the sermon the following Sunday. "I didn't know what would transpire, but I *knew* that God was going to move in a sovereign way. My faith had been fortified."

That Sunday, after preaching, Meador invited those who really wanted to make a deeper commitment to God to come to the altar and to stand together in prayer. About 40 people responded and something happened that Meador had not experienced before. As he went over to the first person and began to pray with him, the man fell to the floor. Pentecostals and charismatics refer to this experience of being so overcome by the Spirit of God that a person can no longer stand as "going under the power" or "being slain by the spirit." Meador went to another person, and the same thing happened. He prayed with another person, and she began to speak in tongues. "No one was receiving the baptism of the Holy Ghost during the first years of my ministry here at First Assembly," he said. "As I continued praying, some five or six people received the baptism and another eight were lying on the floor under the power of the Spirit. Never in my ministry had this happened before!"

The service marked the beginning of what Meador describes as a "three-year revival—glorious years here at the church." He says he still sees the fruits of these revival years in the form of a "caring, compassionate and loving congregation." Although raised with the "signs and wonders" of pentecostal experiences, Meador is cautious and judges them "by their fruits." The fruits of this revival seem to Meador to be lasting ones: "I think today I have the strongest church internally that I have ever had during my 21 years of ministry here. There is a great deal of love and caring for one another. People help one another out—whether it is giving of their time, their goods or their money—without my even knowing about it. God has shown me that I did plant the seeds, and He has brought some of the seeds to fruit."

Meador feels that the church is once again in a period of waiting for God to move. The old divisions have been healed, and now Meador feels the challenge is for the church to move outside its four walls. He talks about his vision. "I feel God is calling us to reach out, not to be a church that is closed in and focusing on itself," he says.

He continued: "That is the challenge I have been speaking through my preaching the last few years. The people do seem to be responding. Over the years there has been a growing concern for the missions and supporting ministries, locally and nationally but particularly in the third world. What I hear God telling me is to pay off our church mortgage and to use the money we normally pay each month to reach out to others, both in church benevolence and to help other local, national and international ministries. I am proud of our facilities; they are very nice. What we have is good, and I am very grateful to God for it. I don't think God wants us to spend money on more buildings and facilities. He wants us to reach out to others in need."

The church has already begun to respond. Missions, both home and foreign, are a high priority for the Assemblies of God, and First Assembly gives generously. The congregation earmarked more than $100,000 annually for missionary outreach. Meador would like to see even more given to this cause. "I don't have any grandiose ideas of a megachurch or a superchurch," he said. "I have an image of a faithful church, of a church that has not forsaken its first love, of a church that reaches out to missions."

Although his feelings about his congregation and its future are basically positive, Meador does have his frustrations. He struggles to understand why many members of his congregation do not share this single-minded way of life. "People have a hard time prioritizing spiritual things, with all of the pulls they feel," he explained. "They feel they have to be successful, they have to have so much money and a certain house, and their children have to do certain things. I was at the other end of the spectrum, so to see these people indulge themselves and their children is a little difficult for me."

In many ways Meador is a classic "marginal man," having grown up in one culture and acclimated to another, but feeling totally at home in neither. He looks back at his childhood of loneliness and poverty. His early experiences have given him what he considers "a great deal of empathy and understanding for people who live in those kind of conditions" coupled with the conviction "that God will always meet the needs of those who put their trust in Him." On the other hand, he has had to adapt to a less personal, more secularized world in which rationality and technical skills prevail. He has drawn from this modern world in developing skills to carry out the administrative role of a pastor.

Meador regards the administrative role of pastor as a "necessary evil." He feels the people of the congregation, experiencing the pressures of a fragmented world, are less likely to serve as church volunteers than an earlier generation. Yet, they expect the church to provide "more and better programs and activities that have to be planned and organized." Meador, who prefers nurturing to managerial tasks, says, "I find myself doing more and more administrative work, and I wish I could change that."

It is a blend of administrative and caring skills that come into play as Meador looks toward the future. His love for missionary work does not stop with encouraging his congregation to write checks of support. He has visited some 27 countries on missionary ventures. Ostensibly most of these visits have been to provide administrative assistance to fledgling Assemblies of God mission congregations. Meador reflected on his motivations: "Some would say, 'Oh, he's just going over there to help them set up an accounting system or something like that.' But there's always much more than that," he said. "Invariably it has been a time of great personal need for the missionaries, and I have been able to encourage them—and in some cases, keep them going. Behind the scenes, I've been able to touch people— to minister while I am there."

Mission activities appeal to Eugene Meador. The simpler faith-filled milieu of third-world Pentecostalism bears strong resemblance to the Pentecostalism of his youth. Unlike the modern world he believes threatens the pentecostal spirit, the less advanced countries provide a milieu for freer movement of spirit and grace. He yearns for what he left behind even as he celebrates his success in a world unlike that in which he was raised.

Rachel Cowan

Filling the Empty Spaces
With Love

by Ari L. Goldman

*"Whither thou goest, I shall go; and where thou
lodgest, I will lodge: thy people shall be my people, and thy God my God."*
—Ruth 1:16

It is a sunny spring day in New York City and a small group of
men and women have gathered in a classroom in an old Manhattan synagogue to celebrate the Jewish Sabbath with prayer
and song. On the walls are the fingerpaintings of the
kindergarden class that meets in the same room during the
week. On this Saturday morning, a dozen worshipers sit in a
wide semi-circle in front of a simple wooden ark that holds the
Torah, the sacred scroll that contains the Five Books of Moses,
the heart of Jewish wisdom.

At one tip of the semi-circle sits Rabbi Rachel Cowan, one
of the most unusual and creative figures in American Judaism.
In her early 50s, tall and trim, she is wearing a billowy navy
blue blouse and pleated beige slacks. Her sunny blond hair is
cut in a page boy style and over it she wears a multi-colored
skull cap known as a yarmulke. Around her shoulders is a
white prayer shawl with black trim. From afar she might be
mistaken for a bar mitzvah boy leading the service for the first
time on his 13th birthday.

The service, one of five going on simultaneously in the synagogue on Manhattan's bubbling West Side, is called the

Learner's Service and is a place for Jews and non-Jews to learn how to be comfortable in a Jewish worship setting. "If you know the words, sing along," Rabbi Cowan gently coaxes. "If you know the melody, hum along. If you don't, fake it. What you say isn't important, it's what you feel."

If you are looking for the cutting edge of Judaism in America, you have found it in Rabbi Cowan. In this intelligent and radiant woman one can observe several major trends of a fast-changing and acculturating faith. Cowan is one of those driving Judaism in new directions while embracing what she and others consider its timeless and enduring values.

The most obvious trend at which she is at the forefront is feminism. In a faith deeply rooted in patriarchy, where men and women still sit separately in many congregations, there were no women rabbis until 1972. Although she was not ordained until 1989, Rabbi Cowan has emerged as a national spokeswoman for the equality of women in Judaism. Women with years of experience in the rabbinate and women who are merely thinking of entering the profession sit down regularly to talk with her.

Another reason Cowan is at the cutting edge is that she was not born a Jew. One of the fastest-growing segments of Judaism today is made up of converts or, as they prefer to be known, "Jews by choice." Cowan is a Jew by choice who has counseled thousands of both gentiles and Jews about the entry points into Judaism. Like many other converts, Cowan's affiliation with Judaism came about through an interfaith marriage. Intermarriage, in fact, may well be the No. 1 trend in American Jewry today. A national survey in 1990 showed that in the late 1980s, a Jew was as likely to marry a non-Jew as to marry a Jew. Two decades earlier only one in 10 Jews married outside the faith.

Rachel Cowan, the daughter of New England Protestants who trace their ancestry to the Mayflower, was actually ahead of the intermarriage trend when in 1965 she married Paul Cowan, the son of assimilated American Jews of considerable wealth and stature. He had built his own reputation as an author and reporter for the *Village Voice*. In the 24 years of their marriage, Paul rediscovered the faith of his ancestors and Rachel discovered that same tradition for the first time. The story of Paul Cowan's religious exploration is movingly chronicled in his 1982 book, *An Orphan in History*. For Rachel, the journey eventually led to her enrollment in rabbinical school.

Paul Cowan died of leukemia in 1989, shortly before Rachel Cowan was ordained a rabbi at the seminary of the Reform movement, Hebrew Union College-Jewish Institute of Religion in Manhattan. During the last years of his life the couple struggled together to combat the disease, as Paul tried painful bone-marrow transplants, chemotherapy and other medical strategies. In the wake of his death, Rachel Cowan has worked with widows and others who sustained profound losses. She insists that she does it as much for herself as for others. Recently, with several friends, she established a think tank called the Jewish Healing Center, which seeks to employ Jewish spiritual practices in the quest for strength and courage in the face of illness.

One more trend that Rabbi Cowan represents is the move away from the pulpit. Ministers of all faiths increasingly perceive their roles as far broader than the confines of the synagogue or church. In Judaism, the title of rabbi has become a credential that has wide currency—rabbis can be found working everywhere from college classrooms to communal organizations to homeless shelters. Rachel Cowan has made a foray into the world of foundations, where she dispenses money to help foster Jewish spirituality. Probably less than 10 percent of her working time is spent in the synagogue.

But when she steps into the synagogue, she makes a profound impression, whether in her small Saturday morning Learner's Service, or on Yom Kippur, the holiest day of the year, when she dresses in white and speaks before 1,000 people from the pulpit of the main sanctuary of the synagogue, Ansche Chesed (People of Loving kindness). "I have been knocked off stride by this holiday season," she said on the Yom Kippur two years after her husband's death. "The memories of the first and last days of Paul's illness, and the deep longing I feel for his presence, have come out of hiding. Busy with the new normality of my life, I forgot that recovery is not a straight uphill journey." People nodded silently in agreement. "How, I now wonder, can we really help ourselves and help each other to feel whole, at one with ourselves? What are the little steps, where are the few pebbles we can place rightfully outside our paths?"

She is memorable because she speaks of a world known to all who hear her; a world of beauty and yet pain, a world of grand plans and shattered dreams. "Most all of us have had our vision of wholeness shattered," she continued. "We fear we will never get it back. But slowly, and with ups, downs, and side tracks, most of us have managed to put together fragments of that whole, and to rebuild structures that give our lives coherence. We have filled the empty spaces with love, with friendship, with books, with work and tasks and causes, with passions and commitments."

Rabbi Cowan spends the work week on the 31st floor of a skyscraper on Third Avenue, across Manhattan from the West Side congregation where she spends Saturdays and the holidays. She is the director of Jewish Life Programs at the Nathan Cummings Foundation, which was founded in 1990 with a $200 million grant from the late philanthropist and owner of Consolidated Foods. Jewish life is only one of four areas of concern for the foundation; the others are the arts, health and the environment. As foundations go, the Jewish portfolio is small; Cowan's department gives away $1.25 million a year to projects relating to spirituality, social justice and interfaith understanding. One of the projects that she funded was the dialogue held in 1990 in Dharamsala, India, between the Dalai Lama, the exiled leader of Tibet, and a group of Jewish scholars.

Foundation work was not exactly what Rachel Cowan had in mind when she enrolled in rabbinical school in 1985. But with her husband's death during her last year of school, she felt that she was not strong enough or independent enough to lead a congregation, especially one out-of-town, where most young rabbis start and where she would not have had her New York support system.

In her Manhattan office, over turkey sandwiches from a local kosher delicatessen, Rabbi Cowan said that she enjoyed the work at the foundation but added candidly that she did not regard the job as long-term. "This is my chance to learn about the Jewish world," she said. But, it was clear that there are other, more pressing issues on her long-range agenda. Here and there on her desk and bookshelves were pictures of her late husband and her two children, Matt and Lisa. Her phone rang incessantly and, before forwarding all calls to her secretary, she spoke to a Catholic woman dating a Jewish man, a neighbor who recently lost her husband and a regular worshiper at her Learner's Service. Matt called from college. And, of course, there were several callers—including one from a woman in Los Angeles who knows the rabbi's sister—seeking grants. "Everybody is looking for funding and, since I know them all, I can't just give them a 'yes,' or 'no,'" she said. The calls about grants seemed to be the ones she enjoyed the least. "We can only fund 5 percent of the proposals we get," she said. "It's really wearying."

The job at the Cummings Foundation was one that Cowan stumbled into in the wake of her husband's death. A friend asked her to come to talk to the board about how the foundation, which had just been created, could focus on spiritual matters that other foundations have overlooked. The board liked her ideas so much, they hired her.

The search for the spiritual has long occupied Rachel Cowan. "Growing up, I didn't have access to a religious way of thinking," she said as she moved away from her desk and telephone and sat in a comfortable cloth chair. "I think this is true of a lot of people today, both Jews and Jews by choice. They hunger for a way to think about and talk about God. Unfortunately, the only thing so many of them have is the God they rejected in Hebrew school or parochial school."

God was only a minor character in her youth. She was born Rachel Brown in Princeton, N.J. in 1941 to parents with deep roots in Christian America who, in line with their countercultural and left-wing ideology, refused to have her baptized. Her father was a civilian mathematician working for the Navy, which meant that the family—Rachel was the oldest of four children—moved frequently about the United States and to Europe. At times, she was sent to live with her grandmother, Rachel, for whom she is named and who was a devout Episcopalian. Her grandmother filled her head with religious ideas—and even tried to have her baptized—but her parents' skepticism appeared to win out.

"While we lived in England, I was sent to an Anglican school," she recalled. "From a very early age, I remember rejecting with fear and anger the image of the crucifixion. It didn't make sense to me that God would have a son, this little innocent baby Jesus who would have this ghastly death on the cross." But the rational approach didn't satisfy her either. "When I was in sixth grade we moved to Wellesley, Mass., an insurance and banking community that was a hard adjustment for this family of non-conformists. One thing you had to do in this town was belong to a church. We joined the Unitarian Church because it was the least objectionable to my parents. I went to Sunday school; I eventually taught Sunday school. I take these things very seriously. Everything we learned was so rational. When the Jews crossed the Red Sea it was because they walked over the mud by foot. Nothing supernatural here. The Egyptians drowned because they were in chariots and the wheels got stuck and sank in the mud."

In his book, Paul Cowan tells how he, an assimilated American Jew searching for his roots, and Rachel Brown, the highly rational Unitarian, met at a civil rights rally in 1963 in Cambridge, Maryland. Paul was in graduate school "avoiding the draft" and Rachel was about to enter social work school. They decided to drive to Chicago together to visit friends. "We stopped at every Howard Johnson's on the turnpike," Paul Cowan wrote. "We felt an immediate, totally unexpected attraction, and wanted to bathe in each other's words. By the time we had driven past the huge Pennsylvania Dutch barns, over the mountain called Snowshoe that terrifies so many truck drivers, through Indiana, with its flat land, its farmers who were harvesting the autumn wheat, we knew that we were in love."

Their religious difference was no difference at all to the young couple. They married in June 1965 under a butternut tree at a farm owned by Rachel's uncle in Williamsburg, Mass. There was no debate over who would officiate; they agreed on a black minister, a civil rights advocate who conducted a secular ceremony that consisted of readings from James Agee and Albert Camus; at Rachel's direction, there was no mention of Jesus. Paul broke a glass underfoot, the only Jewish wedding custom he knew.

Their early life together has the sound of a fairy tale of the 1960s. Early opponents of the war in Vietnam, Paul and Rachel joined the Peace Corps and were sent to Ecuador where they worked in community development and organizing with the poor and unemployed. They moved to Washington where they worked at the Institute for Policy Studies, a haven for political thinkers and activists. Because of his contacts with the anti-war movement, Paul began to write about the movement for the *Village Voice*. He explored the Catholic left and became an intimate of Philip and Daniel Berrigan, two priests who were repeatedly arrested and eventually spent time in jail for their anti-war activities. They introduced him to an entire world of people motivated to social action by their faith in Jesus. Paul listened and wrote eloquently about their beliefs but always felt himself different, the nominal Jew, and one step removed.

When he and Rachel returned to New York in the late 1960s, Paul began to further explore his Jewish roots. He went on a journalistic assignment that turned into a personal odyssey and resulted in a landmark series called "Jews Without Money," about hidden Jewish poverty. As Paul explored, Rachel held back. Earlier in his writing career she often accompanied him as a photographer, taking pictures of coal miners in Kentucky and school desegregation in Boston. But she did not join him in his forays to the Lower East Side and other Jewish neighborhoods. Years later, she admitted that her resistance had to do with the fact that she was a gentile married to a Jewish man and she had feared that she would not be fully welcome among traditional Jews. In their eyes, she knew, she was the blond temptress enticing her husband to cultural genocide.

Rachel's introduction to Judaism was different from her husband's. In some ways, it was her children who brought her along. In the early 1970s child care options in Manhattan were few, and Rachel, intent on pursuing her career in social work, joined other parents in founding the Purple Circle Day Care Co-Op. They heard of a nearby synagogue building that had lots of space. It was called Temple Ansche chesed.

Once a major conservative Jewish congregation, where the rabbi and officers would wear top hats and cutaways on Saturday mornings, Ansche Chesed had fallen into neglect and disrepair in the 1970s. Families with young children had left for the suburbs or the more fashionable East Side; younger people lost interest. Only the elderly remained. Paint and plaster fell from the ceilings and walls of the huge sanctuary and the smell of mildew pervaded the air. A section of seats in the balcony had been cordoned off for fear of collapse. Empty and barren were the classrooms where Hebrew school children once sang the *Alef Bais* (the Hebrew ABC).

This dilapidated congregation was to become Rachel Cowan's spiritual home during the next decade, as an interest in the day care center aroused an interest in Judaism that eventually inspired a career in the rabbinate. It began with Old Testament Bible stories told by fellow day care parents to her pre-school children and their classmates. Gradually she was led to lighting candles on Friday nights, making her home kosher and giving up the family celebration of Christmas. Rachel Cowan, in fact, was far more ritually observant than most American Jews by the time she converted to Judaism in 1980.

But even as a knowledgeable non-Jew seeking to convert, there were few guides or role models. "There was no place to go" to convert, she recalled. "I felt very much alone." The experience shaped her involvement, years later, in working with intermarried couples. Cowan began her conversion effort with the Orthodox, the most traditional of the major branches of Judaism. "That way you won't have any problems," a good friend, Rabbi Steven Shaw, told her. Shaw, who was Conservative, explained that if she was converted by the less rigorous Conservative or Reform movements, the Orthodox might question the integrity of her conversion and might not fully accept her as Jewish. Furthermore, he explained, an Orthodox conversion was the only one accepted in Israel, where the Orthodox rabbis control matters of personal status, such as marriage, divorce and conversion. On Shaw's advice, she proceeded to speak to Orthodox rabbis, but she was unwilling to live by the rules and values they laid out, especially the roles that, to her mind, conferred second-class status on women. In Orthodoxy, women cannot fully participate in the synagogue ritual—they are not called to the Torah and cannot lead services—and cannot become rabbis.

"Steve just sent me off on a wild goose chase looking for a sponsor," she recalled. "It was very hard. You feel very hurt and rejected. Here you want to be Jewish and it turns out you are just a problem. That is how it felt to me. I would cry after all those meetings." Eventually she came back to Rabbi Shaw. "I tried the Orthodox," she told him, "but I'm not an Orthodox Jew." Rabbi Shaw put together a *beth din*—a religious court of three rabbis—who, after sending her to a ritual bath and hearing her declare her commitment to Judaism, accepted her as a member of the Jewish people.

One of the other members of the beth din was Rabbi Wolfe Kelman, who was to become a teacher and close friend of Paul and Rachel Cowan. At the time, Rabbi Kelman was involved in trying to keep the faltering Temple Ansche Chesed open. He enlisted the help of the newest Jew in town, Rachel Cowan. "At about that time I went to a museum exhibit and remember seeing the Nazis make the Jews of Dansk take the synagogue apart brick by brick," she recalled. "And I wondered: 'Are we who live in a free society going to let our synagogue close?' I had a professional degree in social work and experience in community organizing," she said. "I didn't have that much of a Jewish education but I knew I was a good organizer. I moved into a second floor office and got to work." The task at hand was daunting. "The building was so run down and dilapidated and there was no money for anything. But what saved us was what we had—the creativity of the young people and the durability of the old people."

Rachel Cowan became the executive director of Ansche Chesed and was pivotal in bringing it back to life. By the late 1980s it was a thriving congregation that attracted hundreds of Jews, young and old, to a variety of separate services, a kind of shopping mall of Judaism that met a variety of needs. There was a traditional chapel service that attracted the older, established types; a service for college students from Columbia and Barnard; a service for academics, intellectuals and people in publishing; and an experimental service where people often sat on the floor in meditative trances. Later, Rachel Cowan founded the Learner's Service that she led. All of the services were held in an egalitarian atmosphere where men and women participated equally. The top hats and cutaways of an earlier generation were long gone; even the semi-formal wear of regular American synagogue life—tie and jacket for the men, dresses or skirts for the women—seemed to be forgotten by many. People came—and still come—to Ansche Chesed in casual clothes, even jeans and shorts.

The congregation that Rachel Cowan helped revive was not just a Saturday affair, either. As the congregation grew, it got involved in the social agenda of New York, opening a homeless shelter and a food pantry and hosting programs for the elderly. One project that was very dear to her heart was Derech Torah, which literally means "The Way of the Torah" and was begun with her own conversion experience in mind. The program grew out of informal workshops that she and her husband had held for interfaith couples. Derech Torah was an introductory program to Judaism designed to help interfaith couples. In 1983, Rachel Cowan stopped working as the director of the synagogue to devote herself full-time to Derech Torah.

Unlike other interfaith marriage programs begun in recent years, Derech Torah is not just for the gentile partner. Both the Jew and the gentile that he or she is dating must attend. Derech Torah does not promote any one branch of Judaism, but rather introduces the couple to all the alternatives: Orthodox, Conservative, Reform and the smaller Reconstructionist movement. The philosophy reflects that of Rabbi Cowan who was ordained in the Reform movement but considers herself non-denominational. She has learned and grown as a Jew from her encounters with all branches of Judaism, she says, and she does not want to limit the experience of those who she brings to Judaism.

The Derech Torah program is also a departure because it does not necessarily end in a conversion. In fact, conversion is not built into Derech Torah at all. After completing the 30-week course of study, the couple must seek an outside rabbi to perform the ritual.

The experience that Paul and Rachel Cowan had working with interfaith couples became the basis for a book they wrote together called *Mixed Blessings*. When the book was first published in 1987, Paul Cowan was diagnosed with leukemia. Despite hospital stays and chemotherapy treatments, the couple traveled the country giving seminars and lecturing about the perils and pleasures of interfaith marriage.

Today, the Derech Torah program is a mainstay of Manhattan's 92nd Street Y, where it now trains some 90 couples a year. And just as Ansche Chesed spun off Derech Torah, Derech Torah revived another Cowan tradition—the informal workshops for interfaith couples. Typical of the workshops, which are generally closed to outsiders, was one on a spring evening at Rachel's spacious West Side apartment. Before the discussion, people milled about the commodious kitchen helping themselves at the coffee urn or going into the refrigerator to find the milk or snacks. Eventually everyone found seats on the comfortable couches and chairs in the living room. The topic for the night was the Easter-Passover holiday season, just completed. Holidays, when families traditionally gather, are often flash points for conflict when there are interfaith couples involved. The holiday season that year was especially tense and volatile since Easter and Passover fell on the same weekend.

"So how did it go?" Rachel Cowan asked to get the discussion going. After a few perfunctory comments—"nice," "fine," "lovely"—anguished stories began to pour out. One non-Jewish woman, with dark hair and olive skin, told of joining her boyfriend at his family seder on Friday night. "I went," she said haltingly. "I made the effort. But I got nothing in return. . . . They just ignored me." And then the real pain started to flow: "Sunday morning, I said, 'Okay, it's Easter, C'mon now, come with me to church. . . .' " Her voice trailed off in sobs. She couldn't even say the words, but everybody knew. Her fiance refused to join her.

Others reported happier holidays. Stories of acceptance and tolerance were told, but they could not mollify the tales of alienation and hurt. The most joyous story was of a seder that the members of the workshop group had organized themselves, a pot luck dinner at the home of one of the older, married couples in the group. Ritual was kept to a minimum and nobody felt different—all of the couples around the table were interfaith couples.

Although she is a supporter of interfaith marriage—and indeed helps foster it through her programs—Cowan admitted to a certain ambivalence about the whole enterprise. "There are an amazing number of men who want to have their cake and eat it too," she said. "They want a wife who isn't Jewish but they want her to be Jewish. There's a certain amount of sexism in that that annoys me a lot." Nearly all the couples that come to her are made up of Jewish men and gentile women; fewer Jewish women marry gentile men. "This year I have two women who could never be at home in the Jewish community," she said. "I truly don't know why these men are attracted to them. One is a Yugoslavian Jehovah's Witness. Why did he marry her? You can't trust a Jehovah's Witness to raise your children as Jews. What was he thinking?"

The rewards of her interfaith work are discovering women who, as Cowan put it, will be "fantastic Jews." But most, she said, "will be as lukewarm as their husbands." Rabbi Cowan, of course, was one of those rare exceptions, one of those "fantastic Jews," who became as enthusiastic and loving of her Judaism as was her husband. And just as her conversion experience motivated her to help others, so did the experience of losing Paul.

In the first two years after his death, five of her friends lost their husbands, all of them to forms of cancer. "I meet with them individually," she said. "I don't feel that I have a lot of wisdom to impart. But I think what people need more than anything else is a sense that somebody who is a little further down the road survived. I try to model that. I need it myself a lot too."

Like many young people untouched by death, Rachel Cowan said that she had never been able to confront death and illness. As painful as her husband's illness and death was—"apart from all the pain and anger and loss," she said—"there is a very profound teaching that I took with me: The crucial question is not how long we had together, but the quality of how we lived our lives together. I find tremendous solace in the life we had together. We had an incredibly strong marriage, a marriage in which we both grew a lot and changed a lot and I think that gives me the strength not to be defeated by his death. That gives me strength—not peace with it—but strength."

She also has her memories, and a powerful essay written by Paul that was to be his final, brilliant cover story in the *Village Voice*. It was called "A Journey into the Land of the Sick" and was written during one of his periods of remission, before the illness consumed him and he was back in the hospital taking chemotherapy treatments once again. He wrote: "From the day I was admitted to the hospital until the day I left, I felt a small child's joy whenever Rachel arrived in the room, kissed me and began to bustle around as if my hospital room were home."

Rabbi Cowan sometimes uses her late husband's essay in counseling the bereaved. She also uses the Psalms that she studied in rabbinical school, especially Psalm 6. She wrote a thesis about it in her final, painful year at rabbinical school. The Psalmist writes:

I am weary with my moaning;
   every night I flood my bed with tears;
I drench my couch with my weeping.
My eyes waste away because of grief.

She considered the words and then added: "Whoever wrote the Psalm knew what it was like to have your husband die. I felt profoundly connected with it."

In the many facets of Rachel Cowan's career as a rabbi, one role seems to be repeated again and again—that of a role model. When she is introducing her small congregation to Jewish prayer, it is clear that it was not so long ago that she had a similar introduction. When she is working to foster spirituality through her foundational work, her own spiritual search is never far from the surface. And when she is working with interfaith couples or with widows, she can honestly say, "I understand. I've been there." Even when being interviewed for this chapter, she often turned the conversation around so that she was interviewing the interviewer, getting the writer to talk about his own feelings about being a religion writer and the frustrations of being one step removed from fully experiencing religious life. Sometimes, he confided, he fantasized about being a rabbi. "It's a great second profession," she said in her best mentoring style.

Nonetheless, it is very hard to get Rachel Cowan to acknowledge that she is a mentor. When asked about her mentoring roles, she quickly began to talk about the people who have been mentors for her—Rabbi Wolfe Kelman, a powerful influence on her religious life who died of cancer about a year after Paul; Eugene Borowitz, a professor at Hebrew Union College-

Jewish Institute of Religion; Neil Gillman, a professor at the Jewish Theological Seminary of America; and Rabbi Joseph Singer, an Orthodox rabbi with no academic credentials who works with the poor on the Lower East Side.

"I never considered myself as a mentor," Cowan said, "but I think of people whose lives I'm interested in and with whom I stay in touch—students I have had, people in the Learner's Service, people whose weddings I have done. And then there are the many people at Ansche Chesed who have been my mentors, people like. . . ."

The interviewer pointed out that she was again talking about those who served as her guides, rather than talking about those she guided in her Learner's Service, in her foundation work, in her involvement with interfaith couples, in her work with the bereaved, even in the conversation she was now having with a writer. The interviewer suggested that when she went through these experiences—learning about Judaism, searching for the spiritual, seeking a conversion, coping with death, examining the rabbinate as a profession—she acutely felt the absence of role models and that perhaps she had become the mentor for others that she couldn't find herself.

A smile came to Rachel Cowan's face. "Maybe," she allowed. But mentor or role model or guide were words that were too strong, she insisted. A better word, she said, might be "hostess." "Sometimes I feel like I am the hostess at a Jewish party and I am standing at the door and I invite in strangers, but I am always standing at the door. I promise them that there is a really good time inside, but I don't know it myself. Sometimes I think that I should go further in the door also."

Delving deeper into Judaism is Rabbi Cowan's dream. Maybe a few years of study in Israel, maybe further examining the relationship between faith and health, maybe running a synagogue someday. Maybe then, just maybe, she will accept the title of "mentor."

Adam J. Richardson

The Journey of a Teaching Preacher

by R. Gustav Niebuhr

"There are varieties of gifts, but the same Spirit.
There are varieties of service, but the same Lord
. . . In each of us the Spirit is seen to be at work
for some useful purpose.
　　　　　　　　　—1 Corinthians 12:4

Bloodlines alone would have seemed sufficient to put the Rev. Adam J. Richardson into the pulpit. After all, both his grandfathers were ministers. On his father's side, the Rev. Shade Richardson, born into slavery around 1854, became a preacher in the African Methodist Episcopal Church. His mother's father, Charlie Walker, was ordained a Baptist minister at 20 years old and was still preaching at 100. And then there was Richardson's father, too. The late Rev. Adam J. Richardson served nearly 50 years in various A.M.E. pastorates in and around Tampa, Fla., until he retired in 1979.

But when the younger Adam Richardson recalls his boyhood career goal, he says without hesitation that he had every intention of becoming a mortician like his uncle, Clarence P. Wilson. Growing up in Tampa in the 1950s, he used to hang around Wilson's funeral parlor, watching his uncle work and sure he would follow in the man's footsteps. What changed all that was a dream, vivid and recurring, that visited Richardson in the summer of 1961, just before he was to enter ninth grade. These days, as he sits in his office, the pastor's study at Bethel

A.M.E. Church in Tallahassee, Fla., he says it didn't take him long before he was certain it was God speaking directly to him, calling him to the ministry.

Night after night, "I would have the very same dream and it would be about me preaching," he says. He never heard the words to the sermon, but that didn't matter. "All I saw was the preacher and the preacher was me. The vision would begin with me coming around the side of the church, going through the side door and straight into the pulpit." The dream always ended as he heard the congregation exclaim, "Here he is."

These days, there are no disembodied voices that herald Richardson's arrival on the wide platform at Bethel. But a sense of expectation hangs over the 1,200-member congregation when he rises to preach. Standing six-feet, four inches, Richardson dominates the stage, both physically and with the seriousness he projects as he approaches what he regards as the central task of his ministry—preaching.

Clergy familiar with Richardson call him a preacher's preacher, whose carefully-structured sermons are consistently top-notch. They point out that his reputation as a speaker is such that he is in constant demand as a revival preacher across the African Methodist Episcopal Church. "Adam is a person who crafts his sermons," says Dr. James H. Costen, president of Interdenominational Theological Center (ITC) in Atlanta. "I like the seriousness with which he prepares for his work." Costen says Richardson is "very steeped in liberation theology," a contemporary religious philosophy that draws from the Bible an imperative for social change. "But I'd say his theological position is mid-stream," halfway between the liberationists and more traditional views, a position that's reflected in Richardson's sermons, which always contain a core "note of realism, as opposed to pipe-dreaming about what Nirvana might be," Costen adds.

On a particular Sunday, Richardson begins almost reflectively. Early on, he highlights an issue troubling the black community—the tragedy of so many young black men in jail—and uses the latter to encourage Bethelites to get involved in the larger community, through, say, the church's prison ministry or its men's group. The sermon eventually builds to an emotional point as Richardson speaks of his personal experience of God's power and that power's ability to raise up and give purpose to all who seek it. Afterwards, members of Bethel say such sermons give them an unusual three-way combination: an intellectual message, a call to mission and a sweeping emotional lift. "He's not just a preacher, but a teaching preacher," says Mary Newell, an elementary school principal. And indeed, stimulating both the mind and the missionary impulse is what Richardson has tried to do since he became Bethel's pastor in 1978. In north Florida's black community, he says, "you've not had a lot of understanding about what ministry is." The area around Tallahassee is predominantly rural and the creative influence of several denominational seminaries in Atlanta just hasn't seemed to reach this far south. Richardson says that when he came to Bethel, he found many congregants regarded church as simply a minister "preaching on Sunday, . . . maybe having a mid-week service and waiting for the next Sunday."

To counter that thinking, he's made it his goal to inspire a grassroots Christian activism among Bethel's members, to help them discover their places in what he calls the "unordained ministry": volunteer service to the church and the community at large. It is, he says, "the responsibility of the shepherd pastor" to help people discover their gifts and believe they can make a difference. The pastor has tried to lead by example. In his early days at Bethel, he often preached on the importance of voting and political activism. Eventually, he took a run at political office himself, making the run-off for a county commission seat, but losing in the general election to a white candidate. (Voting then was on a county-wide basis, rather than by districts.)

These days, he speaks broadly about how people can effect change by applying their values in almost any situation. In one sermon, he told of a bug exterminator who would whistle hymns while working in clients' homes, thereby creating an opportunity to speak with people about his faith. Richardson has also worked to reinforce this message through ritual. In one service, he held an impromptu altar call, asking all who'd ever felt called by God to social service to step forward and pray with him. In this way, those who felt so inspired were affirmed and the church gained recruits for its outreach programs.

"He definitely has developed a holistic understanding of ministry," says Dr. Jacquelyn Grant, associate professor of systematic theology at ITC and a friend of Richardson's. "Unfortunately, a good portion of the black church has fallen behind its own tradition" of social action, she says. "So a minister these days has to be a teacher" who is "involved in recapturing black church history."

Richardson speaks of community involvement as an obligation for Bethel, which holds a unique status in local black history. The church was founded in 1865 by former slaves at the dawn of their freedom. "That represents a tremendous forward look by a group of people who were recently out of slavery," he says. "I look at these people who are beneficiaries of that original vision. There is a tremendous responsibility on the part of all of us to maintain that heritage."

Richardson was 32 when he was appointed Bethel's pastor. He wasn't a stranger to the place. A dozen years earlier, he'd been a highly visible figure as a right-hand man to the then pastor, the Rev. I. D. Hinson. At the time, Richardson was a student at nearby Florida A&M University. Just before the start of the fall semester in 1965, he'd arrived on campus to practice as a drummer with the university's widely acclaimed marching band. Already, he had plans to spend his Sundays checking out the various local A.M.E. churches; when he found one he liked, he'd join. His second Sunday, he dropped in on Bethel—and ended his search. Hinson, Richardson recalls warmly, was a "fireballing preacher," capable of rousing great emotional response from his congregation. "In the idiom of the black tradition, he would be regarded as a great preacher." Indeed, in that first service Richardson attended, one man became so excited by the sermon, he leapt from his pew, raced to the pulpit and hugged the pastor. "I never got to another church," Richardson says.

Hinson, who knew the young man's father, readily identified Richardson as someone who could help out at Bethel. In fact, young Richardson had already been licensed in high school to preach. So it wasn't long until Richardson officiated at baptisms, helped serve communion, even answered the summons of small, rural churches that would sometimes ask Bethel to provide them with a Sunday speaker. Occasionally, he substituted for Hinson himself, when church business called the older man out of town. Richardson, who doesn't mind telling a joke on himself, says of those Sundays: "The people seemed to like it because I didn't have as much to talk about, so we'd be out of church early."

Trustee Freddie Groomes recalls Richardson cutting a distinctive figure in the church. "At the time, he had a very full Afro," she says. "And he was very thin and very, very tall."

During that period, Richardson says he most admired Hinson for his "zeal in his preaching style" and for the fact that the minister "was not so much intimidated by the array of scholarship in the congregation." (Bethel has long attracted a number of administrators and professors, not to mention students, from nearby Florida A&M.)

The closeness of his relationship with Bethel's former pastor wasn't unusual for Richardson. The latter counts a number of mentors who shaped and directed his early life in the church. First and foremost among them, he says, was his mother, Inez Walker Richardson, a Baptist preacher's daughter who approached church life with a no-nonsense manner. Richardson credits her with instilling in him a discipline about religious duty and personal behavior that in turn helped him develop an awareness of his spiritual self. "I was impressed with my father," he says, "but my mother made us go to church . . . I mean, it was a foregone conclusion that I would be in church on Sunday morning, at Sunday school at 9:30, at morning service at 11 and anything that they would have in the afternoon— youth group at 5 and evening service at 6."

His mother's influence lasted well beyond childhood, helping him understand the responsibilities he'd taken on after he'd accepted his call and been ordained. Richardson remembers one Saturday night, as a teenager, he didn't get back from a date until well after midnight. The next morning, he rose, dressed and went to assist his father in preparing for the day's worship service. But the senior Richardson took his son aside to say that the boy's mother didn't think someone who stayed out so late for personal enjoyment ought to be taking part in leading worship that day. "What it said to me was my mother really took the business of preaching very seriously—some things you can't do and regard yourself as a preacher."

Nevertheless, Richardson makes clear he never regarded church as a place of gray solemnity. It also inspired a sense of play in him as a child. He'd get together with various young friends and cousins to hold mock services in the family home. On those occasions, an upright piano stool in the living room served Richardson as a pulpit. Usually, the service was a funeral—inspired, of course, by the work of his uncle, Clarence Wilson. "Every day," he says, "we buried dolls, we buried balls, we buried Coke bottles and everything." He'd offer the eulogy. Nowadays, uncles and aunts, recalling those games, like to remind him that "even as a kid, 5 or 6 years old, I always preached."

Born in Clearwater, Fla., on Sept. 30, 1947, Richardson grew up in nearby Tampa, where the family moved in 1950, shortly after the birth of his younger brother, Herbert Charles. He says now that during his growing-up years, he had no lack of secular interests—games of sandlot football and enough musical talent to find a place as a drummer in the school band—but he was given to pondering bigger issues, about his life and his relationship to God. "I was as much boy as any boy who has ever been," he says. "I enjoyed my boyhood. But it was intermingled with a real propensity on my part to develop myself spiritually." By the age of 13, Richardson was appointed his church's assistant Sunday School superintendent, a position that involved both the sacred and the mundane, offering opening devotionals and keeping track of pencils, paper and other supplies. He often found himself wondering, what was he "supposed to be about" in terms of his place in the world?

The question shortly preceded his life-changing dream. By the end of that summer, as he was about to enter the ninth grade, Richardson says he had no doubt what had happened: "I felt as sure the Lord had called me to preach as if I had heard a voice." He communicated all this to his father, who cautioned him that he needed to be absolutely certain of a commitment to the ordained ministry. The elder Richardson told him, he recalls, "The last thing you want to do is begin it and not be able to complete it."

By age 17, and then a licensed preacher, Richardson was assigned his first church, tiny Mt. Pleasant A.M.E., near Tampa. The place had strong family associations. The congregation, all of 18 people, consisted mainly of aunts, uncles and cousins of the Richardsons. Back in the 1930s, his father had been assigned that very pulpit and had met his future wife,

Richardson's mother, in the congregation. As an aside, Richardson notes that his own career "kind of followed my father's" for several years. In addition to the experience at Mt. Pleasant, he was ordained to the ministry in St. Paul A.M.E. Church in Tampa, where the elder Richardson had first begun preaching. In his senior year at Florida A&M, Richardson was ordained an elder, a higher grade of ministry in the A.M.E. tradition, at Allen Temple, also in Tampa, the church in which his father too had been ordained.

Richardson smiles at the memory of Mt. Pleasant. The little church, he says, would have fit easily into Bethel's current chapel. But it was a place that saw triumphs proportionate to its size. One Sunday when he was preaching, the congregation voted to take up a special offering and divide it between him and the former pastor's wife. "Thunderous applause went up when they announced the total for the day was $9.20," he recalls. He adds that serving that church "was good, and it has since been good on my resume. And I don't discount that experience of getting four dollars and a half for my services."

One might think—as Richardson did at the time—that all this experience in ministry would be an asset when he began studying, in 1969, for his doctorate in sacred theology at Interdenominational Theological Center in Atlanta, a cluster of six predominantly black seminaries. But rather than offering him a refinement of previously acquired skills, his time there was spent partly in a wrenching reorientation of his preaching persona. It was, he says now, the turning point of his ministry. The source of the challenge was ITC's homiletics professor, the late Isaac Clark, a towering presence on campus and one who Richardson says made it a personal mission to re-make his preaching style. Former students remember Clark hammering home his conviction that "if you ain't got a proposition, you've got no sermon, either." The professor could be brutally blunt in assessing a prospective preacher's skills. Clark told Richardson he was trying to imitate the preachers he'd known as a youth, rather than finding his own voice. "Almost from the very start, he said, 'You started too soon. You've got an old man in you. Get that old man out of you.'"

Clark, it should be said, wasn't the only one who noticed this quality. Alice Peacock, a trustee at Bethel, recalls that when Richardson served under Hinson, "he tried to imitate the pastor to some extent."

Two decades later, Richardson describes his encounters with Clark vividly, testimony to how important the whole experience became to him. But at the time, it was so painful he remembers cursing and crying over some of Clark's comments. "He not just graded my sermons, but degraded them, telling me they were not fit for human consumption."

Yet even early on, the professor was also offering him encouragement—telling him that deep down he was gifted—and dropping hints as to how he could break old habits. After hearing one sermon Richardson preached in class, Clark said, "You don't sound the same as you do in the hallway. You come in here, you want to be somebody else whom you call Preacher." Their rocky relationship reached the showdown stage the day Richardson tried to beg out of preaching in class, saying his wife Connie was about to give birth to their first child. Clark responded that if he didn't give the sermon, he'd get an F in the class.

"I felt so, so down, low, blue about it until I had no energy to try to preach," Richardson says. He carried his manuscript (appropriately titled, "The Making of a Preacher") into the classroom, a place with a glass booth from which the professor could sit and monitor him. Just before he took the pulpit, Clark told him, "Preach good. I'm praying for you." Richardson says he spoke with none of the emotions and gestures he'd learned to practice. He sat down afterwards just feeling weary. Clark, on the other hand, bounded out from behind the glass, shouting, "That's it! That's it! You got it!"

Richardson objected that he hadn't really preached, because he hadn't exerted himself. But Clark told him he'd found his true style. "I think I have discovered my authentic preaching sense," Richardson now says. "But it took that kind of catharsis that was initiated by him."

The two men eventually became quite close, to the point that Richardson, after his graduation in 1973, took Clark's place in the homiletics classroom when the professor went on a semester's sabbatical. And these days, Richardson lists Clark as a personal hero, alongside such distinguished churchmen as Dr. Martin Luther King, Jr., the Rev. Richard Allen, the former slave who founded the A.M.E. Church in Philadelphia in 1787 and the Rev. Daniel Alexander Payne, a great exponent of education and a bishop in the A.M.E. Church. Costen, ITC's president and another of Isaac Clark's admirers, remembers watching the relationship between Clark and Richardson evolve from confrontation to "trusted colleagueship." "Adam was one of (Clark's) favorites. I think he saw Adam's love for preaching," Costen says, adding that at ITC, Richardson's skills evolved in his sermon-writing to where he was "able to what I call 'undress' ideas and get a lot out of them that the average person wouldn't even consider." The latter comment is echoed by members of Bethel, which has a tape ministry to record Sunday services on cassettes. "If you listen to his sermon again, you'll hear three to four sermons," says member Earl Britt.

Even after Isaac Clark returned to the classroom, Richardson stayed on at ITC, teaching a separate homiletics class created when the center decided to expand that part of its program. It was a busy time. Richardson was also teaching a general religion course at Morris Brown College, a predominantly black institution nearby, and was also serving as pastor of Trinity A.M.E. Church in Atlanta.

In all, he spent nearly nine years in the city, liking it so much he planned to settle there permanently. From the start, the place had struck him as wonderfully rich and unlike anything he'd ever experienced. Arriving at the ITC campus, he was nearly overwhelmed by the size of the local black population and by the presence of blacks at all levels of the city. It was two days before he even laid eyes on a white person. This period, the early and mid-1970s, was an unusually exciting time for Atlanta, which was coming to represent the "New South," a forward-thinking place that offered great opportunities to white and black alike. The election of Maynard Jackson as mayor and Andrew Young to Congress marked the appearance of nationally-prominent black political leadership within the city. Richardson saw it up close. While at ITC, he served as a ministerial intern at the Butler Street YMCA, a downtown meeting place for the rising black political and business leadership class. And later, at Trinity, he found himself looking out into a congregation that occasionally included the Rev. Martin Luther King, Sr., who, after retiring from the pulpit of Ebenezer Baptist

Church, liked to drop in on other pastors during their Sunday services.

Richardson's plans to put down roots in Atlanta came to an abrupt end midway through 1978, when his boss, A.M.E. Bishop Harold I. Bearden, suddenly ordered him out of Trinity and assigned him to a church 100 miles away in the small, rural community of Fort Valley, Ga. Bearden's decision came despite the fact that Trinity had been growing (membership had tripled from 200 under Richardson; one regular visitor remembers that those who didn't get to services early wouldn't find space to sit). Richardson had also been selected by the state Chamber of Commerce to participate in Leadership Georgia, a special program for academics, clergy and business people to learn about the state through various seminars. All in all, he fully expected he'd rise steadily in the church in Atlanta. "I guess up to that point, I was pretty naive," he says. "I thought that if you did your work and you succeeded, folks would notice and if there were any rewards, you would get them." He tried arguing Bearden out of the decision, but to no avail. When he went to Fort Valley, he went angry. "I never felt so badly about myself or about my denomination or about the whole system as I did then."

Richardson likens that time to the Israelites' wanderings in the wilderness, a period of hardship and testing of faith in the midst of a more productive journey. As Jacquelyn Grant, the ITC professor, says, that Richardson was able "to survive and come out of it very well" shows his deep commitment to ministry. Of great help then was the friendship of the late Rev. Julius C. Williams, an A.M.E. minister in Atlanta, who told him, "When you become bishop, you'll know what kind of bishop to be." And later that summer, at a church conference in Orlando, Fla., where Richardson preached on how good can come out of struggle (taking as his text Romans 8:28, "all things work together for good to them that love God"), Williams took him aside and told him that the answer to his crisis lay in his own sermon. Richardson remembers responding, "Now all I have to do is believe it."

Richardson's Fort Valley sojourn ended as abruptly as it began. Four months into his ministry there, he received an unexpected phone call from Bishop Samuel S. Morris, whose 11th

District of the church included Florida. Morris asked him simply if he was ready to "come home" and Richardson answered yes on the spot, though without knowing which church the bishop had in mind for him. "I accepted before I knew it was Tallahassee. It was like a door swinging wide and I just stepped through."

Still, being assigned to Bethel was by no means an easy way out. Familiar the church was, but it offered some major challenges. When Richardson arrived, he found more than 1,000 members listed on the church rolls, but a thorough search turned up addresses for fewer than 500 of them. Of those who attended Sunday services, the average age was around 60. Worse, the building was downright decrepit.

As a first step toward revitalizing his congregation, Richardson set out to get Bethel's members more involved in church life. To do this, he decided to find out what they most cared about. "I asked them what they were interested in doing," he says. Building on their responses, he then worked with members to establish a monthly newsletter, arrange workshops on the elderly and on women's issues, and launch new Bible study classes. As church membership began to grow, the congregation proudly adopted a motto, "Bethel is blooming and booming."

The approach Richardson took then is a trademark of his leadership style. ITC's Costen, who gives the pastor high marks for his administrative ability, says Richardson "is enabling without being dictatorial." Bethel's members cite their minister's ability tactfully to encourage them to do things for themselves, to broaden the church's ministries, without trying to push them into it. "He does not appoint people to committees. He allows them to volunteer," says Peacock, the trustee.

Richardson says such restraint doesn't always come easily to him, because at heart, he's a take-charge type. He says he makes himself back off from certain situations, "because I never thought I could do it better than anyone else." But the pastor's activist inclinations turned out to be a decided asset for Bethel when the church faced one of its greatest crises early on in his ministry. Not long after he'd arrived, the congregation moved to renovate their sanctuary, a venerable brick building at the corner of Virginia and Duval streets in Tallahassee's downtown. Services were held in rented space nearby; the work was finished in time for the church to host the annual district A.M.E. conference in 1979.

But it all came to naught in February 1981 when a major beam cracked right in the middle of Sunday services. Bethelites refer to the moment as "the big bang," an explosion that shattered the quiet before an altar call, causing people to jump in their pews. An inspection of the building the next day turned up ample evidence of structural damage and decay. The congregation faced an agonizing choice: Gut the church for a major restoration or sell the historic property and find another site. Many members felt a deep emotional attachment to that location, but with Richardson's strong encouragement, the congregation opted to move.

The building's gone and its site looks puny compared with Bethel's current campus, a seven-acre parcel halfway between Tallahassee's airport and the downtown area. Richardson says the new building—a spacious structure with a glass-fronted lobby—allows the congregation a space commensurate with its growing ministry. And perhaps equally important, the new building appears to have helped Bethel make a fresh start in another area, laying to rest an old reputation as an exclusive place to worship. Richardson says that when he first arrived, "much to my own chagrin about it, there was a kind of at least perception that it was an elitist type of congregation." Then, as now, the church attracted a number of prominent persons from Florida A&M: professors, deans, even former presidents. Many in the congregation insist the silk-stocking reputation was undeserved, that the church has always attracted a healthy crosssection of educational and income levels. Deserved or not, such a reputation can be extremely harmful, Richardson acknowledges. A church "can degrade into a museum," he says. "There must be a continuous reevaluation of where we are and where we're going."

What's also lent Bethel vibrancy is Richardson's personal style. On the one hand, the pastor carries an unmistakable aura of authority. Yet in his interactions with congregants, he comes across as accessible and informal. Jacquelyn Grant, who was in the class behind Richardson's at ITC, says his serious side has always been balanced by a "very fun spirit." Richardson, she says, "has a fantastic capacity for telling stories, funny stories.

It comes out in his sermons." He also has a flair for visual aids, using the occasional stage prop to give his listeners a key to remembering his message long afterward. Once while speaking about Jacob's ladder, Richardson brought a step ladder up to Bethel's pulpit. And some congregants recall a sermon on tithing in which he held up a bunch of 10 bananas, separating one out and displaying the other nine to show how much is left over for the giver after the donation is made. "If you don't address people in their everydayness, it's irrelevant," Richardson says. "And if it's irrelevant, we ought to close the building."

New members at Bethel get a 58-page manual, a thorough guide to the church that covers everything from a basic history of the A.M.E. denomination to the phone numbers of Bethel's lay leaders and the many special dates in the church's year. Dead center is a list of Bethel's various ministries, for couples, single persons, athletes, prisoners, school children and others. The church also offers seminars on basic health, on managing money and—dealing with a subject little discussed in most churches—AIDS. A forum on the disease is now an annual event at Bethel, intended particularly for Florida A&M students, many of whom attend the church during the academic year. Speakers may include someone who is HIV-positive and can talk about the experience of having the virus. "We cannot afford to act as if it doesn't exist," Richardson says. "When every six months or so, students are breaking up and going with someone else . . . it has the potential of being pandemic."

The ministry of which Richardson speaks most proudly is one for the church's men. The Sons of Allen (named after Richard Allen, the denomination's founder) meets Saturdays and sometimes holds longer retreats, bringing men together to share thoughts and prayers over everything from how to stay married and be a good father to what to do about local social and political concerns. The meetings are intended to "develop leadership among men in the context of the Christian faith," says Richardson, adding that this is vital not only to the health of the church but of the larger community.

Bethelites clearly value the group and they credit Richardson with being the type of role model—neatly-dressed, well-spoken, serious yet down to earth in demeanor—that would attract black men to the church. "If he comes into a room, his presence is known," says William Lamar, a member of the Sons of Allen and a steward at Bethel, a position equivalent to that of deacon in other churches.

Members of the Sons act as mentors to a number of Tallahassee's black youngsters, taking them fishing and on field trips. Occasionally, as many as 100 children at a time participate. Once a month, the group holds a party for all those children who have had birthdays in that period. Every encounter offers the youngsters exposure to a moral presence, to people who are ready to talk about faith and values. It is often the first contact these children have had with such adults, Richardson says. "Some of (the children) have never been to church. It's scary when you think about it."

Richardson's congregation seem confident that they can almost always find him around the church. Indeed, a visitor is prompted to ask if he ever takes time for himself. "Sometimes I don't," he replies. Typically, he gets to the office around 10 in the morning and spends the day attending to church business, counseling people and going to meetings of Bethel committees and community groups. Unless he's got a business appointment, he skips lunch. But he tries to take a brief break in the late afternoon, going to his house around 5 ("just to say I got home"), where he shucks off his shoes for a few minutes before heading back to a round of appointments that usually keep him out until 9.

When he talks about his schedule, Richardson allows that he's been known to give a sermon about the importance of taking care of oneself. The main anecdote features a man who goes to his doctor complaining that he doesn't "feel like much." The doctor examines his patient, then concludes, "You probably don't feel like much." The prescription: a hobby, exercise and vitamins. Richardson says he tries to apply the message to himself. He walks regularly. And he likes listening to music. His tastes are wide-ranging, but he prefers classical. Tchaikovsky and Alexander Borodin are favorites. "So I'm able to chill, as the kids would say, just chill." Occasionally, he'll try to get away for an outing with his teenage son, Trey, maybe going to the movies or bowling. (He also has a daughter, Monique, a student at Florida A&M.) Richardson also enjoys traveling, even if it's on business. After an international Methodist conference in Singapore, he returned to launch a campaign in the summer of 1991 for the rank of A.M.E. bishop, joining an already crowded field for a very limited number of positions that would be filled in voting at the denomination's conference the next year.

Among the openings were some of the church's jurisdictions in Africa, positions that A.M.E. insiders say usually are given to newly-minted bishops. In the past, some have regarded service overseas more as a form of paying dues before coming back to a more desirable position stateside. But the thought of going to Africa appeals to Richardson, who says he's hopeful of tracing his roots. Chronologically, the connection to Africa seems tantalizingly close. It was his great-grandfather who was brought over to the United States as a slave, sold to a plantation in south Georgia. As yet, however, family research hasn't been able to pin down just where he came from. When people ask Richardson if he knows his background, he says that given his height, his ancestors must have been Watusis or Zulus, whose members have a reputation for being tall. At Bethel, Richardson has instituted an "Africa Day" (during February, black history month), during which he has preached wearing a traditional Kinte cloth. And throughout the year, he often cites black biblical characters as a way of offering his congregation role models and emphasizing an African presence in the Bible.

A posting to Africa would also fit in with Richardson's sense that once he understood the meaning of his boyhood dream, he stepped out onto a journey, in which God has repeatedly opened doors to ever-greater opportunities to serve the church. He tells a story about how boyhood self-doubt dissolved into excitement and a feeling of adventure, both bound up with the rock-solid conviction that he was about God's business. "I found myself on a bus one morning going into Winter Haven (in Florida), going to preach to a little youth group." Only 15 years old at the time, he suddenly felt struck with incredulity that he'd have anything meaningful to say to anyone. "You're still a kid," he told himself reproachfully. But the momentary fears quickly ebbed. "And I thought to myself, this is it, this is the beginning of something! You're on a bus going somewhere to preach! And that has not ceased. The bus ride has taken me out of the country and all over the country, preaching and doing seminars and workshops. And I enjoy it. I get such satisfaction out of it."

Paul Gallatin

Submitting to the Mystery

by David Nichols

*The apostolically-minded must know how to
wait, and the priest has often occasion to know
how to accept the sense of being helpless; he
must accept the fact of being nearly always
misunderstood.*

—Henri de Lubac, S.J.
The Splendor of the Church

This happened during the fall of 1971, when Paul Gallatin was
40 years old:

He was driving around Tulsa on the freeway when he
looked off to his right and saw a neighborhood that stirred a
memory. Then he saw a particular house he oddly recognized
as the first house he had ever lived in, the house in which his
early childhood took on its final complexion, which was one of
acute aching for someone fate denied him. Gallatin took the
next exit and wound his way back to the neighborhood, parked
his car at the curb in front of the house, and right there in the
light of day wept for the first time over all that had happened
here when he was six years old.

There was the October day in 1937 when Gallatin's baby
brother Patrick, six months old, had strangled to death in his
crib. That had happened here, yes, but the memory was
blocked, the details, the screams that must have ensued when
his mother awoke from her nap to find her baby dead. And

there was the afternoon six months later when Paul and his younger sister, Mary Catherine, had fallen in step with their mother, Esther, as she walked circles around the dining-room table, screaming. What else was there to do but follow mother? How else to begin to comprehend that death had come again to another bedroom down the hall, his parents' room, and that his father lay dead back there, victim of a streptococcus infection of the blood stream?

The screaming and the circular path around the dining-room table stuck forever, but the rest was obscured, denied a reachable place in memory. The wake for his father had been at home, but the details weren't clear. As a little fellow of six he couldn't have been tall enough to stand on the floor and look into the open casket. Had he stood on a chair and looked in? His mother had thought it a bad idea for Paul and Mary Catherine to attend the funeral (why the wake but *not* the funeral?), so there had been no ritual goodbye, no black priestly vestments, no requiem, no incense and holy water and sweet-smelling flowers, no open grave.

In time he began to wonder: What had his father looked like, and had they played together, and what had been the sound of his voice? Later on came the vague understanding that he was expected to become a priest, that his father would have liked that. Never was there any pressure, but the understanding hung in the air, an inchoate summons from a man whose face and voice he couldn't remember.

Paul became the man of the house as he grew older, bringing order to its community life, filling the void left after his father died. He had interceded for Mary Catherine with his mother and even once had given his mother permission to go on a date with the egg man. What was he to do? She'd *asked* his permission. Only two weeks before he left Tulsa for Arkansas, in late summer 1950, did he finally tell his mother he was going to the seminary. He'd made all the arrangements himself. She'd been wondering about his college plans. But she had never asked, probably fearing her asking might spook what she had hoped would be a vocation to the priesthood.

Here, in this house in front of which Gallatin was now parked and weeping, was where all this had been set in motion. And here he was, finally grieving for the infant Patrick and for their father, whose name was Paul, too. A sacramental moment, this, in the life of one dedicated to sacramentality as a life-giving and -sustaining principle—a perfect and poignant example of matter conveying large truth to human flesh and spirit, the hand of God stirring the ashes of memory and letting the fire breathe again.

"My one regret in life is that I'm not a Jesuit," Gallatin remarked some years later in the presence of his bishop and several brother priests. Whimsically, Gallatin had meant to put across that he admired the Jesuits for being tough, wily, intellectually daunting, loyal to the church but more than smart enough to see its human foibles and point them up. That he could so comfortably and casually place himself in Jesuit company was entirely just if a bit immodest. Rather than responding to this mild display of self-confidence, however, the bishop chose to engage in some whimsy of his own. In response to Gallatin's expression of regret that he was not a Jesuit, the bishop said, "That's my one regret, too." It was (and still is) rare for Gallatin to be the victim of such a dry, well-placed remark, and the bishop's comment afforded the other priests present no end of merriment.

Gallatin has never been a member of the Society of Jesus or any other religious order. He's been a diocesan priest since 1958, in effect a general practitioner who ministers to the rank and file, in his case the 4,800 members of St. Charles Borromeo parish, on Oklahoma City's northwest side. Gallatin is the pastor there, having returned in 1989 to head the parish he served as an associate pastor from 1958 through 1965—his first assignment as a newly ordained priest. Gallatin's job puts him at the sometimes-discomfiting juncture between the ideals of the church and the complications of life as it's lived by many Catholics. And he's a patient, forgiving priest who sees others' troubles as a reflection of his own weakness and pride.

Though his whole life has been spent in Oklahoma, save for his time in seminary in Arkansas, and though he has worked most of his adult life as a parish priest, Gallatin seems every bit the worldly Jesuit. He's well-read, well-spoken, well-traveled, thoroughly fractious, insightful to a fault, and sharp-witted—sometimes cruelly so, by his own admission, though much less so since he quit drinking during the 1980s. Among his fellow priests in the Archdiocese of Oklahoma City, Gallatin has a reputation for being an excellent storyteller and an accomplished mimic. Those who revel in these traits of his maintain an informal list of Gallatin's Greatest Hits and, like late-night callers to radio stations, regularly request this or that "oldie." And, like an indulgent disc jockey, Gallatin usually obliges.

At the age of 60 and a height of five-ten, Gallatin is round-bellied and large-chested, with thick arms and big hands. His hair is brown but graying at the temples, and his crown is bald and resembles a monk's tonsure. He wears bifocals that slightly magnify his eyes, which are blue, bloodshot when he doesn't get enough sleep, but always, always alert, scanning the shelves of his bookcases in search of a quotation perfectly illustrative of a point he's making, and squinting when he watches television, which fascinates and repulses him in roughly equal proportions.

Gallatin's is a mobile face whose expression shifts from severity, to impishness, to bemusement, to impassivity with startling rapidity. His voice is vaguely patrician, deep and resonant. When he speaks, Gallatin always supplies italics; there is never any ambiguity about what he wishes to implant in a listener's consciousness. He has a longtime smoker's huskiness and still smokes two packs of Vantage a day, a habit he refuses to surrender. "I have to have *some* addiction," he says.

The combination of Gallatin's expressions, his sense of humor, his comic timing, and his cultured, often-bemused tone of voice call to mind Jack Benny. As with Benny, Gallatin's persona is finely honed, belying as much as it reveals. It belies, for example, his deep insecurity about loving and being loved, the profound empathy he brings to his work, his deep love of God and his fellow travelers in faith whose need for forgiveness is no greater than his own, and his self-doubt over whether he has been faithful enough to the responsibility he's assumed for others' spiritual growth. "I've always exuded more confidence than I have," he says.

Gallatin is an intense man who often spends evenings slouched in a large, well-padded recliner in the living room of his rectory suite. Even at rest, he radiates energy, much as an idling jet does. The man is forever on the verge of an essay; he thinks and speaks in essays. And not modern essays, either. Gallatin's is not the mild, self-effacing gentility of an E. B. White, but the bold, abrasive stuff of Montaigne, with Montaigne's fondness for classical allusion and seamless discursion. Like Montaigne, Gallatin is a lay intellectual ("lay" in the sense that he's not an academician), one of a breed not bent to the confines of academic specialty but still striving toward synthesis, hoping to die having achieved a small measure of wisdom and having made some sense of the world around them. For Gallatin, however, achieving this for himself is not enough. He is compelled to spread that wisdom and that understanding of the world around—in his sermons, in his responses to penitents during confession, and in his celebration of the other sacraments that mark Catholics' lives from birth to death.

The combination of Gallatin's native gifts and his will to use them on behalf of others is a perfect bent for a clerical general practitioner—a parish priest, who, in Gallatin's phrase, "marries and buries" and tries to help his people apprehend, and act upon, life's deeper rhythms.

The buildings of St. Charles Borremeo parish fill an entire city block at the corner of 50th and Grove streets, comprising a large church, an office building (formerly a convent), a school, a rectory, and several smaller structures. The rectory is a colonial-style two-story house with three living suites for priests, one for a housekeeper, and several guest rooms with baths. Gallatin has a full-time housekeeper, Patty Bieber, 63, who cooks lunch and dinner for him and his associate pastor, Joe Meinhart. She also cleans the rectory, and washes and irons their clothes. Unlike priests' housekeepers in the past, however, Bieber does not live at the rectory but maintains an apartment of her own.

At dinner one Tuesday evening, during early December 1991, Gallatin explained to a visitor that he would conduct a penance service for single parents later that evening. He'd already had a busy day. He had met with two parishioners who wanted their marriages blessed (meaning they were not married in the Catholic Church but now wanted the church to recognize the bond), counseled another parishioner, heard the confessions of a class of fifth graders in his parish school, and taught three sessions of a ninth-grade sexual-morality class at Bishop McGuinness High School.

As he spoke, Gallatin struggled to liberate an erythromycin capsule from its bubble pack. He'd had a cold lately, and a parishioner, a nurse, had suspected his ailment might be bacterial and so had dropped off a sample carton of the antibiotic. In Gallatin's view, the bubble package was not only child-proof but adult-proof as well, and of what possible use could medicine be if one couldn't spring it loose from its packaging? Bieber arrived with salads and, seeing his difficulty, came to his rescue, using her fingernail to slice open the bubble pack. Adept at metaphysics, Gallatin often finds the workings of the commonplace physical world unduly perplexing.

The penance service was the inspiration of his associate pastor, Gallatin said, but had been left to him when Meinhart had been temporarily reassigned to an out-of-town parish whose pastor had suffered a heart attack. The service was an experiment, aimed at reacquainting parishioners with the sacrament of reconciliation—"confession," as most Catholics call it—which has fallen out of favor with many during the last two decades. By focusing on a group with similar life difficulties, Gallatin hoped the service would help these parents experience the mercy and forgiveness of God, which is readily available but which is rarely sought these days—sacramentally, anyway. While many priests bemoan the decline of sacramental confession, in few parishes is something done about it.

"Catholics have lost the language of sin," Gallatin said now. "Part of this is because of New Age liberal priests who tell people, 'Oh, you really didn't *sin*. After all, you were raised in a lower economic situation,' or 'You were abused because you're a woman, and, therefore, what you did wasn't a sin.' But as Christians we have to struggle to see things as Jesus saw them. Jesus says to the sinner, 'Go, and sin no more.' He extends an invitation to *repentance*. He engages neither in denial nor retribution.

"And, too, another aspect of the problem is that Catholics believe their pain can't be encapsulated in the language or the form of confession as they knew it in their youth, so they've sought reconciliation elsewhere—in prayer groups, in the Eucharist, in self-help programs. Their approach is still communal, in the Catholic way, but it has bypassed the mediation of a priest. Anyway," Gallatin said, "we'll see how it goes. I've had no time to prepare. I have no idea what I'll say to them."

What he said to them—a group of about 25, some with children in tow—was this: "There isn't a person here whose dysfunction I don't share. I know what it means to want to be touched, loved. I've made serious mistakes as a result of that need. I know, too, what it means to be used, to have high hopes and to end up just being *used*. You know about that, don't you? You also know what it's like to give and give and give, all day long, day after day, week after week, month after month, and have an inner voice telling you all the while that you're not giving enough."

Heads nodded.

"I know about that, too," Gallatin went on. "My *mother* knew all about that. She had to raise me and my sister alone. And I think you can imagine what a job it must have been raising the likes of *me* without much help!"

People laughed at this.

"Why am I telling you I know about these things? Because forgiveness is why we're gathered here this evening. Yes, we're going to ask God's forgiveness for our sins. But we're also going to ask one another's forgiveness—parents of children, children of parents. We're expressing in one another's company what is so hard, sometimes impossible, to express alone. That's the sacramental principle. That's who and how we are as Catholics."

Gallatin then invited all to come forward to receive absolution for their sins. There was no personal confession, no words spoken on the part of the penitents. Gallatin smiled at each as he or she approached. He laid one hand atop the penitent's head and with the other traced a cross on the person's forehead. Then he recited the prayer of absolution, which ends: "Through the ministry of the church, may God grant you pardon and peace, and I absolve your sins in the name of the Father, the Son, and the Holy Spirit."

Afterward, resting in his recliner in his living room, Gallatin said, "I need the same kinds of things they need. A lot of single parents' troubles are sexual, of course, and it's important that they know I struggle with these things, too. I once relied heavily on alcohol to fill my needs. I've pushed people away because I've been afraid of intimacy and at times hurt people who cared for me. There have been times I've not paid much attention to prayer and made my own agenda and action the priority."

Gallatin spent eight years at St. John Seminary, in Little Rock, Arkansas, completing the obligatory four-year undergraduate degree in philosophy and four years of theology. American seminaries during the 1950s were closeted places, harsh by today's standards. Gallatin was a good student who ran what he calls an "underground seminary" with several other like-minded men who wanted to keep abreast of theological currents not addressed in their formal classes. "We gave lectures to one another," he recalls. This won him no favor with the administration. "I never questioned staying, never considered leaving," he says. "But I hardly ever observed the rules. This leads me to submit that my getting through the seminary certainly underscores the presence of grace in religious vocations."

Gallatin was ordained during the spring of 1958 and assigned to a new parish in Oklahoma City—St. Charles Borremeo, whose pastor was Charles Beckman. Beckman was of Irish descent, typical of pastors of his generation. He was a builder and a maintainer, a good, solid priest of the old school. Beckman and Gallatin were destined to clash, and they did. "He was a bright young man with new visions," John Pitt recalled of young Gallatin. Pitt, is a retired aeronautical engineer and a St. Charles parishioner, served the parish as a deacon. "A lot of people here thought Paul was a wild-eyed liberal because of his homilies on civil rights," Pitt says.

Growing up, Gallatin's exposure to blacks had been limited to the maids who rode to and from work on Tulsa city buses. "I grew up in a Southern environment," he says. "I adopted all the stereotypes normal for the time. Racial epithets, however, were not a part of my vocabulary. We were bigots, but *gracious* bigots. Only during the seminary did the injustice of segregation become horrendous to me, compounded by the utter indifference of my Southern classmates. It was so incongruous to me that anyone who believed in redemption could tolerate this wholesale injustice."

There was another matter, too. Gallatin's father had been sick with rheumatic fever as a child. Family lore had it that his life was saved by a black doctor who had made a house call when other physicians wouldn't cross the threshhold for fear of the disease. "I've always suspected hearing that story as a child had a big effect on me," he says.

As the civil rights movement gathered momentum in the early 1960s, Gallatin and other young diocesan priests participated in marches at home and in the South, including the one at Selma, and helped with voter registration. And they frequently preached on the topic, sometimes alienating older parishioners more with their fervor and redundancy than with the substance of their message. Father Beckman was not pleased with Gallatin's protracted leaves. Laughing, Gallatin recalls that he once told Beckman: " '*Your* conscience at this point is immaterial. *I* alone stand up for the truth.' I think he secretly admired me, though," Gallatin says. "He once said, 'I just could not do all that marching around.' And I had to tell him that the people who marched around really *liked* it. People took pictures of us.

"The sixties were *not* a mistake," he says. "Mistakes *were* made. It was a marvelous and courageous address of abuses. But you cannot live out the war story forever. There's a lost generation in the church made up of the civil rights and anti-war people. Their energy is locked into that period, and they're not able to cope with ordinary times. You can't—you *shouldn't* —spend your life on nostalgia. I don't regret any of that—not the mistakes, not the naivete. In fact, I look upon it fondly. I have no desire to repeat it, no desire to relive it. But I love to see young people being imprudent. Youth is when one should do that. That's how young people learn. That's why I get a kick out of young priests, even though I'm hard on them. The church is very comfortable with people who are brash and immature, because it has a belief in growth."

Gallatin sees himself as a recipient of that transforming grace. "Oh, I was really cute," he says of himself as a young priest. After the Second Vatican Council, "I did shocking things, jarring the pants off old ladies. I went around knocking the heads off every statue I could find, purging the church of bad art and distracting images." And yet Gallatin recently installed a statue of the Blessed Virgin Mary on the wall of his church. Why? "What I didn't realize when I was bashing statues was that Catholicism *has* to have some of that affective dimension," he says. "The Church after the council was so cerebral that the affective dimension was lost—with the help of the likes of me! We treated Christ as an intellectual treatise, and virtually ignored Mary and the saints, who are part of our tradition for good reasons. I've discovered that the faith of the people will always erupt in ways they can manage. And that includes *my* faith as well."

Today, Gallatin still preaches against injustice, still participates in an occasional protest, including one at the Oklahoma State Prison during 1990. The state was getting set to execute a prisoner, and Gallatin is vehemently opposed to the death penalty. But, "Paul has far less need to play to the crowd these days than he once did," says his friend Marty Morgan, pastor of St. Thomas More parish, in Tulsa. Gallatin agrees. "We took ourselves too seriously, took *everything* too seriously," he says. "The movement of the sixties lacked levity, humor. I laugh a lot more now. I finally learned that righteous indignation isn't Christian."

Gallatin's Wednesday schedule was lighter than Tuesday's. He celebrated Mass for the school children at 9:30 and had two counseling appointments during the afternoon, followed by a late-afternoon meeting with a woman who wanted her marriage blessed. Gallatin spends a lot of his time counseling people, parishioners and others, including some non-Catholics. "Most people come because they're in a failing marriage, or they feel estranged from God, or because they're clinically ill and need a referral to a doctor," he says. "Many are confused and have no one to talk with. They come because they believe the priest will understand."

Gallatin announced at dinner that evening that he wanted to see a movie. *Black Robe*, about a French Jesuit in colonial Canada, had been playing in town for nearly a week now, and Gallatin assumed it would soon be yanked in favor of a more popular picture. He asked Patty Bieber to look up the showing times in the newspaper as he ate. Bieber reported there were 7:30 and 9 p.m. showings, and Gallatin opted for the earlier of the two. When Gallatin had finished his meal, Bieber stepped into the dining room offering cheesecake or peppermint yogurt for dessert. Gallatin's guest requested the yogurt, but Gallatin resisted moderation and ordered up a large piece of cheesecake. "There has to be *some* compensation for celibacy," he remarked.

The Catholic Church requires that its priests remain celibate (which means unmarried), and the gospel demands that all Christians be chaste, as well—which for a single person means sexually abstinent. Clerical celibacy is not a matter of Catholic doctrine or dogma; it's a practice, a discipline, that came into force for parish priests during the fourth century. Few matters are more hotly debated within the church in the United States these days.

"My mother says celibacy is divinely inspired because it spared some woman *me!*" Gallatin said when asked about his own celibate life. He laughed as he said this, and so did Bieber, from the kitchen. Gallatin stared at the kitchen door, his face the picture of mock severity. "I personally have never believed this state of life is simply some sociological phenomenon in the church," Gallatin said. "I've never seen celibacy as a purely human invention. It is within God's plan for redeeming his people. But, the will of God changes. The church could say that tomorrow we live another gift, and I would have not a minute's problem with that. I *do* think, however, that it would be a tragedy to lose that potent element in priesthood.

"The greatest single pain of celibacy is not having a son or daughter," Gallatin said. He told a story to illustrate this. One autumn when he was in his early thirties, six or seven years ordained, he and some priest friends took a vacation in Maine. They rented a cabin near Bar Harbor. One night, after sleeping fitfully, he got up at dawn and walked along the seashore. It was a cool, crisp morning, and Gallatin was overwhelmed with the natural beauty that surrounded him: the sea, the surf, the sun making its way up the sky. He walked into town and window-shopped. "In one window there was a beautiful blue sailboat, the kind children play with. My first thought was: 'I'll buy that boat and give it to my son.' Then: 'I don't have a son and never will.' I was overwhelmed with sadness, then anger. 'This is obscene,' I thought. 'Any system that would thwart that sharing in creation knows nothing of God! *Nothing!*'"

"Twenty-nine minutes till movie time," Bieber said from the kitchen. Gallatin nodded, in an abstracted way.

"This became a big problem for me," he continued. "Over the next year and a half, I wrestled with this. I concluded—and I believe my conclusion was graced—that *every* human being is called to be generative, that participating in God's life is not just having children; it's being a giver of life. As a celibate male, I could not avoid that call to oneness with the other. Most people achieve that in a singular and coital way. The celibate does so in a non-genital way. The only justification for that is to witness that the genital neither makes nor blocks true intimacy. Celibacy is a witness to non-genital love, a witness that intimacy is possible. That became the model of my priesthood. I had to give the people whatever was in me. I couldn't hide, no matter how exposed or vulnerable I felt.

"But I mourn the loss of that part of life," he said. "I mourn not having children, and there are times I think I'd love to share my life with a woman. (I don't mourn not going to bed with a woman. As a younger man I did, yes.) When I see families, I fantasize, not jealously or wistfully: What would it have been like? How would I have been with my children? The fear is that I would not have achieved intimacy, that I would have been so pedantic with my children I'd have driven them from me."

"*Twenty* minutes," Bieber said.

"Patty, okay," Gallatin said, laughing. "I already have one mother, and I didn't choose to have a *wife*."

Bieber laughed.

"Life is very existential," Gallatin said now. "It has meaning only to the extent that it's *experienced*. Fantasies impute false meaning to existence. I never have fantasies in which my son says, 'Get off my back, you bore.' No, in my fantasies he thinks every morsel that drops from my lips is honeyed with profundity. Fantasy is the ultimate escape. Reality's always better than we think. On the whole, I think I was *called* to be a celibate, and for the most part I receive the gift of celibacy gratefully. But the call is an ongoing process, and it's my conviction that anyone who lives out the gift of celibacy lives in a state of grace.

"Now, whether the church would be enhanced by a married priesthood is an entirely different question," he added. "I think we must first have a genuinely celibate clergy before we can have a genuinely married one. And by that I mean that as celibates we must not live as if we're simply called to be faithful to a promise, but as if we're called to find joy—to know ecstasy through Christ. But we haven't been very courageous in explaining this, and sometimes not courageous in living it. Too many priests see celibacy as a white-knuckled denial of their sexuality."

A couple of minutes later, dressed in black clerical pants, a white shirt and black sweater, Gallatin left for the movie.

The last quarter century has been a tough time in which to be a priest in the United States. Since the mid-1960s, when the Second Vatican Council ended, the priesthood in this country has been plagued with generational polarity, confusion over its role in the church, and, most recently, sex scandals, all duly reported upon in the news media. Perhaps most difficult to endure has been the steady hemorrhage of priests from clerical life. Since 1966, resignations among priests have been legion. Of the nine men from Gallatin's diocese who graduated with him from St. John Seminary, only three remain active priests. Of the others, one is dead, and five resigned from the priesthood.

Confusion among the clergy, however, is symptomatic of malaise in the church at large, as Catholicism struggles to be prophetic in an increasingly secular society whose values it often opposes. While he has had his share of troubles over the years, Gallatin, now serving in his fifth pastorate, has arrived at late middle age with a perspective well-suited to the problems the church is facing in this country. The more unclear things become, the harder Gallatin strives for clarity. He is concerned with orthodoxy and tradition because in both he sees lucidity that could go far toward ordering human experience at a time when disorder has seized the day. Gallatin admires the precision of Catholic doctrine and social teaching and suspects that few of the faithful, clergy included, understand and appreciate it. He believes this owes in part to the failure of the American bishops to regularly preach at the parish level. "Bishops are the primary pastors of the church," he says. "The crying need is for *vision* from the men who lead us, but we don't hear from them. Why? The *Pope* isn't too busy to preach."

Catholicism has as much to offer today as it ever has, Gallatin says, and perhaps more. The clarity of its teaching, its emphasis on the dignity of human life, and its communal, sacramental approach to high mystery are valuable in a culture oriented more toward death and destruction than toward life and redemption. Gallatin sees much of American popular culture as debased and debasing, reflective of a purely material understanding of reality, a view that he believes is as debilitating as it is irrational.

Gallatin sees television as a barometer of the nation's thinking, particularly daytime talk shows, which he tunes in as often as he can. "Those shows amount to truth derived from the emotions of an uninformed audience," he says. "Their hosts are the great apostles of feelings. Look at them closely. Their forum is demagogic, a masquerade of 'openness.' Rarely does one hear from them or their guests language that conveys disapproval. Never is truth the primary object. The primary object is *consensus*. Therefore, all language is aimed at consensus, not truth. As a priest, I, too, perform and manipulate and cajole, but I genuinely believe in God and genuinely hope I speak in his name to my people. But who do the great electronic social arbiters of our society—Oprah, Sallye, Geraldo, Phil—believe in? What roots them in something beyond themselves incarnate in their own technology? We don't know. They don't *tell* the audience what or who they believe in, and they have no creed."

All this notwithstanding, Gallatin encourages his parishioners to maintain the dual vision of a faith that allows the believer to comprehend that what is seen is no more real than what is unseen, and that reality (including Christianity's present suffering) reflects the will of God. He's a hopeful man. "The Spirit will bring order out of chaos," he says. For now, though, he's doing his part by helping his parishioners see that tradition is not something fusty and static but vibrant and alive, its face changing with the times but never the truths it represents. Gallatin sees himself as truly traditional in that he strives to cast Christian verities in contemporary terms—reincarnating, as it were, the truth for contemporary believers without compromising that truth. To this end, he has borrowed liberally from the best of the social sciences (particularly from pychiatrist Carl Jung) without adopting their "impoverished secularity."

In his dealings with young priests who serve as his associate pastors and with seminarians who spend an internship year working in his parish, Gallatin is firm, every bit the teacher and wizened veteran. "Spending a year with Paul was the best schooling I ever had," says Jack Feehily, 50, pastor of St. Philip Neri in Midwest City, which adjoins Oklahoma City. "He would tell me, 'You're not my peer; you are a *disciple*.' I thought that was harsh then, but now I see the profound truth in what he said."

Gallatin sharpens young priests' and seminarians' thinking skills, suggests books they might read to compensate for what he considers the softness of their seminary educations. He is concerned that they have been taught to value emotion over intellect and speculative theology over a thorough grounding in traditional Catholic thought. And he urges them to retain their original enthusiasm for their vocation. "No one, I *hope*, ever becomes a priest because he wants to run a parish," Gallatin says. "The institutional dimensions of the parish priesthood are hardly worthy of the vocation to it. You can get trapped in bingo and lose the prophetic dimension. The priest must constantly ask himself: Am I investing myself in something genuinely redemptive?"

Gallatin's work has not gone unnoticed. He received the 1991 National Federation of Priests Councils' president's award because, as the citation puts it, "his leadership enhances the ministry of others and his words and deeds support the life and ministry of priests: thus he is, as it were, a 'touchstone' for genuine, quality priesthood." His friends agree. "Paul has always been a force to be reckoned with in the life of the priesthood in Oklahoma," says Feehily. "He's always been concerned with a voice for priests." Marty Morgan says, "Priests feel at home with Paul and confide in him about their problems."

Gallatin is proud of the award and displays it on the wall of his office. He knows how unusual it is for a parish priest to receive a national honor, to be pointed out among his peers as exemplary. But as a recovering alcoholic who keeps his "shadow side" in plain view, he believes evil can find especially fertile ground in those who preach the word of God to others—

particularly, perhaps, in those who do this well, as he does. In an age that lusts after "empowerment," Gallatin continually reminds himself that the will to power is the very source of man's fall, that all power is God's, and that any power we exercise is a share in his and is to be wielded according to his will.

Gallatin is conscious of his gifts, conscious to the point of suffering fits of scrupulosity about his real motives as a priest. Does he preach and otherwise minister to point his parishioners toward God, or is his impassioned erudition so much self-display? "The terror of his life is that he might have misled people through his own hubris," Feehily says.

Gallatin began his day Thursday by hearing the confessions of another group of fifth graders from the school. He was late for a staff meeting that morning because the confessions had taken longer than he'd thought they would. ("They're so charming at this age," he said of the students.) Then a priest friend had called saying he needed to talk and asking to have lunch, and Gallatin agreed, forgetting, in his haste, to phone Bieber to tell her he wouldn't be around for the noon meal. Following lunch, Gallatin counseled a parishioner, a woman, for an hour and had a free hour before his next appointment to tend to office work.

Gallatin's second counseling session that afternoon was with a retired air-traffic controller who, a year earlier, had begun spitting up blood. The day after Christmas 1990, this man had undergone exploratory surgery, and his doctors discovered inoperable cancer in his lungs. It was then that he had phoned the church office and requested an appointment with his pastor. "As much as I hoped for a cure, something told me I needed to get closer to my maker," he commented after his meeting with Gallatin.

"I felt I could turn to Father Gallatin after listening to his Sunday sermons. I retained a lot of garbage from the pre-Vatican II years, when religion was a lot harsher. My sense of self-worth was not good, and I didn't feel worthy of God. Father Gallatin has pointed out to me a lot of the good things I've done in my life, and he's explained that maybe my expectations were higher than God's. It's been a very good experience, speaking with him. When you can think better about yourself, when your religious leader says you're not so bad, then you can expect a pretty good reception from God. Father Gallatin is the first priest who's ever known my first name, not just my collection-envelope number. He's indicated great concern for me as a person—and I trust him."

Thursday evening, Gallatin gave a lecture on sacramentality to the parish's RCIA group of about 30 men and women who meet weekly in a large room in the parish office building. RCIA stands for Rite of Christian Initiation for Adults; it's the process by which non-Catholics become Catholics. Though pastors and their associates usually teach segments of the course, it's mostly handled by lay people. Because Oklahoma is an overwhelmingly Protestant state, with Catholics making up a mere four-and-a-half percent of the population (there are only 80,000 Catholics in the Archdiocese of Oklahoma City), and because most of those Protestants are evangelicals or fundamentalists, a thoroughgoing explanation of how Catholics worship is vital to these would-be converts. A great many Protestants express both wonderment and discomfort with Catholics' use of crucifixes, statues, rosaries, and other so-called sacramentals. Charges of idolatry flung at Catholics are as old as the Reformation and every bit as enduring.

"Sacramentality," Gallatin began, "is a viewpoint unique to Catholics. If you had to draw a line, this is it. The vision of the evangelical is radically verbalist, radically spiritualist, and radically *disembodied.*" He stretched the word out: *dis-em-bod-ied.* "We Catholics believe that which is material is the bearer of the truly spiritual, that eternity manifests itself in the physical. The physical reality of life is the way God speaks to us. We're at ease with *things* because we believe God uses all things to approach us. There's ample evidence around us that this is true. There's no image in your minds or mine that did not come to us by way of that which we can taste, touch, see, hear, and so on. There's a driving need within us to reveal ourselves to the other, and we have to use *things* to do that. We look for things that will carry our spirit to the other. God does likewise with us.

"Was Jesus comfortable this way? Yes. One of the first things Jesus does is get baptized with water. He struggles at healing people. He breathes on them, touches them, groans, as

Mark says, with the healing. Jesus uses things, common things —water, wine, food—to communicate his message. Catholics do the same. We set aside some things for sacred purposes. We call these sacramentals. With its deep sense of the created, Catholicism makes no attempt to escape the physical, the mundane, the ordinary. This is a very earthy church, a community of common people, not a community of scholars. We're uncomfortable in places that don't use ritual. When I go to a Protestant funeral, for example, I never know when it's over. It seems sterile to me. Here's grandma's body, and I keep thinking we should *do* something with it: sprinkle holy water on it, incense it, bless it, touch it. It doesn't seem right to ignore the body."

Gallatin: "When I used to drink, I had all these rules for drinking: *I* was in control. I eventually had to face that I was dependent. Several priest friends made an appointment with me to tell me I was an alcoholic. 'I agree with that,' I told them, 'but I don't know what to do with it.' I was paranoid, withdrawn, depressed, caught up in fantasy, wanting to avoid responsibility. I was also insecure. I didn't know if I was bright or not, or articulate or funny, or whether I could pray. The illusion for me was that if I took booze away, *I* wouldn't be there.

"The bishop sent me to St. Luke's Hospital, in Maryland, where they confirmed that I was indeed dependent upon alcohol. On the plane home, I felt dead. I didn't drink anymore, but I continued to feel utterly and absolutely dead. Three months later I went into treatment and spent 90 days at Guest House, near Detroit. I liked it. The treatment was built around the reconstruction of your value system, becoming familiar with a new way of life. I needed that time to look at myself.

"I discovered that I had been selling my soul on the installment plan for laughs and attention. People had encouraged me to drink because I was so funny—and very cruel to those in my presence. I'd generally isolate my victim and key in on some fragile part of him, and in him I would engender hurt, confusion, resentment, and fear. The payoff? If you're clever and bright and witty, people enjoy you; they all laugh, except the person being screwed to the wall. Facing this evil about myself was real liberation. The big sin I had, and which I still struggle with, is pride. I longed to eat from the tree of good and evil.

"When I returned home from Guest House, my people were very accepting of me. That permitted me to take away my crutch for long enough to see that I could walk. I was and am grateful to them for this. The people in my present parish think I'm a good man and a good priest, and that's not an inaccurate assumption. I'm not intentionally pinning anyone to the wall anymore. Ninety percent of the time, I don't pick on the fragile. I'm not a frightened, cruel person anymore. But there's a shadow side they don't see, a tendency toward evil that draws me (and this is true of all of us) to my own resources, would have me believe that what's good in me is not grace but my own: the will to power, something I know all about. If I'm to know God, I *must* know my shadow. Otherwise I could be lost.

"The dark part of us terrifies us, but we shouldn't be afraid of it. It cannot destroy us. It will be separated from us at the harvest. Living facing it will empower God to redeem it and lift us out. I've learned that it's important to look with compassion on your shadow side because that's where you see God. Evil is that reality out there that would blind you to your shadow, wanting you *not* to know God or his love. And you only know evil when you know God. When you *don't* know God, evil comes masked as something else. And that's dangerous—very dangerous, indeed."

Don Wolf, 36, is pastor of Holy Angels, an inner-city Hispanic parish in Oklahoma City. He served as an associate pastor under Gallatin at Enid, Oklahoma, from 1984 through 1986, and has been a member of Gallatin's priest support group since his ordination in 1981. Wolf says Gallatin has taught him a lot about being a priest. "Paul's passions are uncontrolled," he says. "He drank too much, he smokes too much, he eats too much. But St. John of the Cross says that in the evening of our lives the only measure will be the measure of love. I see Paul as a man who has loved with fervor. Yes, he's a man of excesses. But we Catholics fervently believe that's the raw material of sanctity. If we were all modulated, there'd be nothing to be saved from."

On Friday morning, Gallatin drove a mile and a half to Putnam City Convalescent Home to celebrate Mass. He took with him his Mass kit—a chalice, unconsecrated communion hosts, cruets of water and wine, and a small crucifix mounted on a table stand—his vestments, and a lectionary, which contains scriptural readings for Mass and other liturgies. The comingling odors of urine, disinfectant, and recently warmed pastry greeted him at the front door. "The father's here," a man in a wheelchair said as Gallatin walked by.

A group of patients, mostly women, and a sprinkling of family visitors were waiting for him in a room off the main hallway. Gallatin greeted all warmly, in a loud, jocular voice. A small, round table with a pocked surface and a chipped circumference sat in a corner just far enough from the wall for Gallatin to be able to stand behind it. This would serve as the altar. As he spread the contents of his Mass kit on the table, Gallatin bantered with several patients and they with him, but he made eye contact mostly with the silent ones. One woman sat in her wheelchair near the altar, holding a life-size stuffed cat. She had a pleasant though blank expression and the translucent skin of the very old. Gallatin looked closely at the cat, so real did it seem. He smiled at the old woman and she smiled back. "Did you once have a kitty, hon?" he asked, and she nodded 'yes'.

Just before Gallatin began Mass, a woman with a Boston accent spoke. "Father," she said, "don't you think it would be nice if Peter Jennings took a vacation and the Lord gave the news?"

This question sent Gallatin into fits of snorting laughter. He was momentarily at a loss for words, a novelty for him. "Well," Gallatin said, "we know this much: the Lord would tell the truth. Pretty soon we'd want Peter Jennings *back*." His remark met with a vigorous nodding of heads.

Again the woman spoke, "You know, Father," she said, "the longer you're in here"—she made a sweeping gesture, indicating the nursing home—"the more you believe in God."

"Then let's pray to God," Gallatin said. He began, "In the name of the Father, and of the Son, and of the Holy Spirit." And those who could replied "Amen."

During his sermon, Gallatin said, referring to the release of the last American hostage in Lebanon, "Terry Anderson came home this week after all those years of being locked up. But we must pray for those who are locked up but don't know it. *You* may feel locked up sometimes, away from the world, perhaps lonely. You're retired, but you can't retire from *faith*. You must remember: you can do more for the world right here, in this place, with your prayers, than all the presidents and congressmen combined can do."

"The Lord has no hands on earth but ours," said the woman with the Boston accent.

"That's right," Gallatin said. "That's *exactly* right."

That afternoon, Gallatin worked in his office and later met with a man who wanted to marry at St. Charles. He also made an emergency trip to the hospital, to anoint a dying parishioner.

On Saturday, Gallatin celebrated an early Mass, witnessed three marriages, heard confessions, attended a Christmas banquet for senior parishioners in the parish hall, and finally got away for dinner at a Chinese restaurant at 9:15 p.m. He went to bed shortly after 11. Sunday marked the start of the second week of Advent. The gospel for the day was from Luke and centered on John the Baptist's ministry in advance of Jesus' public ministry, as John proclaimed "a baptism of repentance for the forgiveness of sins." Gallatin prepares all week for his weekend preaching, but he makes no notes. Even so, his delivery is smooth, his sentences complete, thoroughly grammatical, and altogether nicely turned. He moves about as he speaks and looks directly into people's faces.

This Sunday's sermon, which he delivered three times, ended with these words: "All life is a preparation for redemption. Each life is grasped and understood. Each of our paths can be made straight. There *is* a relationship between all the events of our lives. Do not despair or think any one event on your journey cancels out your value or that God does not see your life as prophetic for the Kingdom. We are firmly set in the matrix of history, like John the Baptizer and Jesus—the one John proclaimed."

Exhausted, Gallatin retreated to his suite after his last Mass, obviously wanting to be alone. He watched the Cowboys and the Saints play football on TV for a half hour, then emerged refreshed and ready for a late breakfast, after which he would drive to Tulsa to visit with his mother, his sister, and his friend Marty Morgan. "Preaching is a very strange experience," he said. "You cannot preach what you have not prayed. You know at times that God uses you. You could never come up with this otherwise, nor could you ever repeat it. I feel naked. I hold back nothing at all."

Driving down Council Street toward a restaurant he favors for Sunday breakfast, Gallatin said, "I'm often embarrassed when I preach because I get lost in it, so caught up. I let the people see my passion, my own encounter with the gospel. It has to *cost* you. If it does not, it's simply exploitation of them *and* you. The haunting reality for the preacher is falling in love with himself. I know I can play a group; I know I can manipulate God's word. I want my people to know the Lord, I really do. But it's dangerous ground. It makes me nervous. I also know how bullshitty I can be. I could go in to church and read from the telephone book and get a good response. I've practically done that at times." He paused. "I was so *empty*," he said, "and I didn't want them to see that. So I would blow and go, blow and go—and it was shit. I don't do that much anymore."

Is Gallatin ever seized with religious doubt?

"My life is not an even, continual line of unremitting devotion," he said. "Nobody goes around with certitude as a constant companion. There are moments of uncertainty in every life: what does all this *mean*? But if as a priest you hide your uncertainty, you fake what you're doing. And I don't think you can lie for very long. It really gets complicated when you're lying. It's a real mess. Plus, if you fake it, you lose it. So I tell people I'm not sure about this or that. I'm empty. What sustains me is the faith that faith is there. I am willing to submit my energy, my intelligence, my very *being* to the mystery. But sometimes the strain on me is such that all I'm left with is a cry of anguish, an appeal to Another beyond all evidence."

At the Village Inn, on Northwest Highway, Gallatin waited 10 minutes for someone to notice he was there. Finally, the hostess appeared. He said, "Party of two, smoking—tables for which are clearly in view and empty. So why are we waiting?" He said this dryly but charmingly, and the hostess immediately steered him to a table.

In Summary

The fractious and fragile American nation is constructed on a series of small communities. Churches and synagogues, ministered to by clergy who understand the yearnings of Americans, are important building blocks in the archipelago of smaller communities. Attempts to build community, however, often are countered by the strong streak of individualism that is cultivated in the American character. There is a constant tension in the United States between community and individualism.

This distinctive aspect of the American character, a vestige of a nation that seemed to have an endless frontier, sets the United States apart from other countries. More than people in European countries, for instance, Americans maintain that hard work can be a guarantee of success and that people have control over the forces that determine personal success. And, in keeping with this attitude, Americans—to a far greater degree than Europeans—reject the idea that it is the responsibility of government to take care of very poor people who can't take care of themselves.[1]

Robert Bellah and his associates, in their influential books, have written of the limits of individualism and the need for a sense of community.[2] Yet, the American experience, or at least the fictive notion of that experience, has glorified the person, standing alone, who by dint of personal industry pulls himself up by the bootstraps and prevails. This vision helped drive the "Me" generation of the 1970s and culminated in the greed of the 1980s, an era that seemed to be symbolized by the message of "I've got mine and you'll have to worry about yourself." Such a philosophy underpins the marketplace and is the sine qua non of the belief that society is perfected as a result of each entity striving, separately, to prevail. Isn't that what industrialist Charlie Wilson apparently had in mind when he declared during the 1950s: "What's good for General Motors is good for the country!"?

But the selfishness of those who fed at America's trough of riches during the 1980s surely demonstrated that "rugged individualism" has its limits and can, in its most egregious form, be downright harmful to the country. It can mean the breakdown of community, which surely is one of the maladies that afflicts the United States today. The nation has reaped the whirlwind: Don't build the shelter for the homeless in my backyard. Don't tax me to educate poor black kids. The elderly aren't my problem. I can't be concerned about the unemployed middle-class because I have my own job to worry about.

How can the flame of community be rekindled? Where are the connections to be made? Religious congregations can potentially contribute much to these efforts to make caring possible. They can be places in which people learn to go outside themselves and sacrifice in behalf of others. They can be places, in other words, where individualism is tempered and the sense of oneness that any society needs in order to prosper can be fostered. The 1990s, more than any other era since the Depression and World War II, might be a time when Americans come to feel that they are afloat on the same sea.

It remains to be seen whether those entering the clergy today are up to the challenge. What is notable about newer members of the clergy is the extent to which they differ from their counterparts of years past. Joseph P. O'Neill, who has sifted through mountains of statistics on seminary enrollments, says that the changes in the composition of the clergy have been greater in the last two decades than in the previous two centuries.[3] In the future, the diversity among those who become exemplars will be greater if only because women and members of minority groups have gained easier access to positions from which they can be seen as sources of inspiration. The clergy, as much as any career, is characterized by an expansion of opportunities.

Increasingly, too, moral exemplars in the American clergy are apt to be drawn from non-Western traditions. Islam, Buddhism and Hinduism are all growing in the United States as the composition of the population changes. Furthermore, black clergy are more likely to be selected for posts with predominantly white congregations than they were in former years. In 1991, for instance, a black pastor was tapped as conference minister and president of the Massachusetts Conference of the United Church of Christ, which traces its origin to New England's Puritan founders.[4] As a bishop in the Roman Catholic Church, John Ricard appears to have been a forerunner.

The growing role of women in the clergy presents perhaps the most marked change. Women, of course, have not been absent from the sweep of religious history. They have simply been underrepresented in the ranks of official leadership and often not given due credit for their achievements. Even in holy writings there was Judith, a military leader of the Israelites. And Joan of Arc, another woman, found glory on the field of combat and reached sainthood. In our own country, the Congregationalists and the Disciples of Christ were ordaining women in the 19th century. In this last decade of the 20th century, the ordination of women into the Protestant and Jewish clergy is growing commonplace.

The number of women studying for ordination in American seminaries allied with the Association of Theological Schools increased five-fold during the 15 years from 1972 through 1987, bringing their representation to almost one in three candidates.[5] The women profiled in this book are products of that change. Jane Shields, for example, was in her junior year of college before the barriers were removed for her to be able to pursue an ambition dating back to her childhood to become a Lutheran pastor.

Certainly there are profound implications for organized religion in such trends. One must recognize, above all, that the potential of the clergy in the future to provide moral leadership and to serve as an inspirational force for the making of community will be very much shaped by a female perspective. The ways that congregants regard women and the manner in which women in the pulpit project their roles will become crucial to the nation's religious experience and to the extent to which new clergymembers become role models for aspiring seminarians.

A pertinent question therefore is whether the feminization of the clergy will have the effect that it has had on professions that have come to be made up preponderantly of women. Nursing, teaching and social work, for example, are less prominent and less influential fields than they might have been if they were not seen as "women's careers." It is interesting to note in this regard the higher prestige of physicians in the United States than in the republics of the former Soviet Union, where women are the majority of doctors. What is in store for an American clergy in which women may come to predominate or at least achieve parity?

Already it is clear that as women have been entering seminaries in larger numbers, men have been less likely to enroll. That so many seminaries continue to maintain their student rolls is owed principally to the availability of women to replace the men who have been lost. A glimpse at what might have happened in all denominations if women had not taken up the enrollment slack is seen in Roman Catholic seminaries, where enrollments have been sliced in half as women have not been given the chance to fill the slots vacated by men. Paul Gallatin's reflection on celibacy illustrates a major problem of the modern priesthood. Protestant denominations, on the other hand, tend to have more graduates each year than there are positions to fill. There are now twice as many Episcopal clergy as there are parishes.[6]

Yet, Protestant and Jewish denominations that ordain women have been slow to reflect the gender shift in the way that they staff their pulpits. Big congregations are reluctant to hire female clergymembers as their heads. Rachel Cowan, for instance, entered the foundation world rather than leave New York City, as she probably would have had to do to find a position heading a congregation. A benign explanation has to do with the fact that female candidates for these positions tend to have less experience in the clergy than male competitors since most women were ordained more recently. But the impact of sexism cannot be discounted in a profession in which almost all the role models were until recently men. Carol Anderson believes that as women in the clergy get the chance to demonstrate their gifts and skills more of them will prevail, despite sexism.

The black church represents a special case because the advent of female clergy to the head of congregations has been particularly slow and filled with trauma. C. Eric Lincoln and Lawrence H. Mamiya cite an inherent contradiction in this regard:

"Both historical and contemporary evidence underscore the fact that black churches could scarcely have survived without the active support of black women, but in spite of their importance in the life of the church, the offices of preacher and pastor. . . remain a male preserve."[7]

Changes in the clergy of all denominations can be resisted for only so long. Some of the facts about the women who are arriving in the seminaries in ever larger numbers attest to their potential for making breakthroughs. For one thing, they are smarter than the men—at least if undergraduate marks and scores on the Graduate Record Examination mean anything.[8] They also are more apt to come from families in which the parents are better educated.[9] There is growing reason to suspect that increasingly the academic credentials of female candidates for appointments to congregations will be stronger than those of the men and that they may be occupying ever more visible pulpits. In other words, if the clergy is going to produce exemplars and role models in the future the chances are growing that women will be prominent among them.

When it comes to academic accomplishments, however, it must be noted that seminaries generally are not drawing the very best students, be they men or women. The situation is a far cry from that which prevailed a century ago, when many of the leading students at the most prestigious colleges were headed for ordination and a disproportionate number of the professors who taught them in liberal arts disciplines were themselves men of the cloth.

Now, prospective master of divinity students trail by far in their Graduate Record Examination scores those who propose to do graduate work in such fields as philosophy, comparative literature, linguistics and clinical psychology, surpassing only those who are headed for graduate studies in such fields as nursing, education, social work and guidance.[10] The academic quality of male candidates for divinity degrees has declined sharply and it is only because of the new female candidates that over-all scores have remained as high as they are. And, of course, even today, there continue to be large numbers of clergymembers in some denominations who have little or no formal education beyond high school. The modest educational credentials of an E. Eugene Meador and the thousands like him, for instance, pose questions about the connection between higher education and the role of clergy of the future.

A characteristic of the new era of seminarians that is problematic has to do with the life experience that they bring to ordination. In the 1990s, the backgrounds of the men and women attracted to pulpits may uncomfortably resemble, to an increasing extent, the people for whom they are supposed to set examples. Many Americans may be made uneasy when they see an image of themselves reflected in the clergy. Two of every five new members of the clergy, including both men and women, have spent at least 10 years in a previous career.[11] These are no innocent babes. The women, in particular, are older than seminarians of the past and more likely to be divorced and single parents, as well.[12]

Will possessing more experience in the ways of the world make clergymembers, men and women, people with whom congregants can more readily identify? Or does becoming an exemplar depend on having a perceived level of purity that sets the pastor apart from the flock? Somehow, through the centuries, the nation has clung to the Cotton Mather version of religiosity for its clergy, nurturing the image of pastors whose ostensible devotion to goodliness and Godliness knows no bounds.

Regarded from a sanguine perspective, the fact that the shepherds will more closely resemble the flock could be a feature that makes them more "real." Certainly those of the new generation of clergymembers are more apt to bear the mark of human experience than the graduates of cloistered seminaries of the past. Jeb Stuart Magruder's odyssey, as described on these pages, exemplifies—in ways more public than most—the degree to which people may be coming to the ranks of the clergy bearing the weight of transgression. His example in seeking to atone and find redemption is worth observing in an era in which clergymembers generally are more worldly, in ways both good and bad. In New York City, there was the recent example of the Unitarian congregation on the posh Upper East Side that had to decide whether to retain as its pastor a man who left his marriage for the affections of the wife of a parishioner.

It may turn out that despite their blemishes—and perhaps even because of them—exemplars of the 1990s are able to lift the collective communal vision of those around them and, as well, evince a faithfulness to larger truths. This may be, for instance, why Martin Luther King, Jr. and John F. Kennedy remain as sources of inspiration to many Americans in spite of shortcomings in their personal lives.

"Wanderers" and "searchers" are what some of these older, more experienced candidates for the ministry are called by social scientists who study them. They bring with them a deeper experience in the public sphere than those who enter the seminary directly from college. They have had a chance to test their ideals in the cauldron of reality. People increasingly accept as their clergy those whose experiences and circumstances resemble their own. An 87-year-old woman who had made her career as a college professor and psychotherapist was ordained in the Episcopal Church not long ago to minister to those in whose midst she resided: the residents of a retirement home.[13]

This transition to a different sort of clergy is occurring at a time when the clerical estate itself has lost some of its aegis. The controversies that swirl around a more vulnerable clergy have served to yank them into a modern, sometimes contentious arena. Episcopalians, Disciples of Christ and other denominations have argued over whether to ordain professing homosexuals. The Evangelical Lutheran Church has struggled to define its position on abortion. Presbyterians debated the merits of a code of sexual conduct. The ranks of Southern Baptists have been riven by their different interpretations of the literalness of the Bible. Catholics have been under mounting pressure to accept a married clergy. Jews have been divided over the authenticity of patrilineal descent. The pain of a Paul Duke attests to the tribulations brought on by such divisions.

Disagreements involving the clergy have been extended to include such vital issues as euthanasia, genetic engineering and even the environment. The issues may change, but members of the clergy who take stands must continue to be ready to be the targets of the slings and arrows of outrageous misfortune. As the careers of Colbert Cartwright and James Reed demonstrate, clergy who speak out in behalf of principle have long had to contend with brickbats.

There is a very real question of whether America is willing to listen to what the clergy have to say about secular issues. A Richard Manzelmann all too often had to wrap his protestations in the guise of an avuncular oddball in order for his congregants to tolerate his digressions into the secular. People are prepared to compartmentalize the teaching of religion, as if there were no connection to everyday life. Adding to the tendency to exclude the opinions of the clergy is the competition of other—secular—voices on moral matters. Professional ethicists, elected officials, scientists and even movie stars are looked to for pronouncements on a whole range of issues. Amid the cacophony, the quiet voice of religion may not be loud enough to be heard. In order for religion to compete and to overcome this separation, Ronald F. Thiemann proposes that the gospel be restated with a meaning that takes cognizance of the modern world.[14]

Not that members of the clergy don't already have their hands full simply ministering to the everyday concerns of congregants. Divorce, drug addiction, mental depression, poverty, unemployment—all are the daily fare that the clergy encounter. Members of the clergy sometimes find themselves overwhelmed by the mundane. The words are those of Virgil Elizondo, but they could have been uttered by the pastor of almost any house of worship:

"U.S. Catholic culture wants us to be chief handyman, plumber, bookkeeper, and giver of good sermons. We have to change that. People say our sermons have no depth and that's true. But I don't know when the ordinary pastor has time to study. I think U.S. Catholic culture has to recognize that if it wants its priests to be good preachers, to be men of prayer, men of depth, to correlate the Scriptures with what's happening in everyday life, the on-going revelation of God's word, then it needs to give priests time alone. And that is what the American Catholic is not willing to do."

A similar scenario might be outlined for rabbis, as well. It wasn't long ago that the principal role of the rabbi was teacher and scholar. In modern America it is scarcely possible for the rabbi to serve the needs of a congregation and remain immersed in books. The Jewish community, once protected by its intellectuality and its ethnic insularity, was somewhat above the fray. Now, its sense of community is as threatened as that of other faiths. Social problems once unusual among Jews are now very much among the concerns with which the congregational rabbi must contend. The prospect of scholarly pursuit drew a Leonid Feldman to the rabbinate, but he finds himself in a constant battle to carve out time for learning and teaching.

The challenge to the clergy of almost all denominations is to attend to the ordinary while summoning from the congregation that which is noble in the human condition. Americans need such inspiration and they have few places in which to find it. This is a time, says Adam Richardson, when most ministry can take place outside the walls of the church. There is a craving for inspiration. Life needs meaning. People need each other. Many people, even in this age of secularism, want to be spiritually elevated in ways that lead them to contribute to the betterment of society. Billy Graham addressed a throng of 250,000 in Central Park in 1991, in the citadel of the lonely: New York City. Some were simply curious; others were searching.

The traditional bulwarks long ago gave way. The sense of community is teetering and in the big cities it may be shakiest of all. Pastors like Granville Seward have recognized this and have tried to deal with the new realities of the fragmented family even in the midst of the inner city.

What does religion have to say to Americans in an age in which Communism can no longer be cited as the atheistic threat that requires Americans to maintain their faith? Religion in America, in many ways, has a weak support structure and is struggling in the face of new challenges. Church finances are in a state of crisis in many congregations. Voluntary giving to religion has not responded to new needs. Statistics from the Independent Sector show that those who can least afford it give the largest portion of their income to their churches. The contributions of the biggest donors frequently represent but a tiny part of their incomes.[15] Furthermore, there is the question of whether the generosity of the affluent is offered in a spirit of giving and compassion or merely because it makes the donor feel good or feel less guilty.[16]

It is up to the ordained to help lay people understand the significance of faith and good works. There are signs that people still hold religion and those who labor in its vineyards in special regard. A survey conducted on behalf of the *Columbia Journalism Review* to see how the magazine's readers rated the honesty and ethical standards of various professions gave high marks to the clergy. They outranked by far such people as labor leaders, elected officials, business executives, police and lawyers. Only pharmacists rivaled them in the regard in which they were held.[17]

Chances are that regardless of how diligent they may be in filling the prescriptions of the '90s, pharmacists are not apt to be the ones who dispense a more important prescription, that of inspiring fellow Americans to search for the best within themselves. Clergy are uniquely situated for this role and they will be needed more than ever in the 1990s by an American people—aching from economic dislocation, frightened by the disintegration of community, disillusioned by a shortage of heroes and leaders—who yearn to be brought together again and made whole.

Notes

1. "How Americans and Europeans Diverge." Survey by Times Mirror Center for The People and The Press reported in *Christian Science Monitor,* Nov. 22, 1991.
2. Bellah, Robert N. et al. *Habits of the Heart.* Berkeley: University of California Press, 1985. *Individualism and Commitment to American Life.* New York: HarperCollins, 1989. *The Good Society.* New York: Knopf, 1991.
3. O'Neill, Joseph P. "Seminary Students: A Retrospective." An unpublished paper, Sept. 12, 1990.
4. Franklin, James L. "Church Picks New Leader to Raise Its Profile." *The Boston Globe,* June 16, 1991.
5. "Changing Age and Gender Profiles Among Entering Seminary Students." *Ministry Research Notes: An ETS Occasional Report.* Spring 1991.
6. Ibid.
7. Lincoln, C. Eric and Mamiya, Lawrence H. *The Black Church in the African American Experience.* Durham, N.C.: Duke University Press, 1990.
8. "Academic Preparation of Master of Divinity Candidates." *Ministry Research Notes: An ETS Occasional Report.* Fall 1990.
9. Ibid.
10. Ibid.
11. "Changing Age and Gender . . ."
12. Ibid.

13. Goldman, Ari L. "Religion Notes." *The New York Times,* Mar. 9, 1991.
14. Thiemann, Ronald F. *Constructing a Public Theology: The Church in a Pluralistic Culture.* Louisville: Westminster/John Knox Press, 1992.
15. "Poor Flocks Make for Good Donations as Pledge Season Begins." *The Wall Street Journal,* Oct. 11, 1990.
16. Wuthnow, Robert. *Acts of Compassion: Caring for Others and Helping Ourselves.* Princeton: Princeton University Press, 1991.
17. "The Pharmacist Factor." *The Columbia Journalism Review.* Nov./Dec. 1991.

Contributors

Rosemary L. Bray has worked as an editor for *Scholastic, Essence,* the *Daily News,* the *Wall Street Journal* and *Ms.* She is now an editor on the *New York Times Book Review.* Her pieces have appeared in the *Village Voice, Chicago Magazine, Savvy, Black Enterprise,* the *Chicago Tribune, Glamour, Essence, Ms.* and the *New York Times.* She has won awards from the Educational Press Association, Lincoln University, the New York Association of Black Journalists, the National Association of Black Journalists, and the Center for Investigative Reporting.

David Briggs has reported on religion and ethics for the Associated Press since 1988. In addition to his daily reporting and coverage of major religion events, he writes a weekly syndicated column, "Testaments," for AP Newsfeatures. He received his master's degree from Yale Divinity School in 1985. Prior to joining the Associated Press, he was a religion writer for the *Buffalo News.*

Kenneth A. Briggs is a free-lance writer and author of *The Year That Shook the Catholic Church in America.* From 1974 to 1985 he was religion editor of the *New York Times.* Previously, he spent four years as religion writer for *Newsday.* He has taught at the Columbia University Graduate School of Journalism and Lehigh University, written articles for several national publications and contributed to a book, *Reporting Religion.* He has also been a writer and editor at the Gallup Organization.

John Dart has covered religion news for the *Los Angeles Times* for 25 years. He was president of the Religion Newswriters Association, finishing a two-year term in 1992. He is author of *The Laughing Savior,* a popular introduction to the Nag Hammadi Gnostic Library discovery, which he updated and revised in a 1988 edition, *The Jesus of Heresy and History.* He was awarded a National Endowment for the Humanities fellowship for journalists at Stanford University. He was president of the Los Angeles chapter of the Society of Professional Journalists.

Ari L. Goldman is a religion correspondent for the *New York Times* and the author of *The Search for God at Harvard*. The book grew out of a year he spent studying comparative religion at Harvard Divinity School while on leave from the *Times*. He began as a copy boy at the *Times* in 1973. Since becoming a reporter in 1975, he has covered education, state politics and transportation before moving to religion. He has won numerous awards and has lectured widely.

John C. Long has spent 25 years with the *Courier-Journal* in Louisville, Ky., where he is a copy editor and the weekend metro editor. For eight years ending in 1987 he was the newspaper's religion writer, twice receiving the Religious Public Relations Council's Wilbur Award for best expression of religious values in a major American newspaper. He is a contributor on religious subjects to the Lilly Endowment's *Progressions* magazine and edited a report on mainstream Protestantism.

William R. MacKaye, a veteran writer on religion, is editor of *In Trust*, a magazine reporting on theological education. It circulates among trustees, administrators and faculty members of seminaries and divinity schools. He is a former religion editor of the *Washington Post* and a former editor of the *Washington Post Magazine*. He is the author, with Mary Anne MacKaye, of *Mr. Sidwell's School*, the centennial history of the Sidwell Friends School in Washington.

Gene I. Maeroff is a senior fellow at the Carnegie Foundation for the Advancement of Teaching in Princeton, N.J. He spent 16 years with the *New York Times*, where he was national education correspondent. He is the author of several books including *The School-Smart Parent, The Empowerment of Teachers* and *Don't Blame the Kids*. Early in his career he was the religion editor of the *Akron Beacon-Journal*.

David Nichols has edited two volumes of journalist Ernie Pyle's writings, *Ernie's War* and *Ernie's America*. He also has been a consultant to the producers of a film on Ernie Pyle. He is at work on two new books. One is on the lives of diocesan priests. He has worked as a newspaper and radio reporter, edited a corporate magazine and contributed profiles and essays to newspapers and commentaries to radio.

R. Gustav Niebuhr was hired by the *Wall Street Journal* as a staff reporter in 1989 to write about trends in religion for the newspaper's front page. Previously, he worked as a religion reporter for the *Atlanta Journal/Constitution*. He received the Supple Memorial Award for excellence in religion news writing in 1988. He has reported stories from throughout the United States, as well as from Central America, Cuba and East Asia.

Margaret M. Poloma is professor of sociology at the University of Akron. She has served on the councils of the Society for the Scientific Study of Religion, the Religious Research Association, the Association for the Sociology of Religion and the Christian Sociological Society. Among her seven books are two dealing with the Charismatic-Pentecostal movement— *The Charismatic Movement: Is There a New Pentecost?* and *The Assemblies of God at the Crossroads: Charisma and Institutional Dilemmas*.

Roy Reed is a professor of journalism at the University of Arkansas at Fayetteville. He was a national and foreign correspondent for the *New York Times* before returning to his native Arkansas to teach and write. He developed an interest in the civil rights movement while reporting for the *Arkansas Gazette* during the 1950s and 1960s. He is the author of a collection of essays, *Looking for Hogeye*. He was a member of Pulaski Heights Christian Church while Colbert Cartwright was pastor.

Pamela Schaeffer is news editor for Religious News Service in New York, a wire service specializing in news of religion. She assumed her post in 1991 after completing requirements for a Ph.D. in historical theology at St. Louis University. She was religion-ethics editor at the *St. Louis Post-Dispatch*, where her articles were nominated for the Pulitzer Prize. She was on the staff of the *Post-Dispatch* for 14 years and spent 10 years covering religion.